Pantheisticon

American University Studies

Series IX
History

Vol. 98

PETER LANG
New York • Bern • Frankfurt am Main • Paris

Robert Rees Evans

Pantheisticon

The Career of John Toland

PETER LANG
New York • Bern • Frankfurt am Main • Paris

Library of Congress Cataloging-in-Publication Data

Evans, Robert Rees
    Pantheisticon : the career of John Toland / Robert
Rees Evans.
        p. cm. — (American university studies. Series IX,
History ; vol. 98)
    Includes bibliographical references.
        1. Toland, John, 1670-1722. 2. Enlightenment.
3. England—Intellectual life—18th century. 4. Philosophy,
English—18th century. I. Title. II. Series.
B1393.Z7E92   1991   192—dc20   90-41218
ISBN 0-8204-1414-X   CIP
ISSN 0740-0462

© Peter Lang Publishing, Inc., New York 1991

IN MEMORIAM

DAVID SANDLER BERKOWITZ

TABLE OF CONTENTS

PREFACE

John Toland (1669–1722) has been variously understood as deist, freethinker, materialist, monist, literateur, political activist and polemicist by German, Italian, French and, to a lesser degree, British and American writers. It is a career that has never been placed in perspective despite its having been played out amid well-recorded events following the English Revolution of 1688 and its author's claims, increasingly well-founded, to a secure place in the history of modern philosophy. Toland's ideas keep cropping up among latter-day historians and philosophers only to be distorted or adumbrated for want of the patience or time required to interpret his now-scattered writings.

His philosophical system, "Pantheism", has never been so much as outlined. While his influence continues to be felt, no one is able to say precisely why. Known in his day, though elusively, he has fallen into obscurity in ours. His proximity to the powerful—Harley and the Electress Sophia in politics; Shaftesbury, Locke, Bayle and Leibniz in philosophy—points to a once considerable reputation which nearly evaporated. This study will attempt to re-adjust his position within the Augustan and greater European frames by means of a chronological examination of the man and his works.

The method is critical biography, tracing Pantheism's development in the contemporary climate of opinion. From this running commentary, a systematic reconstruction and an historical assessment of Pantheism are hazarded. Sources consulted are in the main original; Williamite, Stuart, Georgian.

Results show Pantheism to have been a revolutionist's ideology and an Enlightment philosophy. As an ideology Pantheism sought to undermine ecclesiastical and monarchical power. Philosophically, Pantheism was an ethical construction in which the Divine Will and the Christian world-view gave way to human reason and physical nature. Once Pantheism is seen more or less clearly, Toland's various writings appear at least quasi-systematically in these contexts either at once or in parallel.

The major conclusion is that the English Revolution and the rise of science were but complementary aspects of an eighteenth century intellectual revolt against the medieval Catholic frame. Toland easily distinguished these great events into separate strands, but consistently sought after their points of inter-connection. Pantheism's language is therefore binary and somewhat lacking in pristine clarity. But his importance to the history of ideas better emerges once Enlightment takes precedence, historiographically, over national politics and scientific discovery. It is also true that studies of Toland are nearly always edifying for students of the time M. Paul Hazard designated as denoting "the crisis of the European conscience". Few concerns of this startling and profoundly transitional period left him untouched.

Cambridge, Massachusetts

September, 1990

Johannes Toland
eigenhändig

Jo: Toland

CHAPTER 1

TOLERATION

John Toland's primary interests throughout his turbulent career lay in the ecclesiastical and civil aspects of the English Revolutionary Settlement. The radical exhortation, "religious toleration and civil liberty!", which occurs most frequently in all his writings, represented for him the Settlement's very aims. His first writings through *Christianity Not Mysterious* (1696) treat exclusively of the ecclesiastical side with its emphasis on toleration. It is proper that we make our beginning examining his personal role in the movement towards religious liberalism after 1688, and with its emerging ideal; that of a complete toleration, bitterly contested first by the forces of Williamite conservatism, then afterward by those of an extreme Augustan reaction under Queen Anne.

The development of Toland's penultimate position is noteworthy. He appeared initially a partisan of Presbyterian, Independent, even Baptist Dissent, and accepted Presbyterian patronage in London from 1690 until 1696. By 1705, however, Defoe branded him "the most extreme for toleration"[1] and by 1713 Toland's plea for the naturalization of Jews[2] proves clearly to us that he had extended the toleration to all save Catholics.

Toland is best known in the world for his religious innovations, his "freethought". Whatever we may think of his philosophical materialism, his party politics and the like, it is usually granted that books such as *Christianity Not Mysterious* (1696) and *Letters to Serena* (1704) are of more than biographical importance. The purpose of what follows will be to show the relevance of Toland's philosophy on three levels of importance: biographical,[3] revolutionary[4] and with respect to the Enlightenment.[5]

It is interesting, though little recognized, that our author had struck his own peculiar coinage for his views rather early on in the pamphlet, *Letter from a Pantheist to an Orthodox Friend* (1705). What the editors of the *Spectator* and *Tatler* termed loosely

"freethought" Toland called "Pantheism". And in view of the importance usually attached to the themes of toleration and freethought
in the history of ideas it is important that we reconstruct what he
meant. Moreover, as Pantheism did not emerge at once but was
created gradually from earlier currents within the stream of religious liberalism, it is necessary that we trace its development before
assessing its systematic result.

Arminians and Latitudinarians

In unearthing Toland anew who cannot take an interest in his initial
period of Dissent or Nonconformity? It involves his youth, his background, and the publication of his famous *Christianity Not Mysterious* (1696), in which are gathered together all the influences of his
early training. Sharply distinguished from Pantheism—Toland later
calls *Christianity Not Mysterious* his "juvenile thots"[6]—this notorious product of his early Non-conformist years nevertheless points
in the direction of the man who in 1705 will be known as "most
extreme for toleration".

   Christianity Not Mysterious might roughly yet correctly be styled
a synthesis of Dutch Arminianism and English Latitudinarianism.
The former was derived from certain arguments and methods of
Presbyterians and Remonstrants with whom Toland had been
associated at Redcastle School in Londonderry, Glasgow University, Edinburgh University, under the Heads of Agreement in
London,[7] and at Leyden University. The latter is patent in the book's
dedication to that paradeigmatic Latitudiarian, Tillotson.

   On the negative side, both Arminianism and Latitudinarianism
may best be defined, even today, as movements of protest against
orthodoxy. Forms of "protestantism", if you will. The Arminians,
early on, had ranked among the heretics of orthodox Calvinism,[8]
and Latitude Men represented Low Church radicals as against High
Church conservatives within the universities and Anglican Church.[9]
Influenced by both, John Toland was, lifelong, nothing if not
opposed to orthodoxy, whether that of Calvin or of the High Church.
Religious persecution in any form—never least if Catholic in origin—drove him when young to violent extremes, and with a missionary fervor against the Catholic House of Stuart.

A brief glance at Toland's background bids fair to explain his hatred of Restoration religious persecution, practiced before 1688, and clarifies his motives for following the Arminian or Latitudinarian lines of protest. Born a Catholic[10] but all-too-thoroughly converted to Protestantism before his sixteenth year, yet with no sectarian affiliation, Toland first witnessed the persecution of Irish Protestants in Londonderry, then, while *alumnus academicus* at Glasgow University, the vicious handling of Scots Covenanters at the hands of Stuart police. With the outbreak of anarchy during the crisis of 1688, following King James II's desertion of the government, young firebrand Toland spoke from the barricades and led a contingent of toughs in a "rabbling" of the Anglican clergy. He paradoxically sought out the Anglican bishop in Glasgow to investigate taking the sacrament, then began frequenting Presbyterian meeting houses while investigating the local cult of Scots Rosicrucians![11] At any rate, the violence of his actions during the Revolution's outbreak suggests he had ultimately made his decision and turned his back on the Establishment. A letter of reference provided him by the newly appointed Presbyterian magistrates of Glasgow is clear evidence that by 1690 Toland was finally and avowedly a Dissenter.[12] He had just received his Master of Arts degree from the University of Edinburgh. Forsaking thoughts of returning to a career in Ireland, torn with strife just prior to the Battle of Boyne, Toland journeyed southward instead to London—a Presbyterian stronghold—his memory fired with images of bigotry, persecution, forced exile, student rioting, and a violent encounter with the King's Troops.

The Defeat of Comprehension

To Dissent forces the Toleration Act of 1689 was small reward for the strong support they had provided the Glorious Revolution. The old policy of insulating the Anglican center against the Presbyterian left and the Catholic right had held firm; the Clarendon Code was not rescinded. Persecution, with exceptions, remained the order of the day, apparently legally, though a period of relaxation was to follow in practice until passage of the Blasphemy Act in 1698. Hopes for a general toleration along Dutch lines had been dashed by the

Declaration of Rights (1689), which, while excluding popish sovereigns or their consorts, nevertheless denied any declared toleration by prerogative. William of Orange favored the broadest possible toleration, but the decision now rested with parliament. Two acts passed ("which were no doubt unnecessary", as one commentator puts it)[13] against the Catholic right, denying them arms and good horses and excluding them from London and Westminster, yet placed parliament in good position to balance this legislation by denying a scheme for the "comprehension" of Dissenters lately espoused by Nottingham and a group of Low Church divines.

The plan for "comprehending" Dissent foundered for two reasons: (1) the terrified resistance suddenly afforded by Tory parliamentarians and High Church divines, and (2) a marked disunity amongst certain ambitious Non-conformists themselves. Whereas the opposition quickly and desperately pulled itself together to block passage in the House of Commons, proponents of the measure fell to debating what sort of Non-Conformist was to be included, and so failed to organize properly. Defeat of the bill was a turning-point in English history: it enabled the government to test its moderating scheme for a Toleration; it provided Dissent with motives for reform and advancement resulting in missionary movements,[14] learned societies,[15] Methodism and other ways of "going it alone"; it helped structure Whig political arguments against Tory insofar as the Whig party continued to draw for strong support upon Dissent. Although John Toland, for the next sixteen years, no doubt fought to turn Toleration into Comprehension while remaining associated with Dissent, it is interesting to note his gradually increasing satisfaction with the Toleration compromise itself. His Memorial of the State (1705) defends it against Dissenter's cries for a Comprehension, and even against the tacit association of Dissent with the Whig party. It is one of Toland's contributions to Whig political theory that he recognized in the success of the Toleration Act[16] a way whereby Whigs might finally disassociate themselves from Dissent without jeopardizing their hold on the Latitudinarian voting managers within the Low Church clergy. It was ever the local clergyman who got out the vote in the districts.

Natural Reason

It is easy to see now that the Toleration Act, wise though its passage ultimately proved, nevertheless could not help but serve to fan the fires of religious controversy in the unstable, near anarchic decade of the 1690s. Not only is a little freedom always extremely dangerous, immediately suggesting the quest for more, but the defeat of Comprehension placed all Dissenters once more in that impossible second-class position under which they had been chafing ever since passage of the Clarendon Code. The meetings of the Heads of Agreement during 1690–1692,[17] to bring Independents and Presbyterians together at least in matters of schools and ordinations, was but the beginning of a protracted, agonizing, political assault by Dissent upon Anglican privilege, for Anglicans alone were now permitted to hold office. In the circumstances, it was natural for John Toland, now a card-carrying Presbyterian, to make use of his good theological training in the Dissenter's cause. From 1690 through 1696 we see him entirely devoted to a single idea: as there was to be a Toleration Act rather than a Comprehension Act, the concept "toleration" must be liberalized so as to include as many Dissenters as possible.

To this end, a common Arminian and Latitudinarian dependency upon "natural reason" suggested the most relevant course. One could not argue with the Established Church nor with parliament concerning the laws of church and state (of which the Toleration Act was one), for these were the authority of the land, and argument is useless against authority. On purely rational grounds, however, one might argue apace and undermine the existing laws with no little effectiveness. It is for this reason that the lapsing of the Licensing Act in 1694 is of such overriding importance; with so many issues of the Revolutionary Settlement still up in the air, it was crucial that some extra-parliamentary means be found to influence public opinion. This was especially the case now, among the Dissent forces deprived otherwise of representation, save for outside lobbying and investment. Toland's *Christianity Not Mysterious*—called by one writer "the signal gun of the deistic controversy"—was to be his major contribution to Dissent's attack upon Establishment orthodoxy, and the boldest use of the public press since the days of Milton and Sir Roger L'Estrange. In great part, the stir it raised was due to the fact that its author signed his name to the second edition (after launching the first as a trial balloon), drawing sudden attention thereby to various dangers and possibilities inherent in a new freedom for the press in England.

If *Christianity Not Mysterious* were re-named in more positive language, it might well have been called *Christianity Altogether Rational*, for such was the understanding immediately purveyed to its readers. Its force lay in the publicity with which it extended the old Arminian and Latitudinarian appeals to "natural reason". Arminians had indignantly reversed Calvin's estimate of reason as a "stinking thing"; Latitudinarians had borrowed Leyden University's Arminian arguments in Laud's time to support their good Thomist contention that "natural reason" was not opposed to grace, but a means to its perfection.[18] Hales, Chillingworth, Whichcote, Jeremy Taylor, and Tillotson, the present Archbishop, had forged a continuous line of defence against any and all detractors of human reason; that is, Anglican traditionalists to the right (who stressed the Stuart ideology of canonical authority, Divine Right and Passive Obedience) and Puritan predestinarians to the left (who placed their belief in the wilful and irrational Sovereignty of God). In defence of the *via media* between Rome and Geneva established in the Thirty Nine Articles, 17th century Latitudinarians, following Hooker, sought to heal the deep divisions which had erupted between Catholic defenders of the Royal Supremacy and their Calvinist opponents throughout the period of the Civil War.[19] In the time of Laud and Strafford this rift had of course widened from mere Separatism to an absolute binary polarization. Chillingworth, the initial Latitude Man, attempted to convince Puritans and Royalists alike that they shared a common "protestantism",[20] appealing in vain to the "rationality" of that position. From this point onward, all Latitude Men dogmatically associated "natural reason" with "Protestantism" (a new term in the language), opposing it evenly to the Genevan authoritarianism of the Republican left and to the "Romanist" authoritarianism of the Restoration right. Toland, dedicating his incendiary book to Tillotson, was rather hypocritically associating himself with this traditional middle road. By 1696, however, Genevan authoritarianism was on the wane after the of witch-hunting ceased at Salem among fanatical Independents to the far left,[21] whereas Romanism and Royalism remained potent forces lurking underground among discredited Non-Jurors and revengeful Jacobites.

Tillotson died in 1696, else he surely would have taken Toland to task for extending "natural reason" beyond his own Latitudinarian position to that of an almost pure naturalism. Naturalism assures us roughly that "Nature is all there is", which, in theological terminology, leaves little or no room at all for such things as Grace, mystery, or miracle. Toland had come very close if not central to a downright worship of reason, a "religion of nature", a deism.[22] The meaning of such a position for politics was hinted at by Peter Browne of Trinity College, Dublin, whose vitriolic animadversions led to the public burning of Toland's book by order of the Irish parliament: the number of Tolands, he says, "grow formidable, they begin to speak out their infidelity and prophaneness as plain as some of them do treason. They are secretly forming themselves into clubs and cabals, and have their emissaries into all parts, which are supported by contributions: and I make little doubt but that their design is at length to show us that all dominion as well as religion is founded in reason".[23] Browne, an insider, knew what he was talking about.

A recent historian of English religious thought teaches us that in William III's reign "the church was divided into two wrangling factions: Latitudinarian Whigs and High Church Tories".[24] Had Presbyterians been Comprehended in 1689 there would no doubt have been three wrangling factions instead of two, for the left would then have been represented in Convocation (the ecclesiastical parliament) along with the center and the right. It is worth speculating whether or not, had this been proven the case, Toland's extension of the old Arminian-Latitudinarian position would have been necessary to belabor at all. The research for *Christianity Not Mysterious* had been financed, at least in part, by the Heads of Agreement.[25] Had the English Presbyterians been Comprehended in 1689, there would have been no Heads of Agreement. It follows that the new naturalism of *Christianity Not Mysterious* owes not a little to the attempt of the excluded Dissenters to stretch and expand the Toleration Act; that is, to promote "protestantism" in the press by argumentative appeals to "the reasonableness of Christianity".[26] Young Toland had been quick to realize that there are no second-class Christians permitted in a naturalist Christianity devoid on either side of Calvinist or of Anglican sources of authority.

The Ideal of a Uniform Christianity

Anterior to Methodism, and a new and exciting idea in John
Toland's time, the conception of a Christianity based on the Gospels
alone had suddenly broken into circulation in the wake of the very
recent Toleration Act. *Christianity Not Mysterious* was one of the first
and best books to systematize this powerful idea,[27] though not the
first to hazard it in the public press. Croft's *Naked Truth*, Bury's *The
Naked Gospel*, and Daniel William's *The Gospel Truth* were well-
known if anonymous publications attempting immediately to seize
the high ground and reintroduce "the Church of Christ". Croft's
piece proposed making the Apostle's Creed sole confession of the
protestant faith in repudiation of all arguments from the early
church Fathers. Bury's and Williams' pieces had concurred, the
former explicitly challenging High Church conservatism in the
Oxford community, the latter the Calvinist radicals of London
Dissent. Croft's anonymity saved him his place on the Bench, but
Bury and Williams were found out; Bury was relieved as Master of
Exeter College in 1690, to face trial in 1694 for an Arian and a
Socinian (an anti-trinitarian), whereas Williams was hotly engaged
by the Independents in that dispute which led to the speedy
destruction of the Heads of Agreement. John Toland had been
directly involved in Dr. Williams' defence, and was, at this time,
under the patronage of certain London Presbyterians led by the
famous parson of Bishopsgate Street,[28] and founder of Doctor
Williams' Library.

There is a confusion in the history of English religious thought
in great part stemming from these Gospel Christianity beginnings in
the 1690s. A number of movements converge at this point, and a
number of other movements radiate outwardly from it. Thus Bury is
called a Latitudinarian and Williams an Arminian, whereas both
were held to be part of the "Arian Movement" and were accused of
Socinian heresy under the Thirty Nine Articles. Moreover, both
Bury's and Williams' books had been printed in the *Unitarian Tracts*,
and have become the special property of the historians of Unitarianism.[29] Obviously there is some point of interchangeability validating
all these claims, for the historians who have made them have
documented well. To say this interchangeability lies in efforts to
widen the Toleration Act of 1689 is too easy, however, and begs the

question. In the present writer's opinion, what is at stake is, in the first place, the above-mentioned appeal to natural reason common to the Arminians and Latitudinarians of the seventeenth century.[30] In the second place, however,—and more basic—lurks the theme of "Gospel Christianity". None of the writers of the 1690's was eager to rouse the authorities through an espousing of an absolutely rational, natural, and non-Christian account of the religious life. Toland was the most radical writer of the decade, but even he is insistent that reason is merely a tool to lead us ultimately back, *ad fontes*, to the New Testament Gospels. This was Locke's thesis in his *Third Letter for Toleration* and in *The Reasonableness of Christianity*; it was Croft's thesis, Bury's thesis, and Williams' thesis. The point of interchangeability appears in their common appeal to these four basic Christian texts. Toland's later attack upon the validity of even these—launched in 1699[31]—is not evident yet in *Christianity Not Mysterious* nor in any writing attributed to him during this, his period of Dissent.

Whatever the theological value of "Gospel Christianity", its political value rested in the support it provided the Toleration, the practice of Occasional Conformity, and the rise of the Dissenting academies. Had the Comprehension scheme not died on the vine in 1689, Gospel Christianity would have justified Comprehension as well. The fact was that a war had begun between the two recognized churches in England: the Establishment[32] might represent the law of the land concerning religion, but a community of scholars was now free to use the Toleration Act and the lapsing of the Licensing Act for the re-founding of the "Church of Christ".[33] Toland's *Christianity Not Mysterious* was to bring this campaign out into the open: the Establishment champion and Tillotson's *protégé*, Bishop Stillingfleet, would then choose to invest John Locke (who had recently re-read his New Testament "without note or comment") with nearly sole responsibility for Toland's outrageous tract.[34] Behind the Locke-Stillingfleet controversy were hidden certain political realities; Dissenter's rights, for example, and "the Church in Danger". Party lines now hardened between Whig left and Tory right, and a policy of reconciliation between these extremes became much more complicated and more difficult to promote for the moderate Whigs and Tories of the Center.

The Commonwealth of Learning

Recent students of the European Enlightenment have rediscovered and plunged into re-studying "the Commonwealth of Learning", sometimes called "the republic of letters".[35] As a movement of ideas, parallel in time with the rise of science, its members, the "Moderns"[36] applied the "new learning" of Baconian induction to the data of history. Its purpose was, in the main, to once for all divest the religious consciousness of "superstition". Oftimes, as in the case of founder Pierre Bayle, the correspondents seemed bent on attacking the religious consciousness itself, rather than its mere distortions. Not content with Toleration or the separation of church and state, these iconoclasts dismissed Christianity as one religious cult relative to the very many of world history. To such proto-anthropologists Christianity was not mysterious, and, though few of them attacked it outright for fear of persecution, their backhanded "defences" infuriated the orthodox in all the countries of Europe.

If one had to trace this movement of letters back to one man or one book Spinoza and his *Tractatus Theologico-Politicus* would spring to mind.[37] A former Jew, holding no brief for mysteries, and rationalist to the core, Spinoza chose to speak for Christianity on moral grounds alone, finding in it the one religion most compatible with his "ethical" and "pantheistic" outlook.[38]

That Spinoza escaped persecution was due mainly to his residing in Holland, chief province of the Dutch Republic, and by and large the most enlightened spot in seventeenth century Europe. Here was the natural center and birthplace for the Commonwealth of Learning: here Huguenot Bayle and Swiss Arminian LeClerc published their annuals, the *Nouvelles de la République des Lettres* and *Bibliotheque Universelle et Historique*, respectively, and here the former had conceived his famous *Dictionnaire* in November, 1690;[39] here English travelers and refugees—Locke, and Second and Third Earls of Shaftesbury, Toland—found refuge at the house of the Whig merchant Benjamin Furly in Rotterdam; here also the great University at Leyden had boasted Descartes and Arminius from among its faculty; here, finally, a technique of "literary correspondence"—so essential later to the eighteenth century—was perfected between Dutch scholars and their foreign counterparts (Spinoza and Oldenberg, for instance),[40] aiding and abetting smooth passage in rough waters of what one writer has termed the "crisis of the European conscience".[41]

Holland's stake in the English Revolution was unusually high, not only because the Stadtholder of the Netherlands Federation and the English King were now one man, but also because a common Dutch-English foreign policy *contra* Louis XIV threatened an imminent exhaustion of Dutch land and sea power. Aware that William III's stiffest opposition came from xenophobic English Tories, Hollanders followed and buttressed the Whig interest with avidity, sometimes in company with Whig merchants visiting or residing in Dutch ports. The development of the Toleration during the early years of the Revolutionary Settlement at once bore the closest scrutiny, for Dissent in this period was directly associated with political Whiggism,[42] and an ever-widening toleration was to the interest of the Dutch state as well as to the "Commonwealth of Learning". From radical Whig and Dissenting points-of-view, the nearly universal toleration practiced in Holland was the true model upon which their own hopes were grounded. In brief, the Toleration Act had given rise to a new wave of letter writing, travel, and general communication between intellectuals and reformers of the two neighboring, protestant countries.

Of particular interest to Dutch Arminians was the current dispute between Presbyterians and Independents in England over Daniel Williams' *The Gospel Truth* (1692). The extreme rationalism of Williams' stance struck orthodox Independents under Richard Mather as Arminian heresy, and threatened the Heads of Agreement a mere two years after its first meeting. The matter was serious, for the Heads of Agreement was Dissent's spearhead in its cold war with the Establishment, and Williams had been forced to a grudging disavowal of Arminianism in 1693 for purposes of party unity. Meanwhile, an abstract of *The Gospel Truth* had been drawn up by young Toland, his then secretary, and sent to Jean LeClerc of the College of the Arminians in Amsterdam. LeClerc printed it in the 1692 edition of his *Bibliotheque Universelle et Historique*,[43] bringing Toland's name to the attention of the European intelligentsia. A *protégé* of Williams, Toland had broken into print in a manner bound to interest the Arminian community in Holland.

Utilizing his connections well, Toland then secured a grant from the Heads of Agreement to matriculate at Leyden University near the end of the year 1692, there to pursue the Doctor of Philosophy degree. As a Master of Arts from Glasgow and Edinburgh and already master of many languages—he claims ten languages in his epitaph—the fiery scholar promised soon to make his mark in Dissent's cause. Little did Williams suspect that his erstwhile secretary would turn his coat by 1697 to become one of Dissent's thorniest opponents!

Leyden had been an Arminian stronghold since the days of the Master's tenure early in the century, but it had also been no stranger to an encroaching secularism and the rise of science. Spinoza had dwelt a few miles outside the walls of the University buildings, and Descartes had taught many Leyden students while in exile. The imposing faculty in theology—featuring famous academic names such as LeClerc, Wetstein, Gronovius, and the younger Friedrich Spanheim—were so dedicated to reason in religion and so opposed to miracle and mystery that their research and teaching appeared to many rather an attack on Christianity than any sort of defence or impartial investigation of it. Tolandian source materials thicken after the Leyden period; close investigation shows the young man's recently acquired Arminianism beginning to unravel if not tear apart as early as 1693.[44] One notable sign of this tendency had been his dismissal from the University before he had completed a single year's residence! Though enamored of the "Commonwealth of Learning"—for he continued to cultivate Graevius and Van Dale by letter after 1693[45]—Toland was now wearying of Calvinism altogether. Benjamin Furly wrote introducing the incipient free-thinker to John Locke in August, 1693: "I find him a free-spirited ingenious man; that quitted the Papacy in James' time when all men of no principles were looking toward it; and having now cast off the yoke of Spiritual Authority, that great bugbear and bane of ingenuity, he could never be persuaded to bow his neck to that yoke again, by whomsoever claimed".[46] Before quitting Holland for England Toland visited with LeClerc in Amsterdam, who gave him a book for delivery into the hands of the Earl of Pembroke.[47] Unlike Furly, LeClerc remained cool to one who had overthrown allegiance to the "spiritual authority" at Leyden.

In one way or another, Toland had made his presence known within the "Commonwealth of Learning" by 1694, and in turn had been influenced through contacts with its members, whether Calvinist, Anglican, or secularist. Furly's letter to Locke in the fall, 1693, made it impossible for the Sage of the Enlightment to ignore the penniless young scholar, so beholden was Locke to the Quaker merchant in whose house he himself had found refuge while in exile.[48] Locke's very angry repudiation of *Christianity Not Mysterious* three years later is a telling point: that part of the "Commonwealth of Learning" to which Toland had been most drawn was the radical wing of Bayle and his followers, not the gradualist school of Locke and the Leyden professors. Radical and unstable by temperament, Toland harbored more of that activist revolutionary spirit reminiscent of the Glasgow barricades than was stirring in Locke.

Scepticism

The author of *Bayle's Relations with England and the English* informs us that "By the time Toland was twenty years old Bayle's *Pensées*, his *Commentaire philosophique*, and his *Novelles* were already widely known", and that "In the case of John Toland, we can point to a close personal relationship".[49] It is certain Toland was a close reader of the quintessential sceptic.[50] The most important similarity between the two, however, was their method of inquiry. This method—derived from Spinoza's *Tractatus*—was called "ecclesiastical history" among practicing members of the "Commonwealth". It consisted of critical examinations of historical data which then were compared, for polemical purposes, to the dogmatic claims of the "priesthood", whether pagan, heathen, or Christian. In Bayle's case the method was openly iconoclastic; "religion" meant "superstition". In Toland's case the spirit was more critical, less damning, yet hardly less polemical. Toland's first essay in the method was *The Death of Attilius Regulus* (1694), penned at St. Edmund Hall, Oxford, while he was reading at the Bodleian. His *Catalogue of Books Mentioned by the Fathers* (1699) made further use of "ecclesiastical history" which, in the words of a student of Voltaire, "inaugurated a new era in documentary criticism",[51] transferring as it did Bayle's sceptical assaults upon authority to the language of English "critical deism".[52] Several other Tolandian works employing this approach were among his most effective. "Ecclesiastical history" was the passionate scholarly concern of the Commonwealth of Learning in Holland. Bayle was king: but Spanheim, LeClerc, Van Dale, Graevius, all assiduously practiced the

technique[53] whereby Lorenzo Valla had originally exposed and excoriated the false Donation of Constantine. "Ecclesiastical history"
subverted the deepest foundations of medieval theology and political theory, whether those of scripture, canon law, dogma, or the
judgments of the Fathers, driving any who sought final authority at
least back to the Gospels alone. Sceptics went further, reducing
Christianity to gross "superstition", an implicit indictment of insti-
tutional religion as such.

Students of Toland have been unwilling or perhaps unable to
credit him with a "defence" of Christianity despite the passion of his
claims.[54] The idea of a rational, completely non-mysterious Christianity appeared monstrous to all but the most liberal theologians
and most educated laymen. A religion without one degree of absolute authority in William III's time was unthinkable to the vast
majority, which, to judge by his astonishing *Commonplace Book*,
included Locke himself.

Yet there is little doubt Toland was seeking some vestige of
authority in his attempts to undermine traditional standards. In
Letters to Serena (1704) and even *Pantheisticon* (1720) he tends to
link the Newtonian system with Natural Law. In *Christianity Not
Mysterious* and *Nazarenus* the link holds between Natural Law and
the Gospels. When all are put together, Natural Law appears
common to Newtonianism and the Gospels, hence a unity, if not
achieved, is adumbrated. All this deserves a discussion unto itself;
here it is enough to say that Toland's scepticism was limited by his
sincere desire, apparently, to uncover a theological rationale for
Christianity which he firmly believed could obliterate protestant
differences and thereby extend the Toleration to that borderline
where a Comprehension must follow.

Ancients and Moderns

It is a truism, vividly apparent at the trial of Galileo, that the rise of
science depended on a parallel movement toward religious toleration. Throughout the seventeenth century in England we may cite
for illustration the distrust shown by the orthodox for "the Sons of
Gresham", or Royal Society, and the bitter opposition of antiquarian
Oxford to the Cambridge of Isaac Newton. "Toleration" also meant

permission to pursue what Bacon had called "the advancement of learning". One of the curious facets of the Ancients and Moderns dispute[55] was its religious one concerning toleration: the Ancients agreed with the schoolmen of medieval times that some *a priori* authority was necessary in all areas of human education, but all Moderns sought to sweep out the Augean stables through an *a posteriori* examination of the data, rebuilding the concept of nature into the new, Baconian "house of Solomon". The struggle of these mighty ideals in the best minds of the English Revolution—Locke's and Newton's, for example[56]—is fascinating to watch. Toland and others of the Commonwealth of Learning were no less affected.

Through "ecclesiastical history" the Commonwealth of Learning sought to subject the data of history to that same scrutiny by which the Royal Society had won so handsomely in the sphere of the natural sciences, and by which Locke had so recently triumphed in psychology. The Commonwealth would enrich the House of Solomon first by securing the proper data (eliminating that great mass proven to be fraudulent), then reconstructing them into a new theology, a new ethics, a new politics. The burning question was whether or not Christianity would stand up under this onslaught. Catholicism, it was assumed, would crumble. *Christianity Not Mysterious* was the beginning of a lifetime attempt to found a liberal theology which (1) would embrace the Modern's findings yet (2) maintain a vestige of authority for the Ancients, grounded especially in the Old and New Testaments. No one can read certain of Toland's later pieces— *Tetrademus* for example (1720) or *Nazarenus*—in another light.

It follows that Toland cannot simply be written off as a sceptic or simple deist. His contributions to liberal theology prove too significant for that kind of dismissal.[57] It also follows (a result more germane to our present topic) that the 1689 Toleration and the subsequent defeat of the Comprehension Bill were to him not merely steps along the road toward a non-religious utopia, in which dreary rounds of pulpit-thundering and persecution would finally have ceased. Toland was never indifferent to religion. His concern for a liberal Christian theology was redeemed for what William James would call its "cash value" in nineteenth century Tübingen, not eighteenth century Enlightment salons.[58] It follows also that Toland was not about to offer either the Toleration nor Comprehension to anyone at all; atheists, Catholics, deists, and others of similar stamp were in these years explicitly excluded.

Toland's Oxford Manifesto

There is ground for suspecting (if not maintaining) that the movement we would later call "liberal theology"[59] was powerfully influenced by Toland, whose *Christianity Not Mysterious* should be read
in conjunction with another document relevant to the "quest for the
historical Jesus"; a letter, or manifesto, written by him while
residing at Oxford, that "delicious spot", in 1694.

Toland had arrived at Williamite Oxford in December, 1693,[60]
just subsequent to his introduction to Locke that autumn.[61] He
plunged immediately into the "antiquarian" movement there and
began, with John Aubrey's help, a *Critical History of the Celtic
Religion and Learning* (published posthumously, in 1726).[62] Of little
direct bearing on politics, Oxford antiquarianism is still of intrinsic
interest to the intellectual historian of Revolutionary times, and
bears something in common with early Tudor political theory (oddly
enough) when Celtic Christianity had provided precedents for
Henry VIII's propagandists *contra* Rome.[63] Toland plunged now
significantly into Roman history, led by "a note of Palmerius upon
Appian" (in the latter's *De Bello Punico*) and a "considerable Fragment of the 24th book of Diodorus Siculus" to demonstrate his
latinity and prowess, arguing the thesis that "the tragical story of
the Death of [Attilius] Regulus is partly invented, partly mistaken,
and altogether a fable". So reads the preface to his *Death of Attilius
Regulus*[64] (1694), which book put to use the various "ecclesiastical
history" techniques he had imbibed abroad. *Attilius Regulus* was his
first *bona fide* publication, and first evidence of that interest in the
Roman republic which, later, linked to Cicero, became an obsession.[65]

Williamite Oxford, subdued for the moment through the exclusion of Non-Jurors and the unpopularity of Jacobitism, remained
nevertheless strictly orthodox when it came to theology and politics,
reason and nature, mystery and miracle, and quashed all innova-
tors such as the luckless Bury, whose *The Naked Gospel* (1690) had
earned him a deprivation. Toland's incendiary presence in this
atmosphere immediately evoked gossip and clerical opposition. A
Dissenting reader financed from the outside somewhere, the young
Irishman born in France with a dubious reputation for reform was
your perfect interloper. Moreover, his connections appeared all to

emanate from St. Edmund Hall, that stronghold for the Cantabridgian causes of Whiggism and the Low Church.

An anonymous correspondent soon took it upon himself to force Toland's hand: "The character you bear in Oxford is this", he wrote, "that you are a man of fine parts, great learning, and little religion".[66]

What the anonymous correspondent meant by "little religion" he made clear in a subsequent letter: Toland was "one who dealt too freely with [religion], a man of aspiring and uncontrolled reason, a great contemner of Credulity, and particularly an undervaluer of the two extraordinary Cures, wrought lately at London".[67] As an antidote to these patent transgressions, Toland is reminded that there is "nothing so forcible as reason *and love*".[68] This same letter provides us the first mention of *Christianity Not Mysterious*,[69] enjoining its author to desist, lest he insensibly fall into "Socinianism, Deism, Atheism, or anything". Opposed to the time-honored Anglican theology of "reason and love" inherited from Aquinas and Hooker, Toland appeared to Oxonian eyes as one who embraced reason while equating love with "credulity" or "superstition"; that is, one of the new breed of sceptics from abroad.

To declare his aversion to foreign scepticism, then, Toland decided to hazard a three-part manifesto in an open letter to the Oxford community, at once affirming his Christianity and protecting his forthcoming book from raising a storm before he had finished researching it at the Bodleian, and to satisfy the seething forces of reaction underneath Oxford's grudging obedience to "yt mongrel King". Nothing in this declaration sets Toland at odds with either the Anglican position or with *Christianity Not Mysterious*. Toland was apparently sincere, if radical, in later calling *Christianity Not Mysterious* a "defence of Christianity".[70] "To what purpose should I study here or elsewhere", he writes, "were I an Atheist or Deist...? What a contradiction to mention Virtue if I believed there was no God, or one so impotent that could not, or so malicious that would not reveal himself"?[71] In *Christianity Not Mysterious*, the moral consciousness, here stated, owed its existence at bottom to divine revelation.[72] Though ever so liberal, Toland is therefore never a mere naturalist, never a complete sceptic, nor wholly Erastian in his view of the Toleration. His Christianity was theoretically unassailable, as witness his "manifesto", quoted at length:[73]

I. I firmly believe the existence of an infinitely good, wise and powerful Being, which in our language we call GOD, substantially different from the universe he created, and continues to govern by his Providence; of whom, through whom, and to whom are all things.

II. Concerning Christ in particular, I believe that he is God manifest in the flesh, or true God and Man, perfectly united without contrariety of will, or confusion of essence. As to his human nature, that according to the Prophets, he was born of a pure Virgin, conceived by virtue of the divine Spirit, and therefore ever free from all the sinful disorders of fallen man. That he rose from the dead the third day after he was crucified by the Jews, and forty days after ascended into Heaven, from whence I expect his coming at the last day to judge me and all the world; and that when he was on earth he not only by his life gave us a perfect example, and by his Doctrine an infallible rule of all that we are to do, suffer, and hope; but also by the sacrifice of his death, reconciled to mercy all such as do the will of his Father, particularly those that believe his word, imitate his works, and accept his intercession. That as well the holy adult deceased before his passion, as children dying before the use of reason, are delivered from death by his merits, so that none can be saved without a Mediator. And lastly, that he is the only Ruler and Legislator of the Church.

III. I believe that we are sancified by the divine Spirit, who worketh in us, and with us, who directs and perfect us. I acknowledge the purity, excellence and obligation of all the evangelical precepts, as they are comprehended under these three heads, to live temperately, justly, and piously; to love God above all things, and my neighbor as myself. This is the sum of my assurance of eternal life, in hopes whereof I am now writing this unfeigned Confession of my Faith.

Having thrown this compression of Christian theology back into his correspondent's teeth, Toland instantly pre-figures its political consequences:[74]

> I dare not confine the Church to the narrow limits of a peculiar Sect, or her Doctrines to the affected phrases of a Party; and because the Gospel teacheth us mutual forbearance and the love of our enemies, I would not be suspected to favour those I cannot abuse with unseemly heat, much less question the truth of what I hold unlawful to impose. All that we have to do is charitably to instruct, and if we can, convince the erroneous. We may pray for the obstinate, and persist in our endeavors, but further we have no commission...and if they slight our exhortations, we must leave them to God. The civil Society cannot be injured by this Toleration, whilst all irregular practices are punishable by the Magistrate...

Toland rests his case on the Gospels. They cannot condone persecution, but they do insist on a full religious toleration. To say that "all irregular practices are punishable by the Magistrate" is certainly to say, albeit obliquely, that no irregular practices are punishable by the Priest.

Christianity Not Mysterious: Text and Episode

The background to the first phase of the politics underpinning Tolandian "pantheism" is now completed. Its foreground emerged in the preparations for *Christianity Not Mysterious*. As a political text, the latter will marshall together techniques, attitudes, and all necessary arguments for the purpose of justifying the broadest possible Toleration. The storm raised by its publication—Leslie Stephen's "signal-gun of the deistic controversy"—elicited the Blasphamy Act of 1698, prosecution by Convocation in 1702, a stir in Ireland hushed only by the attack on Irish woolens, more ammunition in support of the Tory war-cry "The Church in Danger!", from

1702 until 1714, and an echo in every European language not silenced until the middle of the following century.

The text that produced this electric effect purports in itself to carry on for "Luther, Calvin, and Zwinglius" and the "thousands they converted from the superstitions of Rome".[75] This dangerous invocation of the protestant Reformation cannot but have alerted readers to a possible direct attack upon the Established Church. Nor can the sceptical watchword "superstition" have passed unnoticed.

Toland's thesis is couched securely within the language of "ecclesiastical history": "The primitive Clergy upon receiving Mystery, they quickly erected themselves by its assistance into a separate and political body", instituting "Sub-deacons, Readers...Popes, Cardinals, Patriarchs, Metropolitans, Archbishops, Primates, Suffragans, Archdeacons, Deans, Chancellors, Vicars, or their numerous Dependents and Retinue".[76] Herein lies the source of the explosion, even if only by implication. It is declared that (1) there was a "primitive Clergy" or true church; that (2) "Mystery" corrupted this church into (3) a fraudulent church superstructure, which (4) must tumble down once it is proved again Christianity is "not mysterious". The appeal is to a "primitive" state of affairs before Roman acceptance of Christianity by Constantine in 312 A.D. From this reasoning it is not far to Voltaire's "Crush the infamous thing"! No churchman nor self-respecting Tory could blink this open challenge, yet, paradoxically, here was a writer convinced his cause was no less than the latest and best "defence of Christianity"! Toland was of course extending his conception of a fraudulent church to Canterbury, with its "Archbishops, Primates, Suffragans, Archdeacons, Deans, Chancellors, Vicars" and the like. A Dissenter in 1696, Toland stares at the church of the Thirty Nine Articles as he would at any other neo-Royalist institution, mouthing at the Thomism of Hooker, the episcopacy of Laud, the policy of the Stuarts, the Clarendon Code.

Here also flourished the bitter fruit of the Ancients and Moderns dispute. The Moderns, permitted to examine the data of history, and since 1694 to publish them if they dared, were now responsible for *Christianity Not Mysterious*! Few cared to admit it. Locke's *Reasonableness of Christianity*, though criticized,[77] remained within the pale. When Stillingfleet insisted Locke take responsibility for

Toland's piece,[78] Locke temperamentally disowned Toland in an answer[79] which inaugurated that "controversy" best followed in the light of the Ancients and Moderns antipathy; Locke championing the latter party, and Stillingfleet the former.[80]

To support his case for a Christianity anterior to the corruptions of the early Roman Catholic Church, Toland had to defend two sub-theses; the superiority of "reason" over "authority" (hence over "mystery"), and the primacy of Christ and his Gospels over the clergy and its *sacerdotium*. Here also the Ancients and Moderns are reflected, for we have seen the fierce opposition of the former to "reason" and Gospel Christianity at Oxford,[81] that stronghold of "tradition" during the 1690s.

In defence of the first sub-thesis Toland resorted to his Latitudinarian and Arminian training: "I hope to make it appear that the use of reason is not so dangerous in religion as it is commonly represented".[82] This is by no means "rationalism", or the statement that "reason is all there is". It is, however, the insistence—to use Tillotson's words—that no argument will prove a doctrine divine "which is not clearer and stronger than the difficulties and objections against it".[83]

Toland jettisons reason and embraces authority at the last minute: "I am neither of Paul, nor of Cephas, nor of Apollos, but of the Lord Jesus Christ, who alone is the author and finisher of my Faith".[84] This is so because "there is no mystery in Christianity...can be contained in the Gospel", and so forth. Reason is thus no substitute for Faith, but a cathartic by which certain false authorities are to be purged to reveal the true, final, and "primitive" authority of the Gospels. The movement *ad fontes* is here carried to its logical conclusion; beyond the Gospels it is impossible to go. No Christian authority remains prior to their writing. That there must be *some* sort of absolute authority is acknowledged in the statement that religion cannot be private "else there would be full as many creeds as persons", hence it is "always the same, like God its Author..."[85] As to the precise number of years primitive Christianity had remained free of the taint of "mystery", Toland asserts that "the first hundred or century of years after Christ" represented the Golden Age.[86] *Nazarenus* (1717) is evidence this last remark was not lightly made, being an investigation of the "Nazarene" Christians who flourished during that same hundred years prior to the Emperor Trajan.

There is but one reference to the Toleration Act in *Christianity Not Mysterious*, cast in dialogue-form:[87]

> Parishoner: ...Lord, why don't you excommunicate the author [of *Christianity Not Mysterious*] and seize upon his books?
>
> Doctor of Divinity: Aye, sir, time was...But now it appears a man may believe according to his own sense, and not as the Church directs. There is a Toleration established you know...
>
> Parishoner: That Toleration will Doctor—
>
> Doctor of Divinity: Whist, sir, say no more of it; I am as much concerned as you can be, but it is not safe nor expedient at this time of day to find faults.

The emphasis has shifted somewhat since 1691, when the Heads of Agreement met to promote a Comprehension by way of extending the Toleration: now there is a counter-reform movement within the Establishment itself, and Toland appears more content to accept whatever Toleration there is. The contrast between the two "authorities"—a man's own "sense" and "as the Church directs"—is interesting; many English among the upper and middle classes had shifted to the former in practice, yet none before Toland had dared to state it openly in theory. The upshot was an episode even more politically significant than the text upon which it was based.

Toland's book commenced a general war between those defenders of the Church of England and those Dissenters, Whigs, and incipient "freethinkers" who sought to use the unlicensed press to expose the Anglican counter-revolutionary thrust. The Church was destined to lose this war, failing to apply the Blasphemy Act of 1698 in proposed censures of Toland and Bishop Gilbert Burnet in 1702: when the censures passed the Lower House of Convocation, lawyers informed the Upper House that full passage would incure a praemunire, 25 Henry VIII, according to precedents set down in 1689, the very year of the Toleration. In any case, the Whig Upper House was unwilling to censure its fellow member Burnet merely to please the Tory majority below. Deprived of legal power, and legally if ungraciously committed to the Toleration Act, the Church majority fell back upon its formidable extra-legal powers of social ostracism. Church was a powerful political entity during the Revolution Settlement; not only because of certain bishops in the Lords, but also due to the staunch reliability of the lower clergy in getting out the vote during triennial elections. Toland, with Burnet, made a laughing stock of Convocation, but his future chances for a political career in parliament were ruined.

The real issue in the storm over *Christianity Not Mysterious*, not clear until the 1702 debate, was thoroughly involved: its factors included freedom of the press, legal ramifications of the Toleration Act, the reputations of Locke and other Moderns, Whig and Tory religious ideology, the decline of morals since the Restoration, and more. The deepest blood drawn by the young man's outrageous book concerned its relevance to the King's title and to the Stuart political theory of Divine Right and Passive Obedience; that is, to the issues later made evident during the Sacheverell Affair, 1710–1712, when the conservative right—the army of reaction—publicly challenged the Glorious Revolution for the last time. We find hints of this deepmost wound in the animadversions and pulpiteering of certain politically sensitive clergy.[88] Later, in 1699, our harrassed Toland was fiercely engaged and impugned by one Offspring Blackall, later a bishop under Queen Anne, against whom John defended himself exclaiming that the clergyman's attacks were "merely rationalizing the political theory of Passive Obedience".[89] These embittered reactions in combination with Toland's coffeehouse oratory[90] and his Whig publishing activities during the late 1690s (Holles' *Memoirs*, Sidney's *Discourses*, Milton's *Life*, Harrington's *Oceana*) tell us that more was intended within *Christianity Not Mysterious* than a scholarly excursus into Christian theology.

Pantheism: End of the First Phase

In 1697 Toland, notorious, broke publicly with the noble cause of Dissent. The religious first wave in the development of his Pantheism[91] had ebbed away. For the time being, he had said what he had

to say concerning the Toleration and its ever more tedious permutations. Fighting for Dissent, he had gone beyond the Dissenting
position. We first notice the rift in his expulsion from Leyden, in
1693, when Calvinist authoritarianism among the Arminians suddenly offended him. In the following declaration of "a latitude" and
of a general protestantism, excerpted from *An apology for Mr. Toland*
(1697), Toland writes in the third person:[92]

> ...he [Toland] will never deny but the real simplicity
> of the Dissenter's worship, and the seeming equality
> of their discipline (into which, being so young, he
> could not distinctly penetrate) did gain extraordin-
> arily upon his affections, just as he was newly
> delivered from the insupportable yoke of the most
> pompous and tyrannical policy that ever enslaved
> mankind, under the name or shew of religion. But,
> when greater experience...had a little ripened his
> judgment, he easily perceived that differences were
> not so wide as to appear irreconcileable; or at least
> that men,who were found Protestants on both sides,
> should barbarously cut one anothers throats, or
> indeed give any disturbance to the society around
> them: and as soon as he understood the late heats
> and animosities did not totally (if at all) proceed from
> a concern with meer religion, he allowed himself a
> latitude in several things that would have been a
> matter of scruple to him before. That his travels
> increased, and the study of ecclesiastical history
> perfected this disposition, wherein he continues to
> this hour; for whatever his own opinion of those
> differences be, yet he finds so essential an agreement
> between the French, Dutch, English, Scotch, and
> other Protestants, that he is resolved never to lose
> the benefit of an instructive discourse in any of their
> churches upon that score; and it must be a civil not
> a religious interest that can engage him against any
> of these parties; not thinking all their private no-
> tions, wherein they disagree, worth disturbing, much
> less endangering, the peace of a nation.

Toland seldom draws closer to the future 18th century Enlightenment than in this passage. He has separated religion from civil affairs in the modern manner, relegating religion to individual conscience inside a non-political community of protestant churches, branding all religious disturbances between protestants as political in motivation. It was this realization that inevitably shifted his concerns away from theology and worship toward public morality and civil liberties. His interest is now explicitly "civil", "the peace of the nation". Genuine religion, he now maintains, transcends the purely English civil interest in a vast meta-community called "Protestantism". In this intensely personal solution to the Toleration problem, Toland's interest in religion thus temporarily subsides.

Before leaving the topic of the Toleration, however, it is important to compare Toland again with Chillingworth, who much earlier had championed the notion of a common "protestantism".[93] Toland's advance upon Chillingworth lies in this: whereas Chillingworth sought to reconcile Puritans and Royalists, Toland looked forward to a day when all the non-Catholic nations of Europe would be so reconciled. Whereas Chillingworth was conscious of civil war, Toland slowly had become aware of William III's attempts to marshall protestant Europe against Catholic France. In sympathy with William III (as with anyone warring against Catholicism), Toland's travels had taught him that William's cause was hopeless unless all disruptive quarrelling among European protestants came to a halt. Behind Toland's Dissenting experience loomed the spectre of William's first war with France. It is in this new context, then, not in that of traditional latitudinarian thought, that we must interpret Toland's grandiose yearning for "an agreement between the French, Dutch, English, Scotch, and other Protestants".

CHAPTER I

NOTES

1. Daniel Defoe, *Review*, VI, 410b.

2. John Toland, *Reasons for Naturalizing the Jews*, London, 1713.

3. There are six "lives" of Toland: (1) *An Historical Account of the Life and Writings of the late eminently famous Mr. John Toland. By one of his most intimate friends*, London, 1722. (2) *Some Memoirs of the Life and Writings of Mr. John Toland: In a letter to S.B.L. 26 May, 1722., Prefixed to The Miscellaneous Works of John Toland* (Pierre Des Maizeaus, editor posthumous), London, 1747. (3) J.L. Mosheim, *De vita, fatis, et scriptis Joannis Tolandi Commentatio* added to the 2nd edition of his *Vindiciae antiquae Christianorum disciplinae, adversus celeberrimi viri Jo. Toland, Hiberni, Nazarenum*, 1722. (4) *An historical account of the life of Mr. John Toland. An exact catalogue of Mr. Toland's works.*, Part 1 of *The Theological and Philological works of the late Mr. John Toland*, London, Printed and sold by W. Mears, 1732. (5) *An Abstract of the Life of the Author*, Prefixed to *A Critical History of the Celtic Religion and Learning*, London, 1740. (6) Andrew Kippis, entry *Toland* in the *Biographia Britannica*, London, 1751, pp. 3965–3977.

4. Compliments to K.G. Feiling's *History of the Tory Party* remain George F. Sensabaugh's *That Grand Whig Milton*, Stanford, 1952, and Caroline Robbins' the *Eighteenth Century Commonwealthman*, Cambridge, Mass., 1961. Thomas Babington Macaulay's *History of England From The Accession Of James II* remains standard for the decade of the 1690s, supplemented by G.N. Clark, *The Later Stuarts, 1660–1714*, Oxford, 1934, and David Ogg, *England in*

the Reigns of Charles II, James II, and William III, Oxford, 1955. Gilbert Burnet's History of His Own Time, Oxford, 1833 (6v.) is a contemporary account by the Whig bishop who stood censure before Convocation with Toland in 1702. J.P. Kenyon's, "The Earl of Sunderland and the King's Administration, 1693–1695", Bibliog. of Brl. Hist. R71:576–602 O '56 is an investigation into the policy of reconciliation between Whig and Tory prior to the rise of Robert Harley in 1698. The best introduction to the Toleration is Norman Sykes' Church and State in XVIII Century England, Cambridge, 1934, the introductory chapters. See also below, N. 27, p. 69 concerning the Namier school.

5. Many books and articles relate Toland to the Enlightenment, but the following illustrate his recent re-emergence: Roger Emerson, English Deism, 1670-1755, unpublished doctoral dissertation, History of Ideas, Brandeis University; John Hunt, Religious Thought in England, Vol. 11, London, 1871; G.V. Lechler, Geschichte des englische Deismus, Stuttgart, 1841; E. Sayous, Les deistes anglais, principalement depuis Toland jusqu'a Chubb, Paris, 1882; Leslie Stephen, English Thought in the Eighteenth Century, Vol. 1, London, 1876; F.H. Heinemann, "John Toland and the Age of Reason", Bibliotheque des Archiv. die Philosophie, 1950 (4), 35–66. Also the Einleitung (1–53) to the German translation of Christianity Not Mysterious by Leopold Zcharnack in Studien zur Geschichte des neuren Protestantismus, 3 Quellenheft, 1908. Interest in Toland resurged anew after Giancarlo Carabelli's Tolandiana was published at Firenze (1975), answering F.H. Heinemann's call in the latter's Prolegomena. Since then a Toland industry has sprung up in Italy, and, to some extent, in Germany as well. In English, we note two major studies: John Toland and the Deist Controversy by Robert E. Sullivan, Cambridge, Mass., 1982, and John Toland: His Methods, Manners and Mind by Stephen H. Daniel, Montreal, 1987. The card catalogue at Tübingen University, due largely to a monumental project in Christian thought and criticism under Professor Heiko Oberman's direction, has kept up steadfastly with the growing list of Tolandian addenda, desiderata and subtrahenda. A third study in English, Margaret C. Jacob's The Newtonians and the English Revolution, 1689-1726, concentrates heavily on Toland in more ancillary fashion (Ithaca, 1976).

6. See Elisha Smith to Thomas Hearne, MS. Rawlinson, C. 146 f. 17, London, 23 January, 1706. 1706 was the year Toland became an Anglican.

7. F.H. Heinemann, "John Toland and the Age of Reason", pp. 36–39. Also John T. McNeill, *History and Character of Calvinism*, New York, 1954, pp. 364–365. The former links Toland to London Presbyterianism; the latter is a general description of the Heads of Agreement.

8. John T. McNeill, *History and Character of Calvinism*, pp. 262–263, on Arminius at Leyden University.

9. The standard on the Latitude Men remains John Tulloch, *Rational Theology in England in the XVIIth Century*, 2 Vols., London, 1874. His documentation is convincing. See Vol. 1, p. 72 *et seq.*

10. F.H. Heinemann quotes the following in "John Toland and the Age of Reason", p. 40, from the Bodleian Ballard Collection of MSS. V 26 (old foliation), claiming Edmund Gibson, Bishop of London under Walpole, as author: "He [Toland] was born in France, of an Irish father and a French mother: brought up a Papist till ten or 12 years of age..."

11. F.H. Heinemann, "John Toland and the Age of Reason", pp. 37–42.

12. This document, quoted in all biographies, was probably among his papers at the time of his death in Putney, 1722.

13. G.N. Clark, *The Later Stuarts, 1660–1714*, p. 148.

14. The Society for the Propogation of the Gospel in Foreign Parts was founded in 1701.

15. The still-flourishing Society for the Promotion of Christian Knowledge was parent organization to the missionary movement, founded one year before its offshoot.

16. Toland, *The Memorial of the State of England*, 1705, comes out against Comprehension in defense of the Toleration, joining moderate Whig opinion to Harley's policy of reconciliation, thereby balancing Tory attacks on the Toleration with Dissenting attempts to expand it.

17. G.N. Clark, *The Later Stuarts, 1660–1714*, pp. 148–150, sees the Heads of Agreement as a counter-attack by Dissent against the defeat of Comprehension.

18. The burden of Thomas Hooker's *Laws of Ecclesiastical Polity* is pure neo-Thomism within the context of the Thirty Nine Articles; Latitude Men conjoined this text with Arminian arguments to sieze upon a compromise between Nature and Grace, hence their centrist "latitude".

19. The intellectual history of this division resulting in Separatism has been evaluated by Sandra Rudnick, *From Created to Creator; Conceptions of Human Nature and Authority in 16th Century England*, unpublished doctoral dissertation, History of Ideas program, Brandeis University, 1963.

20. William Chillingworth's *Religion of Protestants* (1637) initiated this, so important to Toland's politics.

21. The Salem witch trials in the Massachusetts Bay Colony expended much of this former intensity after 1692; Richard Mather's leadership of London Independency, in its antagonism to Presbyterianism, reflects it best from 1690 through 1694. See John T. McNeill, *The History and Character of Calvinism*, pp. 364–365.

22. Roger Emerson's definition of deism, based on George Berkeley's understanding in the *Alciphron*, centers around "naturalism", or the substitution of an absolute Nature for the Thomist ontology of Nature and Grace in combination. *English Deism, 1670-1755, passim*. Toland avoids the pitfall, though consensus of opinion follows Berkeley in the belief that he did not. Toland is more akin to Arthur Bury, whose *The rational Deist satisfy'd by a just account of the Gospel* (an enlargement of his *The Naked Gospel*

(1690)), printed in 1703, joins deist arguments with Gospel protestantism in a third, Liberal-Christian stance.

23. Peter Browne, *Letter in Answer to a Book entitled Christianity Not Mysterious*, London, 1697, pp. 172–173.

24. G.R. Cragg, *The Church and the Age of Reason, 1648–1789*, London, 1960, p. 61.

25. F.H. Heinemann, "John Toland and the Age of Reason", pp. 37–38.

26. Toland goes beyond Locke's position in the latter's book of this title, published 1695; broadly, the difference lies in Locke's maintaining separation of the two powers, one natural and the other supernatural, in comparison with Toland's collapsing them into an essential immanence, common to both.

27. Locke's *Reasonableness of Christianity* (1695) was systematic insofar as it sought to reconcile the Gospels with natural reason.

28. The cases of Bury and Williams attest to the common rationalism shared by Latitudinarian Anglicans and Arminian Presbyterians during the seventeenth century. The Gospel movement amounts to a virtual coalescence of these two related strands of English thought.

29. See J.H. Allen, *Unitarianism Since the Reformation*, New York, 1894, pp. 139–143; also E.M. Wilbur, *A History of Unitarianism*, Cambridge, Mass., 1952, Vol. 11, p. 226. Though there is no logical connection between antitrinitarianism and Gospel Christianity, both are part of a drive toward simplification of the Faith. Arthur Bury is held by Wilbur to have reduced Christianity to two maxims—"believe and repent"—in which the Trinity had no place. Attacks on the Trinity were surely political, as was the return to the Gospels; High Anglicanism depended on trinitarian dogma to help keep the Toleration in hand; all Dissenters under the Toleration had to swear to it. Arianism and Socinianism are logically connected to Unitarianism by their anti-trinitarianism, but not all Arians were

Unitarians in the early 1690s, for Firmin's movement had not yet formed a separate church. See Roland N. Stromberg, *Religious Liberalism in Eighteenth Century England*, Oxford, 1954, Chapter IV.

30. Leslie Stephen, *English Thought in the Eighteenth Century*, I, p. 111: "Christianity is being gradually transmuted by larger infusions of rationalism".

31. Toland's attack is in his "A Catalogue of Books", (attached to *Amyntor*) London, 1699.

32. "Established Church" means that of the Clarendon Code as amended by the Toleration, descended from the passage of the Thirty Nine Articles in 1664.

33. The Locke-Stillingfleet controversy, begun over the terms "reason" and "mystery", soon devolved into a discussion concerning the Trinity. Defenders of the Gospels appeared to Stillingfleet *eo ipso* Unitarians. Edward Stillingfleet, *Discourse in Vindication of the Doctrine of the Trinity*, London, 1696.

34. For the fundamental, general treatment, see Paul Hazard, *The European Mind: The Critical Years (1680–1715)*, New Haven, 1953; Frank Manuel, *The Eighteenth Century Confronts the Gods*, Cambridge, Mass., 1959. Two monographs of importance are L.P. Courtines, *Bayle's Relations with England and the English*, New York, 1938, and Norman L. Torrey, *Voltaire and the English Deists*, New Haven, 1930. C.M. Crist's *The Dictionnaire philosophique portatif and the French Deists*, Brooklyn, 1934, is a supplement to Torrey. Two articles are noteworthy: Rosalie Colie's "Spinoza and the Early English Deists", *Journal of the History of Ideas*, XX, 1, Jan. 1959, pp. 23–46; Christopher Dawson, "The Historic Origins of Liberalism", *Review of Politics*, 16(3), 1954, pp. 267–282.

35. This aspect remains to be investigated with any clarity; R.F. Jones, *Ancients and Moderns*, 2nd ed., St. Louis, 1961.

36. Rosalie Colie, "Spinoza and the Early English Deists", relies heavily on Matthias Earbury's pamphlet, *Deism examined and*

confuted, London, 1697. Spinoza's book, Earbury maintains, turns its reader into "a perfect Deist", p. 3.

37. Frank Manual, *The Eighteenth Century Confronts the Gods*, *passim*, treats of Bayle, Van Dale, Toland, Graevius, Bekker, Le-Clerc, and Fontenelle as a "circle". The reason this group has been long ignored is the philological basis of its learning, he says, imposing and befuddling to most modern scholars.

38. Ernst Cassirer, *Philosophy of the Enlightenment*, Princeton, 1951, p. 206. Pierre DesMaizeaux, editor of the *Dictionnaire* in England, was Toland's editor-posthumous as well. Bayle cites Toland in the 1703 and 1710 editions of the *Nouvelles*. Cassirer believes the *Dictionnaire* devoted itself initially to continuing Father Richard Simon's work; Simon, a fountain of the "Commonwealth of Learning", is cited by Toland in several places. Descent from Spinoza was avoided, however.

39. For example, Toland to Graevius, Van Dale, and Leibniz in his *Miscellaneous Works*, 1747, pp. 331–337, 383–402; Toland also corresponded much with a German nobleman, Baron Hohendorf, concerning *arcana literaria*.

40. Paul Hazard, *The European Mind: The Critical Years (1680-1715)*, *passim*.

41. See Macaulay, *History of England*, 2, pp. 270–271. He says of Low and High Church that "Indeed the line which separated them deviated very little from the line which separated the Whigs and the Tories". As Dissent could never reconcile itself to High Church, Macaulay develops his *History* according to the assumption that a Tory and a Dissenter were as oil to vinegar; true until a reconciliation party of "King's Servants" under Robert Harley rose in 1697. Dissenters were Whigs.

42. Jean LeClerc, *Bibliotheque Universelle et Historique*, Tome XXIII, p. 505.

43. F.H. Heinemann, "John Toland and the Age of Reason," pp. 41–42.

44. Toland, *Miscellaneous Works*, 11, pp. 331–337.

45. Lovelace Collection, Bodleian Library; see F.H. Heinemann, "John Toland and the Age of Reason", p. 41.

46. F.H. Heinemann, "John Toland and the Age of Reason", pp. 41–42.

47. The standard biography of Locke has been until recently H.R. Fox-Bourne, *Life of John Locke*, London, 1876. Locke spent two years with Furly, and a considerable time at Leyden.

48. L.P. Courtines, *Bayle's Relations with England and the English*, pp. 148–151.

49. His *Adeisidaemon* (1709) tangentially attacks Bayle for alleged slights upon Livy.

50. Norman L. Torrey, *Voltaire and the English Deists*, pp. 199-200.

51. *Ibid.*, p. 15: "*Christianity Not Mysterious* clearly and emphatically marks the beginning of English 18th century critical deism".

52. The arguments of Luigi Salvatorelli, in "From Locke to Reitzenstein" support this allegation of systematic bias. *Harvard Theological Review*, XXII, 4, October 1929, pp. 263–369; see especially pp. 263–264.

53. See Toland, *Apology* (1697), *passim*.

54. See below, pp. 17–18.

55. Locke's *Discourse on Miracles* (1706) and Newton's religious works are far more conservative than those of the deists, in startling contrast to their modernity in epistemology and science.

56. Save for John Hunt, *Religious Thought in England*, 1871, and J.M. Robertson, *A Short History of Freethought*, 2nd edition,

London, 1906. The opinions of Stephen have oversimplified Toland's role and contribution, usually in one or the other of these
directions.

57. David Patrick, "Two English Forerunners of the Tübingen
School: Thomas Morgan and John Toland", *Theological Review*, LIX,
October 1877, pp. 562–603; the anonymous author of "The English
Freethinkers", *Theological Review*, V, November 1864, p. 496ff;
Leopold Zscharnack, *Einleitung* to *Christianity Not Mysterious*,
1908.

58. The burden of Patrick's "Two English Forerunners of the
Tübingen School" (see n. 57) is that Toland was ground up and
transmuted by the Halle theologians under Semler into grist for the
mill of the great Christian Baur and certain of his pupils; Harnack,
for example.

59. "Liberal theology" is ambiguous, blurring several stages of
meaning and growth; it stands mainly for the beginning of the
present de-mythologization of Christianity begun by certain Tübingen Hegelians, in which the quest for the "historical" Jesus, Paul,
John and others was begun, as in Harnack's *Dogmatics*.

60. Toland, *Miscellaneous Works*, II, pp. 292–294.

61. This we infer (1) from Furly's introduction of Toland to
Locke, dated August, 1693 (above p. 12), and the acquaintanceship
of the two some time prior to 1696. Locke to Molyneux in 1697
(*Works*, Vol. IX, London, 1823, pp. 421–431) mentions Toland
entered "my chamber" but not "my heart and affections".

62. Toland, *Miscellaneous Works*, Vol. 1, p. 2.

63. See Edward Foxe, *De vera differentia*, 1534.

64. Reprinted in Toland, *Miscellaneous Works*, Vol. II, pp. 28–
47.

65. There is that emphasis in Toland on Cicero so as to suspect
the former of patterning his life on the latter.

66. Toland, *Miscellaneous Works*, Vol. II, p. 295.

67. *Ibid.*, p. 309.

68. *Ibid.*, p. 312, emphasis added.

69. *Ibid.*, pp. 312–313.

70. Toland, *Apology* (1697), p. 24.

71. Toland, *Miscellaneous Works*, p. 302. This precise characterization of "deism" by one supposed to be an arch-deist has long been overlooked.

72. Toland revives the Stoic epistemology of the "common notions", (of *Synderesis*) in *Christianity Not Mysterious*; reason is a blending of divine and animal, not only noetic but moral in the union; a "moral sense" theory of knowledge.

73. Toland, *Miscellaneous Works*, Vol. II, pp. 303–304.

74. *Ibid.*, p. 305.

75. Toland, *Christianity Not Mysterious*, p. 176.

76. *Ibid.*, p. 170.

77. Toland, *Miscellaneous Works*, Vol. II, p. 315.

78. Edward Stillingfleet, *Discourse in Vindication of the Doctrine of the Trinity*, London, 1696.

79. Locke, *Letter to the Bishop of Worcester*, London, 1697.

80. Locke accepted Stillingfleet's scholastic terminology, then bested his opponent. Stillingfleet is said to have died from mortification. See H.O. Christopherson, *Bibliographical Introduction to the Study of John Locke*, Oslo, 1930.

81. Above, pp. 16–19.

82. Toland, *Christianity Not Mysterious*, Preface, viii.

83. Quoted by Leslie Stephen from Tillotson's *Sermons*, Vol. 1, p. 225, in *English Thought in the Eighteenth Century*, Vol. 1, p. 78. Toland's book was dedicated to this famous Latitude Man.

84. Toland, *Christianity Not Mysterious*, Preface, xxviii.

85. *Ibid.*, p. xiii.

86. *Ibid.*, p. 168 ff.

87. *Ibid.*, p. 113 f.

88. Blackall was translated in 1706, much to Whig disgust. Browne became an Irish bishop. Toland said of Browne the latter's attacks on *Christianity Not Mysterious* "made him a bishop".

89. Toland, *Amyntor* (1699), conclusion.

90. William Molyneaux to John Locke, Locke's *Works*, Vol. IX, p. 421.

91. Above, pp. 1–4.

92. Toland, *Apology* (1697), pp. 18–19. Leopold Zscharnack thinks this passage the key to all Toland's works (*Einleitung* to *Christianity Not Mysterious*, p. 4), whereas F.H. Heinemann focuses on the first of the *Letters to Serena* (1704) ("John Toland and the Age of Reason", pp. 42–46). The *Apology* is important: the present writer sees in it an end of the first phase of Tolandian "pantheism".

93. Above, p. 6.

CHAPTER II

CIVIL LIBERTIES

If *Christianity Not Mysterious* sums up the initial religious phase of Toland's pantheistic system, *Anglia Libera* (1701) concludes its initial secular phase. We have split into two the battle-cry "Religious Toleration and Civil Liberty!", plotting toleration up to 1696, then civil liberty from 1696 to 1701. This is not artificial, for in fact, with only one exception, Toland's writing is religious in emphasis through 1696, and secular in emphasis between 1697 and 1701. Only in *Amyntor* (1699) and, to some extent, the *Life of Milton* (1698), are matters such as Toleration, church government, and ecclesiastical history even reintroduced. The storm raised by *Christianity Not Mysterious* had broken over its author's head. It was wise to let it subside for a time. When the altercation with Blackall occurred in 1699, Toland's notoriety took yet another bound. When he arrived in Hanover with *Anglia Libera* under his arm in late summer, 1701, he was something of a celebrity.[1]

Accepted as "the most extreme for toleration" by 1705, Toland was known earlier to have also been perhaps the most extreme for the fortunes of the Whig party. Only John Tutchin, future editor of the *Observator*, slain in front of Westminster at the time of the 1707 Church riots, was perhaps the more radical.[2] Toland's Whiggism proves as complex as his religious free-thought; both were adaptive to a complex and unstable period of history. It is for this reason that a study of Toland, from a peculiar and interesting angle, is a study of the Revolution itself. Locke's *Two Treatises of Government*, so important to the Whig imagination after 1714, had not yet been canonized; Tutchin, Trenchard,[3] and Molesworth[4] were sporadic in output. Only Toland, whose impressive editions of Holles, Sidney, and Harrington stood next to his *Life of Milton* in the course of this period, seemed Whig and unpredictable enough for the events of the day. His appointment by William III to Lord Macclesfield's train as it proceeded to Hanover in 1701 attests to his momentary significance in the party structure. Though his fortunes sank following the death of William and the accession of Queen Anne, he was, until this moment, someone to watch. Attached from the beginning to the influential Robert Harley,[5] Toland gave every sign of ascendancy. The untimely death of William III was the fateful turn which made it necessary for him to lay aside politics for the consolations of philosophy. Haunted always by the desire to play a significant role in the affairs of state, he was never able to regain his initial patronage.

Rise of the Fourth Estate[6]

The lapsing of the Licensing Act in 1694 created the "institution" of Grub Street. Astute politicians were quick to seize advantage of the possibilities for propaganda afforded by the change. The careers of Toland, Defoe, and Swift depended largely on this development. All were employed at one time or another by the enigmatic Robert Harley, without any indication they were aware of each other's names on the Harleian payrolls. Each represented a divergent position on Harley's own political spectrum, enabling the ubiquitous "trickster" to assume whatever public posture he might.[7] Though creatures of the professional politician, they have now to be conceded a political role of no small significance. The impact of Defoe's *True Born Englishman*, Davenant's *True Picture of a Modern Whig*, Toland's *Memorial of the State*, and Swift's *The Conduct of the Allies* is a matter of record.

Toland was quickest to publish under the new dispensation, bringing out *The Death of Attilius Regulus* at Oxford (1634), a translation of Davanzanti Bostichi's *Discourse on Coins* (1696),[8] and, in that same year, *Christianity Not Mysterious*. The enormous sales of *Christianity Not Mysterious* established a working relationship between author, printer, and bookseller. By all indications, however, the financial return for the author was a poor one,[9] still it was more than compensated for by possibilities for notoriety and influence. Before the death of William III it is certain Toland was writing for Harley and the Third Earl of Shaftesbury,[10] and it is probable that the already fabulously wealthy Duke of Newcastle (and equally wealthy Sir Robert Clayton) were among certain of his new-found patrons.[11] Although a few politicians, such as Lord Somers and Robert Walpole, preferred to do their own writing and publishing,[12] the less energetic and more impatient had sooner or later inevitably established connections with Grub Street. It was not long before Tutchin, Davenant, and Defoe were writing, editing, and publishing serial-magazines for the Whig and Tory party machinery.[13] Toland longed to do the same, but never succeeded in raising enough money for a journal,[14] nor indeed for other perhaps more worthy literary undertakings.[15]

Part and parcel of a writer's popularity under these conditions was the list of patrons he was known to represent. Toland was read in King William's reign because readers *knew* his patrons, hence, sought to know the views that they wished made publicly known. The use of the "dedication" in a pamphlet was precisely to render one's patron's name exquisitely clear. Public relations campaigning was nothing new in the seventeenth century.

Toland's output in this Golden Age of propaganda was not inconsiderable; in 1697 *The Militia Reformed*; in 1698 an edition of Sidney's *Discourses on Government*; *The Memoirs of Denzill, Lord Holles*, also edited; *The Danger of Mercenary Parliaments*, written for Shaftesbury; *A Letter to a Member of Parliament*;[16] in 1688–89 *The Life of Milton*; in 1699 *Amyntor*; in 1700 *The Art of Governing by Parties* (buttressing Harley's current policy); the poem *Clito*; the truly splendid folio edition of Harrington's *Oceana*; in 1701 *Anglia Libera* and *Propositions for Uniting the Two East India Companies*; in 1702, *Paradoxes of State*. Each publication tells us something concerning its author's civil liberties predilections under the new constitution. What Milton had heralded years before in *Areopagitica*[17]—the now-realized freedom of the press—gave without cost to intrepid journalists a readership envied by many a practicing politician.

The anonymous *Letter to a member of parliament, showing, that a restraint on the press is inconsistent with the Protestant religion* (1698) has been ascribed to Toland's *animus*. Style, familiar praise of Locke and Burnet, and an attack upon standing armies all tend to re-enforce this guesswork. The central argument—that the only excuse for licensing is blasphemy—was an implicit concession to the violent Tory reaction against a free press, then at its height, and to recent passage of the Blasphemy Act (1698).[18] In view of the effect engendered by *Christianity Not Mysterious* a year or so earlier, concessions were in order. The argument of the title, however, had been aggressive rather than conciliatory. Invocation of a universal "protestantism" is the strongest indication of Tolandian authorship,[19] and sudden linking of this concept to Whig insistence for a free press was a most interesting development.

As we have seen, Toland's argument in the *Apology* (1697) for "latitude" being "so essential an agreement between French, Dutch, English, Scotch, and other Protestants" implied, in the negative, a resolution "never to lose the benefit of...any of their churches", but did not imply an attack "against any of these parties". Licensing or censorship favoring the Anglican minority—a "private interest"— was therefore inconsistent with "protestantism", the general religion.

The interesting development was Toland's apparent identification of "protestantism" with this time-honored canon of the Whig party. For Toland, latitudinarians were now Whigs, and Whigs latitudinarians. Whigs and latitude-men professed the freedom of the press in the manner of *Areopagitica*, whereas Tories and Anglicans traditionally had insisted upon licensing and censorship. Passage of the Blasphemy Act in 1698 was less a Tory attack upon blasphemy than an oblique foray against the unlicensed press. Everyone knew this. There is no greater indication that the Whigs were the party of revolution than this reactionary subterfuge to curtail the press. Convocation's attempts to prosecute Toland and censure Burnet in 1702 were but a continuation of this feral aggressiveness. Failure during Convocation's proceedings was a turning point: thereafter the Tories perforce must organize their own press although they were running seriously behind. The careers of Davenant and Swift begin with this decision, post-dating by almost a decade the careers of the prominent Whig writers.

The arguments in *A Letter to a member of parliament* are reiterated in a passage we now know to be Toland's, the one concerning *Areopagitica* in his *Life of Milton* (1698–99).[20] Note the rhetoric of white-hot Whiggery:

> And certainly, there's nothing deserves more wonder
> than that any wise People should suffer a small
> number of injudicious Fellows, always ready to

suppress whatever is not relish'd by their own Sect or
the Magistrate, to be the sole Masters and Judges of
what should or should not be printed; that is, of what
the Nation is to know, speak, or understand: and I
need not hesitate to affirm such a Power in the hands
of any Prince (the Licensers being always his Creatures) is more dangerous even than a standing army
to Civil Liberty; nor in point of Religion is it inferior
to the Inquisition.[21]

There is evidence Toland was the first to have planned a literary
journal under the new freedom to speak out. In his *Project of a
Journal Intended to be published weekly* (1704–5)[22] he tells us "Tis
very surprizing that something of this nature has not been thought
of before in our country, or, if any had formed such a design, that it
was never yet executed". True, the journal he had in mind was to
have been no mere party organ—his models were Bayle's *Nouvelles*
and LeClere's *Bibliotheque Universelle* rather than *Heraclitus Ridens*—
still its reason for existence was purportedly to promote "the Law
and the Gospel";[23] that is, to reaffirm the twin causes of "Toleration
and Civil Liberty".

An important, ironical passage from *Project of a Journal* gives us
perhaps the best expression of Whig opinion concerning press
freedom:

Our Laws, it's true, enforce the observation of moral
and social Duties, and tis acknowledged, even beyond the seas, that our Divines are the best Preach-
ers in the world. But as all Duties come not directly
under the cognizance of the Laws, nor all the different circumstances of any Duty whatsoever; so the
Magistrate is but half obey'd by those, who can elude
the intention of the Legislators, either in point of time
or place, or in any particular not foreseen at the
beginning: and he's often not at all obey'd, by such as
know no other reason of the Law, but only the
authority that has given it a sanction, which they
regard as a meer force, that might as well have
appointed the contrary...But when these very men

> perceive...that the good of all persons indifferently is
> the scope of the Laws...then a more cheerful and
> sincere obedience will be yielded by them to the
> Laws, and the Magistrate be better imployed in
> distributing honor than inflicting of shame. This is
> likewise as true of the Divines...[24]

In brief, Whig political theory held a free press necessary on
grounds of political *education*, scorning "passive obedience" while
appealing to the sure knowledge of issues daily set forth. Thus
dignified, intrepid Grub Street denizens seriously conceived of their
calling as little less than a fourth estate, and a new power in the
political universe, which, indeed, it had become.

A Whig Party Crisis

Near the end of his life, writing about Shaftesbury,[25] Toland hazarded the opinion that the Revolution, "in itself the best cause in the
world", had been subverted and corrupted from within during the
reigns of William III and Queen Anne. The villains were not Tories so
much as "apostate Whigs". A former Junto leader, Halifax, was
singled out in particular.[26] Sometime before William III's death,
Shaftesbury, leader of the "Old" or "Real Whigs", had been forced by
ill health to resign his power to certain opportunist "Modern Whigs"
of the cabinet. The crisis resulting in this splintering has been until
quite recently imperfectly recorded.[27]

The source for the confusion had been a nagging predilection to
think of the Whigs and Tories of the 1690s as a "two party system".
In such a system the majority in Commons and the Lords, alongside
its cabinet ministers, must of force face a minority "opposition", as
indeed later was to be nearly always the case. During the dark days
of Whiggism, from 1698 until 1700, however, the situation proved
radically different. Government was paralyzed by factions; ministers of the Junto, Williamites, High Tories, moderate Whigs and
Tories under Harley, Old Whigs. The Junto party machinery was
good enough for its time, but hapless after 1698 because consistently unable to muster its majority. The "opposition", a rag-tag of
factions assembled by Harley,[28] brought the Junto down casting

suspicion upon its honesty and splitting Whig membership. The crucial alignment emerged as a coalition of Williamites; Junto or Modern Whigs as against another one of Tories, Old Whigs, and Harleian moderates. The latter side came gradually to predominate. King William, His government threatened by what seemed to him a congenital, even perverse English ingratitude, threatened to abdicate.[29]

Not one, but a series of issues had divided the ambitious Whigs. At bottom lurked a belief that the Junto and its adherents, after four years of governmental power, had betrayed their sacred Whig political theory while currying favor with minister Sunderland and his cabal of "Williamites".[30] This alleged clandestine interest favored government for King against Commons for purposes of mere place or personal gain. Sunderland himself, who had served James II and had survived the fallout of that King's desertion, was justifiably an object of universal distrust. In brief, Harley suddenly succeeded in pitting Old Whigs against Modern Whigs, convincing the former that the latter had been corrupted in office, and had decided to turn their coats in support of the King's incessant warmongering. Insofar as Whiggism meant nothing if not the control of King by Commons, even Old Whigs fell reluctantly in line behind their new leader. Harley, one must never forget, had himself been elected in 1688 as an ardent Whig of the country, and seemed to this extent forever trustworthy. If later he, too, was to support Queen Anne against Commons, to preserve whatever seemed to him a sacred *balance* between these two powers,[31] he was nevertheless committed, in 1698, for Commons against King William III. In 1698, the Peace of Ryswick signed, Harley deemed it at once necessary to strip this King of his wartime authority, and to bring the Throne to heel in a general way in accordance with the Bill of Rights. What now commenced was the underlying constitutional struggle of the Revolution Settlement, put off by the war of the League of Augsburg.

There is a final preliminary to be considered before coming to grips with the events of the political struggle itself, one launched by William's understandable but ill-advised attempt to keep his wartime army.[32] A division as deep as party had concomitantly arisen during the attainder proceedings against a certain Sir John Fenwick in 1696–97, resulting in an electoral war between the country squirearchy and several grandees of the realm whose interests had begun to coincide with wealthy traders of the City and a number of aspirant lawyers of the Temple. Without going into the affair in any detail[33] its upshot was that Whig loyalties, ruptured or badly shaken over resolution of the Fenwick episode,[34] finally split those at Court from those in the Country immediately subsequent to the elections of 1698. A "New Country Party", made up of squires, Whig *and* Tory, pledged their attack against all courtiers, placemen, standing armies, and any measures taken smacking of ministerial gerrymandering.[35] There could be no clear-cut majority in the new Commons under these conditions. With this wedge, Harley, long disassociated with party and now the leader of the squires, severed Old Whigs from Modern Whigs and decisively wrecked Sunderland's cabinet Junto. Since the days of Harrington Old Whigs conceived the franchise to have been based on the ownership of land, and this was to become the rallying cry, naturally, of the squires. Modern Whigs of the town, however,—merchants, grandees, lawyers, owners of East India Company stock—likewise naturally favored the newer franchise based on income. The Achilles heel of the party thus lay in this deep division of landed and moneyed elements and it drove the country forces, by their very principles, into the arms of the upstart Harleian "opposition". There was little confidence in the Junto; its fall was imminent.[36] Toland's "apostates", then, were assuredly Sunderland's Modern Junto Whigs yet in power at this time.

William III's Standing Army

Toland's accusations against Sunderland's "apostate Whigs" reflected a split which could not heal, but remained to be endured until the Whig Supremacy under Walpole. Embarrassment was acute: a rent in the majority might be tolerated, even understood, but a rent in the vaunted Whig political theory was the Fall of Man itself, edging on tragedy. Tories had no viable political theory after 1688; all Whigs knew this and revelled in the fact. "Divine Right and Passive Obedience" might rise again briefly to haunt England after 1710, but too much water had gone under the bridge for anything to become reinstituted in law. The genie was finally out of the bottle. Whig theory was the theory of the Revolution, and the Revolution was legally a success after 1701. All Whigs were fiercely proud of their "principles", forged during and after the Civil War.

Yet a flaw had been detected. Theory started to transcend practice. Idealists in the party were accusing its practical politicians of corruption in office and betrayal of Commons. Old Whigs, entrenched in their "principles", had had little access to wealth or favor under the new constitutional monarchy, whereas Modern Whigs, loose of "principle" but holding either office or seats in parliament, were openly finding ways to grow prominent and rich. Toland's "apostate Whigs" were Whigs grown fat and morally flabby. Ministers and placemen were especially culpable. It was no secret that office had become the quick, easy path to wealth and status.

The first, most telling indication that the Whig political theory was in trouble—descending from its Harringtonian heights in quest of the more modest Lockean plateau—occurred when Old *versus* Modern Whig writers squared off over the question of the army, in autumn, 1697. Even as Country that winter and spring had divorced itself from Court, (over the Bill for Regulating Elections) so now Old Whigs were about to divorce themselves from Moderns once the joyous message from Ryswick set bells tolling and bonfires blazing up and down the Thames. Foremost among Old Whig pamphleteers then was John Trenchard,[37] inspired by Harley and his "new country" partisans. Foremost among Modern Whig pamphleteers, however, was none other than grandee John Somers,[38] then Lord Keeper of the Great Seal and Lord Chancellor to His Majesty the King. Trenchard urged disbandment, Somers maintenance. Trenchard opposed the King, Somers supported the King. Both, in the grandiloquent Whig manner, appealed to history in defence of their respective positions; Marius and Sulla, Caesar and Augustus, Rome and Carthage, Osman and Sforza, Cressy and Poitiers, Star Chamber and Shipmoney were serially involved. Tories rubbed their hands at last at the prospect of a sudden Whig disaster. Harley had virtually ensured that disaster (and Sunderland's resignation) by proposing in a pretended spirit of compromise that a small force of regulars equal to the military establishment of 1680 he retained. This made light of both Trenchard and Somers: the former had lost a great "principle" by his motion, as the latter had failed to control the parliament for his King. Harley's motion was carried by forty votes, in the form of "a resolution pending final count". The Mutiny Act, retaining the army, was then allowed to expire in 1698, with only three hundred and fifty thousand pounds set aside for a remaining skeleton force.

A pamphlet war ensued until the following year's parliamentary resolution to reduce William III's forces to 7,000 men, all Englishmen. John Toland's *The Militia Reformed*[39] sought to mitigate the storm for liberty, law, and property which had broken over the heads of William III and his now-provisional ministers. When considered as a compromise between three contending Whig positions—those of Trenchard, Somers, and of Harley—his pamphlet must be regarded as intrepid, a remarkable piece of work. Moreover, it gives us an immediate indication of its author's approach to the party crisis. His optimistic belief in "reason"—by which he had sought previously to solve the mind-boggling problems of medieval theology and of the Toleration—again is evident in this high-flown synthesis of Whig factions.[40]

For Trenchard and the Old Whig squirearchy of the country, *The Militia Reformed* advocated the disbanding of the army as then understood, thus saving Trenchard's sanctified Whig principle opposing all "standing armies". Implicit in the full title—*The Militia Reformed, or an Easy Scheme of Furnishing England with a Constant Land Force Capable to Prevent or to Subdue any Foreign Power, to Maintain Perpetual Quiet at Home Without Endangering the Public Liberty*—was Trenchard's contention that a militia was in fact at least competent domestically, and that foreign mercenaries trained in war were a burdensome, disruptive luxury. A Harringtonian rotation-scheme[41] for training and service sounded musically to Old Whig ears. The distinction between "regulars" in the militia who were "men of property", and their "auxiliaries" who were their "servants" could not but assuage Trenchard's fury.[42] The Old Whig interest was flattered further by propositions permitting the "auxiliaries" to advance to the rank of "regular militia" if and when, one day, they too acquired property;[43] to exempt no Englishman from the draft because of titles or wealth; to pro-rate each officer's rank according to his property (and to "index" that rank if his property increased or diminished); that no person under eighteen could hold governmental posts "of honor or profit" without having served in at least two campaigns "by land or sea"; and, finally, that all foreign levies might be "auxiliary" only, and never "regular militia". This last measure satisfied the pangs of xenophobia some Old Whigs shared with Tories anent William III's Dutch Guards.

Toland now offered reassurances to Somers and the Modern Whigs, ingeniously proposing that the *cadre* of the militia be none other than that skeleton army of regulars retained by parliament following Harley's motion of 1698; that is, precisely those 7,000 officers and men left over from yesterday's war with France![44] A rigid training program involving inspections and war games was proposed at quarterly intervals each year; a force of 60,000 men was to be evenly distributed from throughout the north, middle, and west of the country based on county-wide periods of induction and dismissal; a draft, enabling the government to call on all males from ages eighteen to fifty: these recommendations,[45] taken together, purportedly scotched Somers' arguments against the effectiveness of a mere militia, should a French attack materialize on behalf of James II,[46] or any other of the exiled Stuarts.

Whether or not Toland wrote *The Militia Reformed* on a commission from Harley remains a matter of conjecture, but that Harley was pleased to see his compromise legislation defended in so ingenious a manner is proven when we consider the latter's patronage of the young Irishman from that moment forward. This patronage—in great part the burden of our story—was to prove considerable over time. Certainly Harley's was in excess of other patronage, whether that of Shaftesbury, Sir Robert Clayton, Newcastle, or Molesworth. Tolandian understanding of Tory legerdemain especially must have pleased Harley, whose idea of coalition (against the Junto) and its relation to the regal power depended upon an Old Whig-Tory *rapprochement* in terms of "country" *versus* "court". *The Militia Reformed* cleverly enlisted Tory support for a militia-army by its emphasis on land rather than money in matters of "property"; the above-mentioned exclusion of foreign levies from the "regular militia"; a remarkable passage advocating the protection of noble and landed families, stating no man ought to be required to serve abroad "during one year after his marriage"; that no family should suffer all its sons to fight abroad at once, and, finally, that an only son might never fight abroad without parental consent.[47]

Toland's Latitude Regarding Party

Reaction to *The Militia Reformed* is testimony that the curse of party
had in truth endangered civil liberties. Sunderland's advice to
William III that he now govern through the Tories under Danby,
then later through the Whigs under Somers, Montague, Orford and
Wharton had resulted in the grudging resignation of the "cabinet
maker", and in William III's alienation from Old Whigs and Harleian
moderates in the Commons. The acquiescence of "apostate Whigs"
to Sunderland's policies in the ministry and in the Lords had, when
the chips were down, resulted in schism. Not only were the floun-
dering Whigs now hopelessly divided; lines of communication and
trust quickly atrophied between Commons and its own ministers.
Harley had succeeded in reducing the army to 7,000, native-born,
on the 17th December, 1698. This broke the ministry once for all.
The admiralty was attacked on 29th March, 1699, and Orford's
resignation on 15th April threw the "apostates" into near chaos.
Approaching the end of April, Commons sent up a bill "making the
militia of this kingdom more useful". On 19th April the question of
Crown lands held by William's favorites in Ireland had been opened,
making the administration a laughing stock,[48] and providing Harley
with yet another mammoth issue with which to pillory Crown and
Court. The tide was irreversible, some Modern Whigs even deserting
their leaders to vote against the Court: "I do not see", wrote Vernon,
"how they can ever rise again".[49] William III was now isolated.

Toland's *Militia Reformed*, it may be said, played a not insignifi-
cant part in this rout. If nothing else, his account of the militia-
question brought him to the attention of Sir Robert Clayton, one of
the pre-eminent Whig town merchants, and among the wealthiest
commoners in England. The pamphlet *Modesty Mistaken* (1702),
penned by an anonymous Tory, is acidulated evidence that Toland
had the gall to place an advertisement in a daily declining acceptance of Clayton's purported offer that he sit in parliament from the
latter's pocket borough, that of Blechingly in Surrey.[50] Toland's
dedication of the magnificent *Oceana* folio to Clayton in 1700 and a
letter dated December 4, 1693,[51] establish this patron-client relationship at the very time the standing army issue was all the talk.
These facts in themselves would seem little, were it not that Sir
Robert Clayton, in 1697, had loaned William III thirty thousand

pounds for the maintenance of His Dutch Blue Guards.[52] At that time Clayton led the powerful London merchants in support of Somers and the Modern Whigs. Though it is quite possible Clayton donated his thirty thousand pounds for gain or favor, his support of Toland after publication of *The Militia Reformed* indicates a nimble coat-turning to the camp of the Old or "real" Whigs. Toland had convinced at least one important Modern Whig to cross over. Clayton's change of heart cannot but have swayed certain others to follow his example.

The question of the army concealed a nagging dilemma facing free-wheeling Whigs merchants such as entrepreneur Robert Clayton. Loyal to party and principles, they nevertheless opposed war with France, and they insisted upon a moderately strong deterrent of soldiery so as to discourage the cosmic, jesuitical ambitions of Louis XIV. In theory they concurred with Trenchard, in practice with Somers. They opposed standing armies—the bane of Stuart *and* Cromwellian rule—and they required a protectionist mercantile policy for their vast interests abroad, especially against those of England's Dutch allies! To this end they had created the Bank of England—a Modern Whig institution—and had reinstituted Cromwell's Navigation Acts. Toland's solution to this dilemma had been a strong militia, Harringtonian in composition, low in cost. Clayton appears at some point to have been won over, or he caved in, after first supporting William III. Eminent Whig historians may sneer at the impracticality of a militia;[53] the fact remains the idea was by no means impracticable at the time. Had war with France not broken out once again over the Spanish Succession, parliament's bill "making the militia of this kingdom more useful" would certainly have been realized, and the first Partition Treaty might well have forestalled the war's outbreak. No one, of course, was prepared for the death of the nine year old Elector of Bavaria,[54] least of all Louis XIV.

The disputes over the standing army unveil a pattern in Toland's political behavior. His point-of-view had emerged at once thoroughly anti-party yet thoroughly Old Whig. There is no contradiction in these two seemingly inimical conceptions, though how Old Whigs—undoubtedly a party—might remain a party yet assume the posture of anti-party requires some explanation. Obviously, the usual spectrum-thinking, whereby opposition between the extremes of left and right balanced by moderates at the center had in some sense been violated.

The Old Whig position had been first defined with reference to a so-called Tory party, then second with reference to its own offshoot, the Modern (or "apostate") Whigs. Old Whigs in 1698 thought themselves the original Whigs of the Exclusion Crisis,[55] and valued such as John Trenchard and Anthony Ashley Cooper—after 1699 Third Earl of Shaftesbury—as "favorite sons"—direct links to the party Fathers.[56] During the Exclusion Crisis these originals represented the Country as opposed to the Court interest, whereas Toryism was stained indissolubly through its long association with the Stuarts, all true Court Tories thereafter being automatically suspected of Jacobitism. It is this country interest of the original Whigs—in 1698 shared by many Tory squires—which marked off Old Whigs from Modern. Old or Real Whiggism was anti-court, anti-monarchical, constitutional. Old Whiggism yoked together Commonwealthmen and Cromwellian Republicans with supporters of the present constitutional monarchy. Supporters of Divine Right and Passive Obedience—Court Tories and later Jacobites—were "excluded". Enemies of Old Whiggism during the Revolution Settlement were not only the embittered Jacobite minority, but any and all Tories who supported the King's prerogative in individual issues as they emerged after the 1689 Bill of Rights: standing armies, place bills, triennial parliaments, the independence of the judges, whatever. As one writer puts it, the decisive struggle of the Revolution Settlement was between King and Commons,[57] each issue forcing the general and mortal showdown anew. Tories stood traditionally for the protection of King's rights, Old Whigs for the rights of Commons.

How, finally, had the Old Whigs, purportedly for purposes of place and gain, switched their allegiances to support William III on this issue or on that, compromising the long-range ideals of the party? To the Old Whigs, the have-nots of the Settlement period, this surely had jeopardized the Revolution as such. Modern Whig support of the Crown on any issue at all meant betrayal of principle. Sunderland's Junto, forced to work hand-in-glove with William III, had created this intolerable situation. Modern Whigs were therefore "deviationists", to borrow a term associated with another revolution of more recent western history. Old Whigs were "hard-line". Any Old

Whig who changed his principles on any single issue for any reason was thereby branded a "Modern Whig".

Yet Toland, now spokesman for the Old Whigs, excoriated party and had sought to pacify all factions in *The Militia Reformed*. We discover his true position, and the Old Whig position in consequence, when we ask ourselves what he was for in the Revolution, and what he was against. In answer to the first question—"What was Toland for?"—we say he was for a *latitude* enabling all save Jacobites to have their way in the matter of the army. In answer to the question "What was Toland against?" we say he was opposed to Jacobitism, which would permit the King full prerogative were He a Stuart. In 1696 Jacobites, who had never legally recognized William III, also opposed an expensive standing army, the King's defence against an invasion by their favorite.

Toland was, then, a "latitudinarian" in matters of civil liberty as well as he was in religion.[58] As an Old Whig he sought to reconcile warring factions in the name of the "revolution", even as he had previously sought to reconcile sects and Low Church within a common "protestantism", the brotherhood of all non-Catholics. For Toland, Old Whiggism meant a *latitudinarianism in politics* and it embraced Englishmen of all parties save Louis XIV's Jacobites as genuine proponents of the Glorious Revolution. Old Whigs now sought to offer the populace a broad program for purposes of keeping the faltering Revolution on a straight track as it lurched unevenly toward passage of the Act of Settlement.

The Art of Governing by Parties

Toland's political latitudinarianism is pinpointed best in two works, both dated 1701: *The Art of Governing by Parties* and *Anglia Libera*. The former is a description of English politics in negative vein, ascribing to party all the evils of the time, whether in religion, parliament, on the bench, within the ministry, or in foreign affairs. The latter is a positive complementary description in a happier mood, subsequent to the triumphant passage of the Act of Settlement. Both are important tracts for students of the period, inasmuch as they reveal with merciless clarity and in some depth the political conditions of the day.

The statement for the Revolution in *The Art of Governing* is quickly evident: "There can be no balancing in preferring a Whig to a Tory; that is, a free government to arbitrary power; the Protestant religion to Popery, England to France, and if I may add one thing more, King William to King James".[59] In concert with this secular manifesto is the latitudinarian element, elevating the good of the state above that of any party: "Twas never known that such meetings produced any good effects, where the antagonists, like so many gladiators, eagerly contend for victory, and mind nothing less than the search for truth. Each party misrepresents the other in accounts they give of their proceedings..."[60] The paradox implicit in *The Militia Reformed* is thus made explicit in *The Art of Governing*. Granted one party alone for the Revolution, Toland is thereafter opposed to any party! The art of governing by party—practiced openly by William III and Sunderland as an instance of *divida et impera* through the usual Tory machinery in 1690–94,[61] and again through bureaucratic Whigs in 1694–98—had been preeminently a Stuart invention, whereby Charles II in an earlier day had almost succeeded in dividing and conquering the entire legislative branch.[62]

After reaffirming (Chapter II, *Art of Governing*) the latitudinarian thesis of the *Apology* in which "protestantism" had nearly been wrecked by various contending churches and sects, and reasserting the undoubted truth that Charles II had attempted successfully to poison the Restoration clergy with his own aversion to presbytery, Toland proceeds to discuss civil liberties under William III with a naive candor never forgiven him in later years.

Charles II, he begins (Chapter III, *Art of Governing*), not only poisoned His clergy with talk of "presbytery"; he poisoned also His loyal Royalists with talk of "Commonwealth".[63] The upshot of this dividing and conquering in politics was now Whig *versus* Tory, and their accursed offspring. Opposed in principle to the latter, as we have seen, and convinced Tories as "the principal Agents and Instruments of the Court, ought in my opinion to be excluded out of all Trust",[64] Toland admits nonetheless that, now, "the Liberties of England are not a little beholden in this Reign to Torys"![65] Furthermore, "...the apostate Whigs of our time deserve to marked with Infamy".[66] These apparently inconsistent judgments are in fact consistent with the official Old Whig position from 1697 until 1702. Once again, the *Art of Governing* made clear and explicit what was, in *The Militia Reformed*, veiled and implicit. A new "country party" had emerged to protect landowning squires from the corrupted Whigs and unregenerate Tories of the Court. Toland was enunciating Harley's future position, that of Old Whigs and moderate Tory squires in combination. It was a heady time to be engaged.

The curse of party in parliament (Chapter IV) began with the corrupting of elections. Charles II, never content with making bishops and judges, tried to shape parliament as well, providing his pensioners with liquor and money with which to ply the local freeholders. Elections by 1700, Toland says, were "a sort of Civil War" raging in the land between two "sides": "Pensioners, Officers, and Tories on this;...Republicans, Whigs, and Dissenters on the other".[67] That these "sides" should ever develop into a "two-party system" was anathema to him, no less than the legalization of "Civil War". Much better to pass a Self-Denying or Place Bill, "so often talked of, and as often dropped every Sessions",[68] or, better, when the "House of Commons thus abounds with Officers" and "private pensioners", to abjure the Triennial Act for annual parliaments.[69] The Crown, ministers, and party managers might find annual elections at the least financially embarrassing, not to say ruinous. Should they cease trying to buy elections, sitting members in parliament would be immeasurably benefited, for "all those who buy their elections sell their votes". Much better also to abolish rotten boroughs,[70] and to create new corporations for "Leeds, Halifax, Manchester, Newbury, and Croydon", empowered to elect their own representatives.

The later Stuarts had also ruined the Bench, buying "the most stupid, immoral, and illiterate they could rake out of the Inns of Court", who were "rather Parties on the Bench than indifferent Judges". Chapter V of the *Art of Governing*[71] informs us, although Hales and some others were commendable, that "the Tories supported these Judges as long as their cruel and illegal proceedings were confined to the Whigs". Monsters such as Jeffries justified this acidulated comment. The remedy is "an Act to ascertain some fund for the salary of the Judges" giving them their independence from Crown support. Here was yet another direct reference to the future Act of Settlement, in which the "independence of the judges" clause formed its own separate landmark.

Nothing Toland wrote did his career more harm than Chapter VI of the *Art of Governing*, pertaining to the ministry. Here the "apostates" of the Junto were brought under fire, and indifferently called "Evil Counsellors, Cormorants, Bloodsuckers, and Harpies", or "Locusts in their Palaces"! Somers, Orford, and Halifax (the first two now currently under impeachment) were all but named.[72] Obviously Toland and his patrons looked upon any future "cabinet system" with as much disfavor as upon any incipient "two-party system". The ministers' trimming, their subsidization of spies and pamphleteers, their influence with the King, their deals with the Old and New East India Companies, their gerrymandering of elections, their reliance upon the King's general pardon if under impeachment by Commons; all these smacked of unscrupulousness and the abuse of public trust. That worst of all blinds—the "reason of state"—had cloaked the ministry in an aura of conspiratorial government *a la* Richelieu. The roles of Somers and Orford in the two partition treaties, ever justifiable in the eyes of the classic Whig historians, were clandestine, and contributed much in their way to the success of Harley's opposition program.[73] Fear and hatred of "reasons of state" are elaborated upon in Chapter VIII, on foreign affairs, in which the Harleian attack upon the King's favorites, notably Portland, predictably received Old Whig support.

What is the remedy for all this burgeoning corruption, Toland asks his reader?[74] It can only be, he answers, "a Parliament equally constituted". Our author has wrapped himself in the mantle of *censor* of the republic. Beginnings can be made, he asserts, through reviving the Qualifying Bill of 1697, passed in Commons but rejected in the Lords. Under this measure a residency of five hundred pounds per annum in the shires, and two hundred in the boroughs were required before one might stand for parliament. We have returned to the financial problem of free elections. Men of party might think twice before supporting straw-candidates at those prices!

Anglia Libera

Perhaps no better exposition of Harley's coalition program remains available to historians of the Settlement than *The Art of Governing by Parties*. Faced with the task of discrediting the King, yet somehow never implicating the great Savior of the constitution Himself, the book was an admirable, limning justification of the actual legislation soon to follow, the Act of Settlement. Almost every point broached in the *Art of Governing* was raised for discussion during the debates.[75] The book was itself part of a sure, deadly attack unleased upon King and Junto by the "new country party". Toland's place in the Harleian machinery seemed assured. With passage of the Act, in 1701, it fell naturally to the writer who had played such an important part in its development to herald its achievements. *Anglia Libera* (1701) is the Act's official account, clause by clause. For writing it Toland was rewarded by William III and sent to Hanover.

In the *Art of Governing* (and in *Anglia Libera*) a climax was attained in the series of editions and writings proclaiming a political program.[76] One part is purely Old Whig: the defence of liberty, religion, and property dating originally from the Exclusion Crisis. In another, however, the Old Whig point-of-view had been merged with that of the "new country party". Specific issues, arising in the 1690s, had ameliorated this admixture of political oil and vinegar. Triennial parliaments, the Fenwick assassination attempt, William III's veto of a crucial place bill in 1694, the Peace of Ryswick and the foreign danger; all these had hardened and articulated the program of the "old country party" of the first Earl of Shaftesbury and his Exclusion Whigs. The fact that William III was a near autocrat in foreign affairs and equally indulgent in domestic affairs did much to create the Harleian line, and stiffen the Act of Settlement's terms. If the original Whig interest had lost its "Modern Whigs" to the Court and to the town, it had gained its majority elsewhere by conversion of hundreds of country Tories to anti-regal principles. This new majority might admire William III in war, even in peace, but the Act of Settlement is eloquent proof it was determined his like should never rule England again. Likewise, it determined to scotch any sudden influence from the new moneyed interest in the City. The "Pensioners, Officers, and Tories" representing this newest bloc in parliament threatened the constitution through their egregious policy to throw the balance of the "King in parliament" permanently toward the King. It was an "evil design" held to have been concocted by men in high office, the so-called "ministry", at one time predominantly Tory, afterwards predominantly Whig.

There are two important meanings of the word "liberty" expressed in *Anglia Libera*. The first was traditional in Whig theory,
that of "natural rights" based on "Natural Law", a great Stoic
conception revived in Grotius for specifically modern conditions. It
is this classical conception in Sidney, Shaftesbury, and Locke
which was again set forth to justify the power of parliament against
lingering Stuart pockets of power. By this token, "Divine Right" and
"Passive Obedience" were held "unnatural" when compared with
Natural Law, hence "tyrannical" and ultimately in violation of
"natural rights". English constitutionalism was so dependent on
this premise, and the literature of the times so suffused with it that
it remains a truism to restate it here.

With the advent of Harley's "new country party", however, a new
and second sense of "liberty" begins to surface. Perhaps John
Toland was the first to herald this epiphany in the *Art of Governing
by Parties* and in *Anglia Libera*? If so, they are important books. In
this new sense, "liberty" has come to mean any person or society
generous enough to entertain opinions and actions of as many
different "parties" as intend no harm to the country when it is
considered as a whole.

We found a strong hint of this second sense in the almost
dilemmatic handling of the Whig-Tory relationship in the *Art of
Governing*. On the one hand, it was stated "there can be no
balancing in preferring a Whig to a Tory"; but on the other, it was
also stated, equally absolutely, that "the Liberties of England are not
a little beholden in this Reign to Torys". The answer to this seeming
dilemma is easily found out when we realize that Toland wrote the
Art of Governing simultaneously in two contexts; that is, Old Whig
and "new country party". An evolution of sorts had transpired. The
Whig program—soon to be enshrined in the Act of Settlement—had
enlisted Tory squires after 1697, who had crossed party lines. As
such, a new criterion had emerged by which an Englishman's
political position might be judged, unrestricted by the traditional
Whig-Tory opposition. This new, shining criterion was precisely
"*Anglia Libera*", a new understanding of "liberty", which seems to
have burst upon Toland's mind with great force in 1701. *Anglia
Libera* and the poem *Clito* this same year were paeans to
"liberty", conceived not as natural rights dependent on Natural Law,
but rather as the capacities of the "new country party", with its

parliamentary majority, to transcend and legislate above the always anticipated Whig and Tory strife.

Returning to the first conception of "liberty"—the natural rights of parliament *contra* Crown—there was little in *Anglia Libera* and nothing in the *Art of Governing* to please King William. The "liberties of parliament" were anathema to him! He had nearly abdicated in 1698 rather than stay on to rule over this ungrateful body! Yet *Anglia Libera* is nothing if not an account of limited monarchy, and, insofar as it is recounted in the Act of Settlement point by point, it is a stunning criticism of William's reign. The clauses that, after Anne, the King must be Anglican in religion,[77] that all foreign wars must be by consent of parliament,[78] that the regal person might not travel outside England, Scotland, or Ireland without parliamentary consent,[79] that all legal and even customary questions were to be decided in Privy Council,[80] that all offices, grants, pensions, and seats in Privy Council were to be henceforward exclusively limited to English, Scots, and Irish,[81] the place cause,[82] abolition of the royal pardon,[83] and the ornamental final clause rendering the King a parliamentary appointee[84] were each and all reproofs of the Dutchman! Toland not only articulates these reproofs in *Anglia Libera*, he hymns them, chapter by chapter, in strict order. A superficial reading of his book provides not one reason why William III was so pleased with it that forthwith he sent it ceremoniously to Hanover on a cushion, appointing its author as his ambassador's secretary.

Why then *did* King William cast his blessing upon *Anglia Libera*? There is only one answer. Its importance for William III lay not in its references to the Act of Settlement but to something else; namely, that rejection, finally, of Sunderland's attempts to rule through both the Whig and Tory party organizations, and the King's own acceptance of Harley's "new country party" coalition joining Old Whigs and Tory squirearchy. Had he given England up for a bad job, and hoped only for easy passage of his annual money bills now that another major war with France was underway?[85] Harley, firmly in charge of raising the fifth parliament of William III, might help or hinder the war effort, therefore it was best to placate him? Toland was Harley's man. The latter's political strategy for a "new country party" to reconcile Whigs and Tories, once blessed by the King, proved perfectly timed to events, and was therefore useful. The prorogation of his fifth parliament in December, 1701, and the return of a war parliament (if barely under Harley's control) more than satisfied William III as payment for his generous acquiescence to the Act of Settlement the year before. He was in the field again, ready for a second clash with his lifelong enemy, Louis XIV, or so he thought. The valiant King fell from his horse and died before the Grand Alliance had been ratified.

Summing up, we may say William III blessed *Anglia Libera* pragmatically and expeditiously, caring little for Harley's "new country party" as a domestic political ideal. Whig, Tory, coalition; it did not matter to him. But regardless of the political coil from out of which Harley's coalition emerged, we may say that its justification in political theory, and for the Enlightenment, was the extension of "liberty" beyond mere "natural rights" to that of a certain "liberalism", the ideology of the later eighteenth century.

It is certain that Toland never used the word "liberalism". Ismatic words were not common in his time, generally speaking; even "Protestantism" appeared more often than not as "the Protestant religion". Still, "liberty", "latitude", and "liberty of conscience"[86] appear henceforward throughout his political writings. At best, perhaps, we may ascribe to the Toland of *The Art of Governing* and *Anglia Libera* a certain "liberality" or generosity of spirit, whereby not only all Protestant churches or sects, but also all political parties were granted equal recognition and respect once it was agreed their aims were not opposed to the commonweal? But does not the term "latitude", perhaps a trifle dry, precisely cover this meaning or case? The answer is that it does, and that it would be improper to equate "latitude" with "liberalism" out of hand, much as each of their usages suggests the other.

Propositions for Uniting the Two East India Companies (1701)

Drunk with coalition, Toland hastened to apply his new-found "latitude" principle to the then-raging struggle between the two East India Companies, proposing their merger into a bipartisan third. Animosity between the old and new companies threatened suddenly to tear Harley's coalition apart. The struggle was postponed, and a merger eventually did take place in 1708. Toland's plan proved prophetic, though we cannot give him full credit for it: behind the political back loomed the tremendous figure of the rising Harley, whose power in parliament as Speaker gave Toland's writings at this time an air of *fait accompli*. More important was the latitude principle itself, the desire and policy to conciliate. As in *The Militia Reformed*, party is transcended in an effort tailored to adjust Tory, Old Whig, and Modern Whig interests within a single context, over-arching each particular interest in a dialectical, centrist plan of eminent practicality.

Complex as the economic situation had become during the 1690's,[87] it is clear that the success of the Junto in renovating England's trading and finances under Montague's direction—who, as Baron Halifax, was impeached for corruption in 1700—had thrown open vast new markets to the Whig merchants and their friends, and thereby made of English, Irish and Scots trade a political football. If for no other reason than that it was Montague who had created the Bank of England and the New East India Company, Tories and Harleian moderates were up in arms. Harley had sponsored an abortive Land Bank in 1696 with Tory funds to counterpoise the Bank of England's monopoly on credit. The Old East India Company under Sir Joshua Childs frantically lobbied parliament to buy seats to protect its Tory stockholders from injurious legislation and from declining profits. The great wealth of the new City Whigs soon was disbursed toward a similar packing of Commons. By 1701 Toland is able to assert that party strife may be "briefly comprehended under the names of the New and Old East India Companies"! This division is bad for the country, because splendid for speculating politicians.[88] Here we assume his target once more to have been those "apostate Whigs" of the Junto whose plans and money had created the New Company, and whose practices, in 1701, were under the close scrutiny of the impeach-ment committees investigating Somers and Orford.

It is interesting that Toland's "latitudinarian" solution to the East India question in no way prefigures the 18th century liberal economics of *laissez faire*. His known patrons, Sir Robert Clayton among them, were mercantilist. The "third" company was to have had the usual monopoly consonant with the inherited protec-tionist system. The motive for merging the Companies is classically mercantilist: "less money", Toland says, "will be exported out of the Kingdom".[89] It is obvious that Toland's personal interest in the East India question was more political than economic. He is concerned not with countering certain novel economic writings by Charles Davenant or John Pollexfen,[90] so much as exposing the corruption of "mercenary parliaments". Whig and Tory competition for control of the fabulous East Indian trade was also, to be sure, dangerous for Harley's coalition at home.

The Commonwealth Idea

By commission or by self-appointment, Toland appears to have been the designated keeper of the Whig canons prior to the death of King William. In the midst of the titanic parliamentary struggle, from 1697 until the spring of 1702, he somehow found time and money to edit and have published Holles' *Memoirs* (1698), Milton's *Life* (1698), Sidney's *Discourses* (1698) and Harrington's *Life and Works* (more often referred to as the *Oceana* edition (1700)). Obviously, the young freethinker saw little or no contradiction between classical Whiggism and the program of Harley's "new country party". Old Whigs belonged to the "old country party", which had opposed Charles II in Exclusion days, hence the "new country party", its Tory members to the contrary notwithstanding, was but a modern-day revival of the hard line of the English Revolution, with Harley determined to push through an Act of Settlement before the "good old cause" might find itself again subverted from within.

Toland, if keeper of the canons, by no means acted alone. There were many Williamite intellectuals drunk with revolutionary fervor at this moment, all of them known to one another from Oxford and Cambridge to London. Their circle usually met with John Aubrey at St. Edmund Hall, Oxford,[91] or in London at the famous Graecian Coffeehouse under the sponsorship of the younger Trenchard or of Robert Molesworth.[92] The ideology imbibed at these meetings—circumscribed as "the Commonwealth idea", as they themselves were called "Commonwealthmen"—was no mere student brew of slogans or rhetoric, but the most sophisticated product of the new English humanism. The learning of the members of this "Commonwealth Club" rivaled that of Bayle and his Holland circle, the so-called "commonwealth of learning". It is interesting to note that, as far as we know, only John Toland belonged to both scholarly circles.[93]

The Commonwealthman's passion was first and last the "good old cause", the English Revolution. His conception of the nature of the English Revolution he had inherited from two previous generations of scholars, poets, and statesmen. These revered ancestors—Harrington, Milton, Marvell, Neville, Sidney, Shaftesbury, Holles—are names to conjure with in any history. The ideology they shared, however, even until recently, has fired the imaginations of but few historians,[94] and in consequence is little appreciated in its depth and scope. Much of Toland's pantheism is drawn from his passionate understanding of the Commonwealthman's frame of mind.

True to the humanist scholarship from out of which it arose, the Commonwealthman's Revolution was rooted not in an idealistic vision of the future, but in a profoundly romantic vision of the past. In this regard, 1688 stood not as a break, but rather it was a *return*, even as the earth, in its "revolutions" about the sun, "returns" to the point, relatively, from whence it came.[95] There was a circular, classical vision of history stirring the Whig imagination. Milton's *Paradise Lost* and *Paradise Regained* are certainly not detached from the Commonwealthman's vision of the Glorious Revolution. Harrington's *Oceana* had, in great part, been a tying together of the English experience with the rest of European history as comprehended in his day. *Plato Redivivus* was a title both revealing and seriously intended by its author, Henry Neville. The Whig mind had become long, vast, and cyclical. Granted requisite learning, the Whig frame turned unassuming scholars and gentlemen into converts and fanatics, in all probability capable of regicide. Certainly the presence of the Stuarts not far off in France, biding their time under the protective wing of the then most powerful Monarch on earth, and encouraged at home by a small but seething minority, rendered the Commonwealthman's coffeehouse gatherings regular, necessary, even urgent. The rise of Harley and Foley in the Commons, and their now predictable opposition to Crown in the cause of Country, seemed to the Club members a providential resurgence of the faltering, now betrayed Revolution. One must correlate its members' impressive literary output—works by Molesworth, Trenchard, and Toland especially—with a final, conclusive attempt to close the revolutionary ring.

As the seventeenth century unfolded, and the Whig view crystallized, the focus of the Commonwealthman became, in a word,
Ciceronian. Of all governments provided the earth by the God of
fortune, the Roman Republic suddenly seemed the most desirable,
the nearest to perfection.[96] There is thus a vital distinction, often-
times lost, between the Utopia of the Commonwealthman and that
of the Augustan. If, in the 1690's, the Commonwealthman hoped
that 1688 might redeem his classical *republic*, imagine his confusion when, under Queen Anne and George I, it became ever more
apparent that "Great Britain" was instead a return to the imperial
Golden Age of Augustus Caesar![97] In accepting this compromise
with history, the "eighteenth century Commonwealthman" became
the invisible, forgotten man of his time. His chance, suddenly, had
come and gone. For ordinary Whigs of the Supremacy were more
than content with the Settlement compromise, and, hardly remem-
bering the sacred canons of the luminous republic, they chose to
amass wealth, read John Locke and build houses.

Toland's writings from 1698 to 1702 show him ever attempting
to reconcile those actual events of the Revolution Settlement with
the lofty "Commonwealth Idea". In constitutional terms, this meant
reconciling the reality of an Augustan limited monarchy with the
disappearing ideal of a Ciceronian or, better still, a Catonic republic.
In point of fact, the Act of Settlement failed to secure the Revolution.
A few cogs of historical time had slipped in Harley's negotiations
with the country Tories and yet powerful Modern Whigs. The return
went beyond its appointed degree by precisely the number of years
it had taken the Roman republic to pass into Augustus' *Pax
Romana*. Radicals had failed to achieve the best, having secured the
better. However, they may not have begun to lose all hope until
1714, any more than did Jacobites at that moment while supporting
Bolingbroke. But with the triumphant passage of the Septennial Act
of 1716, the Commonwealthmen were driven underground, their
message reserved for another, more successful "revolution" less
than a hundred years hence in America.[98]

The significant writings on the Commonwealth theme from
Toland's pen during the crisis years were two: the "Dedication" and
"Preface" to the folio edition of Harrington's *Oceana* (1700) and his
poem, *Clito* (1700).

Toland was at great pains to reconcile King and Commonwealth
in 1700, as witness the "Preface" to *Oceana*; it is the aim of the

English government, he says there, "to find out the Secret of so happily uniting two seemingly incompatible things, Principality and Liberty". This is precisely "Augustanism". By this token, the English constitutional monarchy was already a Commonwealth in comparison with the French monarchy, and King William III, as Augustus, was a Commonwealth's King.[99] It was a line of reasoning fairly undercut by the "Dedication to Sir Robert Clayton", however, in which the Corporation of London is reckoned more admirable than the nation itself by virtue of its toleration of all save Catholics, its rotation-system for electing officers, its general grandeur. London, not England, is "New Rome in the West", and Clayton, not King William, is "Father of the City, as Cicero...was the first of all Romans called the Father of his Country". There is an inconsistency between this "Dedication" and the "Preface", envisioning London the perfect Commonwealth, whereas England under William III had apparently yoked "Principality and Liberty" violently together.

That Toland was deeply disappointed by those concessions made to the Crown during the negotiations prior to the Act of Settlement we infer from his rustic poem *Clito* (1700), the most personal statement of these maturing years. The following, which is frankly seditious, shows us how clearly and secretly he separated revolutionary strategy from revolutionary tactics:

> ...When I perceive that Oracle fulfilled
> Which was to me pronounced by men divine
> That *all goes well when Whig and Tories join*
> I'll sing the triumphs of the good old Cause
> Establish Justice, re-enthrone the Laws
> Restore the nation to its perfect health
> Then power usurped destroy, and form a
> Commonwealth.

However this reads as "poetry", it is a near perfect statement of the Commonwealth Idea. Symbolically, Toland sees Harley's "new country party" of Whigs and Tories as Adeisidaemon, *Clito*'s hero. Laws, not the King, are to be "enthroned"! As Harrington insisted, "a government of laws and not of men" is the basis for any "natural" government. Such had been the motto of the "good old Cause". A "Commonwealth" is a nation restored to "perfect health", naught less. Here we have cornered and trapped for an elusive moment and true, radical Toland, who, in the prime of his life, once each year drank to King Charles I's execution at the annual meeting of the Calves-Head Club.[100] Here indeed is the hard line of the Old Whig.

In *Clito*, then, we discover the reason for Toland's hatred of monarchy, "constitutional" or otherwise. It is an institution, he says, resuscitated by the Counter Reformation at Trent; that is, a conspiracy against the state by the Catholic Church:

> No longer thus the world shall be misled
> By him that's falsely called unerring head
> His triple crown I scornfully will spurn...[101]

Hatred of Catholicism is the negative corollary to veneration of republican Rome in the classical Whig philosophy of history. There is a dark and debilitating side to the immense revolutionary cycle, a nadir to be reached before the apex of regeneration occurs. Between the Golden Age of the classical republic and the Revolution of 1688 there had been a Miltonian descent into the depths, a Fall of Man, a loss of paradise. Adeisidaemon, Clito's interlocutor, inveighs against the enemy, "superstition", in a language all Whigs of the time knew and understood:

> Nor will I here desist; all holy cheats,
> Of all religions, shall partake my threats;
> Whether with sable gowns they shew their pride,
> Or under cloaks their knavery they hide;
> Or whatsoe'er disguise they chuse to wear
> To gull the people, while their spoils they
> Share.

The drum-like, Miltonic line is to say the least imperfectly represented.[102] But it should be clear that hatred of superstition lay not only at the base of Toland's quest for a Toleration, but at the base as well of his quest for Civil Liberties. Both were one in the Whig philosophy of history. Between the "ancient" Golden Age of the Roman republic and the "modern" Golden Age of *Anglia Libera*, mankind had been dragged into the depths by that "Son of the Morning", the luciferic Catholic Church. Toleration had given way to Inquisition, and civil liberty to Monarchy. Any vestige of the latter, with its "Divine Right and Passive Obedience" sloganeering, derived its authority ultimately and logically from Catholicism.

Is the power of the Whig philosophy of history throughout the Revolutionary Settlement in any way derived from the Miltonic fervor for a classical republic resurgent after the Peace of Ryswick? Why did Toland edit and publish an entire series of Republican works, penned earlier in the century, at precisely this time? It would seem that the problem of the Succession loomed on the horizon once more, with no one but the Stuart Duke of Gloucester or the Stuart Princess Anne presently in line. Radicals among the Commonwealthmen felt obliged to raise the question of a republic, and to put as much pressure as possible on the government to pass an Act of Settlement to ensure a Protestant Succession. Measures within the Act must guarantee control of Crown by Commons, according to the Bill of Rights. Toland revered the great Republicans of the past, as had all Whigs who did not number among the "apostates". It is possible that he envisioned, along with a few others, a classical republic entirely stripped of Crown and of Church for the not-too-distant future.

CHAPTER II

NOTES

1. J.P. Erman, *Memoirs*, Berlin, 1801, pp. 198–199; F.H. Heinemann, "Toland and Leibniz", *Philosophical Review*, September, 1945, Vol. LIV, No. 5, pp. 194 and 439.

2. Tutchin had been a 1688 firebrand, not without cause. A victim of the Bloody Assizes under Jeffries, Tutchin had been whipped almost to death. See *D.N.B.* article.

3. John Trenchard, the Commonwealthman pamphleteer, came to prominence in the disputes over the Mutiny Act at the time of the Peace of Ryswick, and later collaborated with Thomas Gordon as author of *Cato's Letters*, a Whig journal. Not to be confused with his father, Sir John Trenchard, Secretary of State during the early years of William III. See Caroline Robbins, *The Eighteenth Century Commonwealthman*, Cambridge, Mass., 1961, pp. 88–91.

4. Author of *An Account of Denmark* (1693–94), and translator of Hotoman's *Franco-Gallia*, Molesworth led the Commonwealthmen in the 1690s and remained Toland's staunch, consistent patron until the latter's death in 1722. See Caroline Robbins, *The Eighteenth Century Commonwealthman*, Chapter IV.

5. Harley, later Lord Oxford, looms large in any history of the Revolutionary Settlement: parliamentarian, speaker, Secretary of State, finally Treasurer, his policy was consistently one of "reconciliation" between Whig and Tory, Chapel and Church. K.G. Feiling's *History of the Tory Party, 1640–1714*, Oxford, 1924, p. 333 ff., interprets this wrongly as the neutral position adopted by "King's Servants".

6. Thomas Babington Macaulay, *History of England*, Vol. III, J.M. Dent edition, London, 1946, pp. 528–539; from the Tory point-of-view see K.G. Feiling, *History of the Tory Party, 1640–1714*, p. 294, in which the matter is barely discussed. Macaulay is evidently in disagreement with G.N. Clark (*The Later Stuarts, 1660–1714*, pp. 149–150, who says "There was no discussion about it [the lapsing of the Licensing Act]: parliamentary opinion had simply ceased to regard ecclesiastical and administrative censorship as a guarantee for the public peace".)

7. The list should extend to "economist" Charles Davenant, who, prior to Swift's conversion to Toryism, served Harley right of center. See K.G. Feiling, *History of the Tory Party, 1640–1714*, p. 354.

8. Bostichi was a Florentine "academician", whose work had been antiquarian rather than economic in emphasis, though it is reasonable to assume Toland edited it because of an interest in the new mint, established in 1696, and the founding of the Bank of England.

9. Isaac D'Israeli writes: "In examining the original papers of Toland which are preserved, I found some of his agreements with booksellers. For his description of Epsom he was to receive only four guineas in case 1,000 were sold. He received ten guineas for his pamphlet on naturalizing the Jews, and ten guineas more in case Bernard Lintott sold 2,000..." See D'Israeli, *Calamities of Authors*, New York, 1881, Vol. 1, p. 254 n.

10. See *Miscellaneous Works of Toland*, Vol. II, pp. 227–228, and the publisher's note to the second edition of *The Danger of Mercenary Parliaments* (1721). See also F.H. Heinemann, "A Prolegomena to a Toland Bibliography", *Notes and Queries*, Sept. 25, 1943, pp. 184–186, and Anna Seeber, *John Toland als Politischer Schriftsteller*, Freiburg, 1933, pp. 4–8.

11. *Anglia Libera* is dedicated to Newcastle, Lord Holles' nephew, who was appreciative of Toland's publication of his uncle's *Memoirs* in 1698. The magnificent folio edition of Harrington's *Oceana*,

printed in 1700, was dedicated to Clayton, then Lord Mayor of London.

12.   See Thomas Babington Macaulay, *History of England*, Vol. IV (Dent edition), p. 328 ff. for Somers *contra* Trenchard concerning the standing army question; see J.H. Plumb, *Sir Robert Walpole*, London, 1956, pp. 183–184. For a general account of political journalism during the Revolution Settlement; W.T. Laprade, *Public Opinion and Politics in Eighteenth Century England*, N.Y., 1936.

13.   The *Observator*, *Examiner*, and *Review*, respectively.

14.   See Toland, *Miscellaneous Works*, Vol. II, p. 201.

15.   *Ibid.*, Vol. I, p. 231 ff. on Toland's plan for a complete translation and edition of Cicero, then a *desideratum*.

16.   Attributed to Toland by a former owner of the Defoe collection, Boston Public Library, W.P. Trent of Columbia University. It might generally be noted here that the bibliography for the Revolution Settlement period (begun by W.T. Morgan of Indiana University) is far from completed or stabilized. The rash of anonymous publications during the years of freedom of the press must be traced to authors individually, usually by dubious exigencies of internal evidence.

17.   An appeal to this Whig canon by Charles Blount in his *Just Vindication of Learning and of the Liberty of the Press* (1693), reprinted by his editor, Gildon, in Blount's *Works*, (1695) had much to do with the disgrace of the Licenser, Edmund Bohun, in 1694. See Thomas Babington Macaulay, *History of England*, Vol. III (Dent edition), p. 533 f. A free press became a Whiggish "natural right".

18.   See Roland N. Stromberg, *Religious Liberalism in Eighteenth Century England*, Oxford 1954, p. 35. The Blasphemy Act affected Toland, whose *Christianity Not Mysterious* had been widely interpreted as anti-Trinitarian. This especially by Stillingfleet, who laid Toland's anti-Trinitarianism at Locke's door in 1697. Convocation thought Stillingfleet had been bested, and indicated the

weakness of its position by inducing parliament to ban the topic. The Act failed to stem the tide, however. It was a dead letter from the start.

19.   Chapter I, above, p. 25. Toland's *Defence* (1697) as well as his *Apology* (1697) stresses Chillingworth's initial discovery of a universal "protestantism".

20.   Toland, *Life of Milton*, edited by Helen Darbishire in *Early Lives of Milton*, London, 1932, pp. 127–133.

21.   *Ibid.*, p. 133.

22.   Toland, *Miscellaneous Works*, Vol. I, pp. 201–214.

23.   *Ibid.*, pp. 201–203.

24.   *Ibid.*, pp. 202–203.

25.   Toland, (editor) *Letters from the Earl of Shaftsbury to Robert Molesworth, Esq.*, 1721, pp. vii–viii.

26.   *Ibid.* The third letter of the collection shows Charles Montaque, the future Halifax, to have been Shaftesbury's political rival. Montaque was a "modern", Shaftesbury an "old" or "real" Whig.

27.   The three standard works in the confusing area of party history during the Settlement are, from the point-of-view of the Junto, Macaulay; from the Tory point-of-view, Feiling; from the Commonwealthman's point-of-view, Caroline Robbins. See Robbins, *The Eighteenth Century Commonwealthman*, 86–87. The so-called Namier school has fairly cleared the matter up: see Robert Walcott, *English Politics*, 1956; G.S. Holmes, *British Politics in the Age of Anne*, 1967; W.A. Speck, *Tory and Whig*, 1970. Also, J.H. Plumb, *The Origins of Political Stability*, 1967.

28.   In collaboration with another Cotswolds squire, Paul Foley, and with moral support from his aged father, Edward Harley. The latter was dedicated especially to the "old" Revolution, and the interest of the "country".

29. See Thomas Babington Macaulay, *History of England*, Vol. IV, (Dent edition), p. 432 for the King to Heinsius, December 20/30, 1698.

30. This last "faction" has been brilliantly established and analyzed by J.P. Kenyon, "The Earl of Sunderland the the King's Administration, 1693–1695", *Bibliographies for English History*, R71:pp. 576–602, October, 1956.

31. Harley's early biographer, E.S. Roscoe, and K.G. Feiling both misconceive Harley as a "Tory"; G.M. Trevelyan emphasizes Harley's "policy of reconciliation" between the parties: see *England Under Queen Anne*, Vol. II, Chapter V, *passim*.

32. William's dilemma was his need to keep a strong force should his secret negotiations with France over the Spanish Succession break down, else he must make these negotiations known to parliament to justify keeping his troops, losing the benefit of secrecy with regard to Austria, the major pawn in His and Louis' game. Disbanding the army in 1698 had weakened William's power of negotiation with France, and may have influenced Louis toward final recognition of the Old Pretender, September, 1701.

33. Thomas Babington Macaulay, *History of England*, Vol. IV, (Dent edition), pp. 294 ff.

34. The loss of Godolphin, a moderate Tory, was complicated by the resignation of Shrewsbury, a strong Whig and a scrupulously honest man whose very presence might have averted suspicion in the years to come.

35. Historical Manuscripts Commission Report, Portland, viii, p. 54, also Toland, *The Militia Reformed* (1698), p. 7.

36. In this sort of situation, any ministry of a later date would immediately have resigned. That it did not occur to the Junto to resign is proof there was as yet no "two-party system". The impeachment proceedings directed soon against Halifax, Somers, and Orford no doubt had much to do with the birth and development of such a

"system". This was a poor way to run a government, with impeachment the only alternative to inefficiency.

37. His *Short History of Standing Armies in England*, 1697, opened the floodgates.

38. See Macaulay for the arguments *pro* and *con* in detail regarding the Trenchard-Somers dispute, *History of England*, Vol. IV, (Dent edition), pp. 328 ff.

39. One of the few books by Toland found in Thomas Jefferson's library; see the *Catalogue of the Library of Thomas Jefferson*, Library of Congress, Washington, 1959, numbers 2678, 1597.

40. In calling Harley in effect a Whig I refer more to his party origins than to his later shift to the right, made definite in his coalition with St. John after 1710. This is defensible in any account of the 1690s.

41. In the *Oceana*, a "*rota*" was introduced as a scheme for parliamentary representation and place. The cult of property before Locke began with this scheme insofar as higher office had been correlated in Harrington with greater holdings in land.

42. Toland, *Militia Reformed*, p. 18.

43. Toland, the "Preface" to Harrington's *Oceana* (1700), p. xix; it is held important that "the passage to Preferment is open to Merit in all persons", regardless of birth. Aristocracy of merit was a revered principle of the Enlightenment, but was new in 1700.

44. Toland, *Militia Reformed*, p. 31.

45. Propositions 3, 4, and 5 of *Militia Reformed*, pp. 32 ff.

46. A rumor bruited about after Sir John Fenwick's confession in 1696. An "association", after the manner of a similar measure in Queen Elizabeth's day following the execution of Mary, Queen of Scots, was formed to protect William III from assassination, the

breaking of the oath signifying immediate attainder. Some high
Tories refused the association on grounds that swearing would
imply recognition of William as legitimate sovereign, negating the
sovereignty-by-conquest fiction agreed upon in Stuart political
theory. William did not press for the association, recognizing the
impasse.

47. Propositions 1 and 6, 10, and 9 respectively in Toland's
Militia Reformed.

48. For these develoments, Feiling, *History of the Tory Party,
1640-1714*, pp. 331-333.

49. *Ibid.*, p. 338. Vernon spoke from the inner councils of the
Junto as Shrewsbury's *protégé*.

50. Toland's advertisement in *The Postman* read: "There hav-
ing been a public report as if Mr. Toland stood for Blechingly in
Surrey, it is thought fit to advertise, that Sir Robert Clayton has
given his interest in that borough to an eminent Citizen, and that
Mr. Toland has no thoughts of standing there, or any where else".
See Andrew Kippis, "Janus Junius Toland", *Biographic Britannica*,
Vol. VI, pp. 3970-3971. Toland was in hot water and abroad at this
time. Laughter must have been uproarious in several quarters.

51. Toland, *Miscellaneous Works*, pp. 316-324, 325-331.

52. *D.N.B.* article, "Sir Robert Clayton".

53. Macaulay's bias against Trenchard and his defence of
Somers in the army dispute places him thereafter in the Modern
Whigs' camp against the Old Whigs. *The History of England*, Vol. VI,
p. 328 ff.

54. No one anticipated the death of the Elector, upon whom
Louise XIV and William III had agreed to rest the Spanish Succession in the first Partition Treaty, October, 1693. Of the many ironies
in the history of monarchical politics attendant to the problem of
kingly succession, this was surely one of the most tragic.

55. See J.R. Jones, *The First Whigs*, London, 1961, *passim*.

56. The first Earl of Shaftesbury was, if not the founder, the foremost leader among the Exclusion Whigs. Toland wrote *The Danger of Mercenary Parliaments* (1698) and *Paradoxes of State* (1702) (see F.H. Heinemann, "Prolegomena to a Toland Bibliography", *Notes and Queries*, September 25, 1943, pp. 185–186) for the Third Earl, his sometime patron among what remained of the Old Whigs.

57. Betty Kemp, *King and Commons*, London, 1959.

58. Toland, *Art of Governing by Parties* (1701), p. 118.

59. Toland, *The Art of Governing by Parties*, p. 54.

60. *Ibid.*, p. 27.

61. Although Sunderland's biographer, J.P. Kenyon, insists Sunderland's intention was Harleian or "Williamite" in his attempt to neutralize party, it appears best to follow Feiling when he says that the second Danby ministry was "in a Tory direction", with William at that time convinced that Whiggism, which he feared for its revolutionary bent, was inimical to monarchy. There were too many Tories in this ministry for it to be "neutral".

62. Toland, *Art of Governing by Parties*, pp. 7–8.

63. *Ibid.*, p. 31.

64. *Ibid.*, p. 54.

65. *Ibid.*, p. 53.

66. *Ibid.*, p. 54.

67. *Ibid.*, pp. 60–63. "Officers" were those discontented favorites of the King dismissed from the army in 1696.

68. The purport of these two bills—the ministerial point-of-view *versus* that of parliament—was that Crown appointees, receiving Crown monies, could not pack parliament by maintaining their absentee seats, nor vote while in office.

69. Toland, *Art of Governing by Parties*, pp. 65–70; also *Danger of Mercenary Parliaments* (1698, 1721), *passim*.

70. One of the boroughs mentioned as "rotten" in the *Art of Governing* was Blechingly in Surrey, for which Toland declined to stand in 1702.

71. Especially pp. 83–90.

72. Toland, *Art of Governing by Parties*, p. 111.

73. These treaties, one preceding and the other following the death of the Elector of Bavaria, represented William III's major effort to contain Louis XIV by diplomacy. See William L. Langer, editor, *The Encyclopedia of World History*, Cambridge, Mass., 1963, p. 445, for a succinct account.

74. Toland, *Art of Governing by Parties*, pp. 164–167.

75. K.G. Feiling, *History of the Tory Party, 1640–1714*, pp. 343–344: "The party significance of this great constitutional measure, for which Harley was the first to move, was that it represented the constant programme of the "country" party since the Revolution". A comparison of the *Art of Governing*, *Anglia Libera*, and the Act itself (reprinted in easily available form in the *Edinburgh Source Book*, edited by Basil Williams, London, 1933) shows Toland working for Harley almost point by point regarding the debates in committee.

76. The inception and terribly long *denouement* are marked by *The Militia Reformed* (1698) and an edition of the Third Earl of Shaftesbury's *Letters* (1720), respectively.

77. First clause of the Act of Settlement.

78. Second clause of the Act, reflecting parliamentary distrust of William's secret diplomacy through Dutch favorites (Portland and Heinsius) and the Junto.

79. The third clause of the Act. William III's trips were annual.

80. The fourth, rescinded in the Regency Act, 1706.

81. The fifth, aimed at William's Irish grants to Portland and Elizabeth Villiers in particular.

82. Sixth clause, rescinded in 1706, as the ministry had by then stabilized.

83. The ninth clause, aimed at Somers' attempts to escape impeachment for his role in the Partition Treaties.

84. Also an *ipso facto* ratification of the Bill of Rights above William's signature.

85. There is evidence to support this view. William's major concern was always protection of the Low Countries against the French; seldom the domestic welfare of England.

86. There seems little difference in the following between "la-tiitude" and "liberalism":

> The *Liberty* of the understanding is yet a nobler Principle than that of the Body...and where there is no Liberty of *Conscience* there can be no civil Liberty, no encouragement for Industry, no proper Means of rendering the Country populous, no Possibility of Men's freely informing themselves concerning the true Religion, nor any refuge or Protection for the Distressed, which is the greatest Glory of free Governments. (*Anglia Libera*, pp. 99–100)

As this rule applies to the reader as well as to the writer, it would seem that the *individuality* of liberty is here asserted. Moreover, the principle applies not only to religion, but to politics and society, hence a step beyond the connotation of "latitude" Toland had earlier employed in his *Apology* (1697).

87. E. Lipson, *The Economic History of England*, Vol. III, London, 1947 (the 4th edition) for the best survey. Also the first four chapters of John Carswell's *The South Sea Bubble*, Stanford, 1960, on the relation of the great Companies to party and ministerial politics.

88. Toland, *Propositions for Uniting the Two East India Companies*, pp. 1–2.

89. Toland, *Propositions for Uniting the Two East Companies*, p. 6. There are two elements: (a) the bullion or specie theory of value, and (b) the "balance of trade", whereby more bullion or specie must come into the country than goes out.

90. Tory and Whig economists, respectively, and great rivals in the contemporary pamphlet warfare. The former noted for his *True Picture of a Modern Whig* (1701).

91. John Toland, "Preface" to Harrington's *Oceana* (1700).

92. Caroline Robbins, *The Eighteenth Century Commonwealthman*, Chapter IV, *passim*.

93. One reason for this was Toland's extraordinary gift for languages. The theological peregrinations of the "commonwealth of learning" required Hebrew, Greek, and Arabic (Toland had Aramaic as well), whereas "Commonwealthmen" could get along with Latin, English, French.

94. Notably the Whig line from James Mackintosh and Malcaulay through G.M. Trevelyan.

95. I am indebted for this definition—omitted in the *O.E.D.*—to J.H. Hexter, who brought it to the attention of the Conference on British Studies biannual meeting, March 21, 1964. See also J.G.A. Pocock, *The Ancient Constitution and the Feudal Law*, Cambridge,

1957, Chapters I and II: the concept of the "ancient constitution", and a return to it, is developed consistent with the conception of a return to the "classical republic".

96. Zera Silver Fink, *The Classical Republicans*, Evanston, 1945, *passim*.

97. Cf. Toland to Harley, *Miscellaneous Works*, Vol. II, p. 220 seq.

98. Based on acceptance of Caroline Robbins' thesis, *The Eighteenth Century Commonwealthman*, concerning English sympathizers with America in 1775.

99. Toland, "Preface" to *Oceana* (1700), p. viii.

100. Ned Ward, *Secret History of the Calves-Head Club*, 1703, p. 9: "J.T.", who authored "Milton's Life" has a collection taken up for himself after quaffing a bumper to the death of Charles I. Also Swift's *Toland's Invitation to Dismal*, 1710, in which Nottingham is satirically invited to dine there with Toland.

101. Toland, *Clito*, p. 14. The papacy is intended, and the counter-reformation.

102. George F. Sensabaugh, *That Grand Whig Milton*, Stanford, 1952, Chapter V, *passim*: the tremendous vogue for Milton after 1694 is brought to its peak by Toland, 1698–99, with publication of his *Life of Milton* and an attributed edition of *The Works of John Milton*, 1697. Toland's *Amyntor: A Defence of Milton's Life*, kept the fires blazing until the Act of Settlement. This Miltonic craze fitted nicely into the program of the "new country party", which, in the last analysis, ran parallel in time to the elevation of the Junto. Milton appears to have been adopted as standard-bearer *posthumous* by the Old Whigs, who did well to contrast his republican idealism to "apostate" corruption.

CHAPTER III

PANTHEISM

The Commonwealthman's Program

The first two phases of Toland's career, summed up in *Christianity Not Mysterious* and *Anglia Libera* respectively, while introducing to us his lifelong concerns for Religious Toleration and Civil Liberties, were premature. In the first instance, he had made up his mind not to cast in his lot with organized Dissent, and so deserted that important cause in 1697. Likewise, in the second, his fervor for the Commonwealth Idea diminished palpably after the death of William III, a watershed in English politics marking the reversal of so many fortunes in either party. 1701 through 1706 were to become the years of his maturity. In this span of time his thought crystallized into systematic, manageable form; in 1705 he distinguished his own point-of-view from all others, or so he thought, dubbing it "Pantheism". More importantly than even this, however, was a final decision to trim his tautly stretched idealistic sails and to come to terms with contemporary *Realpolitik*. Maturity for Toland signified disillusionment as well as system. Pantheism would allow for more understanding of human failure than had the Miltonic, idealistic fervor of 1700 and 1701.

Before embarking upon the sea of these events, however, it will be instructive, by way of contrast, to dwell a moment further upon the Club of Commonwealthmen. This cause, short and relatively stillborn, was yet an important and interesting element of the Revolution Settlement, akin, if less violently so, to that of the Hebertist left during the early 1790s in France. What Toland as "Clito" may have lacked in following he tended to make up for in agitation, and (in company with his counterparts on the extreme right of the spectrum) he assumed his place at center stage in moments of tension and crisis.

In this context Toland's pen was responsible for an important if little remembered pamphlet trenchantly revealing the conversations and thinking of the men at the Graecian just prior to the Act of Settlement's becoming law in 1701. In this remarkable summation—*Limitations for the Next Foreign Successor, or [a] New Angle-Saxon Race Debated in a Conference between two Gentlemen*—idealism, while obvious in tone and in style, gives way in specific issues to more hard-nosed, practical considerations. An entire political program emerges, so extreme when compared with the actual Act of Settlement legislation that it can only be considered incendiary. For all that, it was not at the time unrealistic, given the viewpoint held by the majority of Commonwealthmen; it was valid for the times, if extreme, when placed upon the political spectrum. Molesworth, Shaftesbury, Neville, Fletcher of Saltoun, Trenchard, even Toland had their measures of influence in special quarters. The Act of Settlement existed to resolve the crisis in constitutional politics just antecedent to the death of the King; the logical moment for Commonwealth voices to be heard had arrived.

The message of *Limitations* was that "post-Reformation" dream for a universal Protestantism espoused in the *Apology* (1697), in which all manner of Dissenters and Established Churchmen, being Protestant, ought to follow Chillingworth in "comprehending" their differences. Toland had always conceived of this as the next step to be taken within the ongoing Protestant Reformation, and he labored on its behalf to place himself in the reforming traditions of "Calvin, Luther, and Zwinglius".[1] The same appeal in *Limitations*, however, is geared less to the Dissenters than to the Act of Settlement itself, and, following that, to the problem of Union and the approaching war with France. In the strongest terms, the Commonwealthman spells out to his Tory interlocutor the necessity for an anti-Catholic solidarity among all the "protestant" allies. The arguments are penetrating, even prophetic, prefiguring actual situations postdating King William's death prior to the Act of Union in 1706. They are keynoted by this statement of the Commonwealthman's *raison d'etre*: "I am for an Arbitrary Power in Parliament.....tho I be against it in Kings..."[2]

"Arbitrary Power in Parliaments" is the Commonwealthman's radical solution to the Ciceronian-Augustan problem of "Principality and Liberty"[3] then confronting the English nation. The Tory

interlocutor, shocked, considers it tantamount to abolishing the
kingly office entirely, a proposition the Commonwealthman is at no
pains to deny.[4] *Limitations for the Next Foreign Successor* is good
evidence that the Commonwealth Club at the Graecian was, relatively and in secret, a neo-Cromwellian organization whose front
was mere progressive Whiggism. In 1701, they emerged as an
activist group, a party. Toland assures us they were defunct by
1716,[5] after the burning issue of the Succession had finally and
successfully been resolved. The height of their agitation may well be
marked by this very pamphlet, dated 1701, which had obviously
been written and published just before the committee debates were
resolved surrounding the Act itself. "We may talk without doors",
says the Commonwealthman, "but they [parliament] must deter-
mine within doors". No legislation since 1688 had meant more than
this Act. The more liberal the Commonwealth Club might make it by
their intense lobbying, the more justified their enterprise. Tacti-
cally, having thrown all their support behind Harley's "new country
party" in order to bring the Succession issue to a debate at all, their
strategy or overall design was now to secure as many "limitations"
upon the royal successor to Queen Anne, as possible. If this
analysis is correct, as the evidence suggests, the Commonwealthmen of 1697–1701 were the spearhead for the republican element
inside Harley's coalition.[6]

Comparisons of the "limitations" demanded by the Commonwealthmen with those that were actually achieved vividly illustrates
the extent of the compromising taking place "within doors" between
Old Whigs and Tories, let alone between the coalition entire and the
adamant Tory right wing. The Whig left came off very badly in the
long run, especially after later modifications to the Act of Settlement
were passed as part the Regency Act of 1707.[7] The following
"limitations" in Toland's piece were apparently not acceptable
"within doors", if indeed they were ever discussed there at all.

First, the demand for annual parliaments, as in *The Danger of
Mercenary Parliaments* (1698): Toland, Shaftesbury, and Fletcher of
Saltoun considered the Triennial Act a woefully insufficient guarantee against the Crown's ministers bribing and packing the Commons.[8]

Second, an end to Crown prorogations of parliament. This
element of the prerogative, vastly limited (by the Triennial Act) since

certain abuses under the Stuarts as early as 1641, was not even mentioned in the Act. Indeed, less than six months after its passage Toland was himself actively promoting William III's prorogation of the Latter's fourth parliament.[9] But true Commonwealthmen considered it gospel that even limited prorogations were a flagrant breach of civil liberty because, in times of crisis, they always proved of great advantage to the King.

A third demand listed was to put an end to any sudden creations of peers of the realm by the Crown's ministers. Whether ecclesiastical peers as well as secular were intended is not clear; presumably they were, for no differentiation is made. William III had packed the Lords with Latitudinarian bishops, but this could hardly be considered contrary to Commonwealth interests. More likely the possibility of this predominance being undermined by the future Queen Anne, or the possibility of a sudden creation in order to affect a specific act of legislation (such as occurred in 1711–12 on New Years Day when the Queen created a dozen in one day at the behest of Harley and St. John) was the loophole under scrutiny.

The royal power of appointment had always been a Commonwealthman's target. "Evil counsellors", bad generals, atrocious judges and absentee bishops were all held attributable to the Crown, and governmental corruption attributable to the power of appointment itself. Toland's Commonwealthman asks for (1) the future appointments of the Lord Chancellor, Lord Treasurer, and Lord Admiral to be ratified by parliament alone (a reflection upon the Somers, Halifax, and Orford impeachments), (2) consultations with parliament over all church, army, navy, and militia appointments, and (3) a joint power of appointments to be shared by the Crown with Parliament concerning field officers, especially during wartime, to prevent some modern General Monck turning the upcoming War of the Spanish Succession into an invasion for the Pretender.

The remaining demands were radical and equally pertinent: a parliamentary committee for elections and for foreign policy; an end to the royal veto over acts of parliament; the formal election of all monarchs to replace the time-honored succession-principle; control of military pay and parliamentary drafts; *referenda* among freeholders to ratify any and all constitutional changes, and abolishing the custom of the "King's Speech" at the opening sessions of new parliaments.[10] Each of these "limitations" were justified by real abuses dating back as far as James I. Failure to correct them might yet subvert the Revolution, or so it was maintained.

Of these extraordinary measures none of them was written into the Act of Settlement! Some, presumably, may have been discussed "within doors" as bargaining counters. Another "limitation", not recounted above, was indeed incorporated into the Act; namely, a place clause to prevent all sitting members of Commons from accepting Kingly appointments. It was this precise clause, however, which was later repealed in the Regency Act of 1707. If Toland's "limitations" reflect the Commonwealth point-of-view, then that point-of-view had been virtually ignored. What limitations there actually were in the Act were more than acceptable, one must conclude, but originated with Whig and Tory moderates, not the Club of Commonwealthmen. The Protestant cause remained in danger, after all. The Act of Settlement's dead letter—referring "all matters and things relating to the well governing of this kingdom" to the nearly obsolete Privy Council—effectively parried all subsequent, sporadic Commonwealth runs at the Augustan Establishment.

On another front, however, Commonwealth agitation fared better. The "limitation" of the Act of Settlement restricting government posts (other than that of the Crown itself) to English, Irish, and Scots citizens alone, although deceptively couched in the language of Tory xenophobia, suggested an irreversible step toward the subsequent Act of Union. Reasons for a Union as early as 1701 are penetratingly evaluated in *Limitations*, and reveal the dangerous complexity of the situation at that time. That Ireland was even mentioned alongside Scotland may well have been a concession to Whig (and Commonwealth) fears that, should Ireland be excluded, the chances for a Catholic uprising in that country after an invasion by the Pretender would certainly flare up. The case for Ireland in Toland's pamphlet is unrealistically strong; prejudice against the Irish in England had always been more than a little stronger.

The best argument for a Union, Toland writes, is the civil war which must surely ensue should England invite in the Hanoverian Elector independently of Scotland. The Stuarts had been Scots, and Scotland had borne the depredations of that House with patience. Why ought they to accept a damned Hanoverian as their ruler because he had been chosen by the English?

> Have not they [the Scots] as good a Right to chuse
> their Prince, and appoint their Terms as we?...Is
> Justice grown partial...? You may contemn the *Scots*
> as you please, but I think it will [not] be prudent for
> *England* to come to a final Conclusion either as to the
> Terms or Person without the Concurrence of
> *Scotland*...their resentments are come to a great
> height.[11]

The disaster of the Darien Company had only served to sharpen the old resentments: "Suppose that we shall without them chuse the Elector of *Hanover*, and that they chuse either a Native of their own or any other Foreigner; it will infallibly issue in a War".[12]

Toland paints an interesting picture of foreign affairs should a German prince enter the country before the upcoming Union with Scotland:[13] the Scots reacting in opposition would at once ally themselves with the Dutch, who, resenting the mushrooming of German interests about them, would likewise seek a coming to terms with the Scots. This would provide the latter both with trained mercenaries and a strong navy in a war against England! Meanwhile the Scots, keeping their Throne open (by parliamentary stopgaps of one sort or another), might then invite in the Pretender, given a little time in which to dicker with Louis XIV. Ireland, always discontented, would opt for Scotland rather than England, and England's "balance of Europe" would have evaporated merely in consequence of its having alienated the Scots!

To prevent this all-too-realistic possibility from occurring Toland suggests that "an indissolvable Union should, if possible, be formed betwixt the two Nations". He cites precedents for a Union from ancient "British" history, then revealingly turns to the Dutch Republic for his current model: "It's the like as to the Seven United Provinces; they are so many distinct Sovereigntys, yet this does not hinder their Union nor make any difference as to Privilege among their respective Subjects".[14]

In projecting the future "Great Britain", presumably common talk among the Irish and Scots intellectuals frequenting the Graecian, Toland envisions the foreign situation anew, this time presupposing Union, and suggests the following set of alliances for a transcendent and "Protestant" Europe:

So that *England* and *Scotland* might easily be united
in general for Offence, Defence, and communication
of Privileges, without intrenching on one another
Sovereignty as to what relates to their particular
Constitutions; these also in time would come to
cement, as have those of *England* and *Wales*. This
would make *Great Britain* easy at home, and formidable abroad. The Parliaments of both Kingdoms,
like the Provincial States of Holland, might continue
as they are for the security of their respective Liberties; and a proportionable number of both might
under the direction of the King regulate all matters
concerning the Union, as the States General do, but
always with a *salvo Jure* to the Parliaments of both
Nations, whose advice they should take, and to
whom they should be accountable. In order to this,
it were requisite that the Names of *English*, *Scots*,
and *Irish* should be diffused, and that the distinction
should be South, North, and West Britains.

Realizing that the equal status of the English with the Irish would
be too much for Tory stomachs to digest, he added the following:

As for Ireland in particular...it's unreasonable that
our own Offspring who conquered that Country, or
our Children or Brethren who from time to time
transplant themselves thither, should be looked
upon to be in the same condition with the native Irish
whom they conquered, and lose the Birthright of
Englishmen: Therefore a Temperament ought to be
found out, to remove those causes of disgust which
that Nation complains of, and to prevent the like for
the future. The better conditions we allow our Neigh-
bors, the more we assure ourselves of their Friendship; and as the case now stands, we have more need
of securing our Old Friends, than to make them our
new Enemies. It's an unnatural and impolitik defect
our Administration hath hitherto labored under,
that instead of joining these three Nations in one

common interest, their Differences seem daily to
increase.[15]

Here again, ever moreso, is Toland's trademark; the role of the
"healer" of differences. This time, however, there is a justification
appended befitting a Commonwealthman and classical scholar:
"*Plato* and *Aristotle*", he says, "who had nothing but human Reason
to direct them, had a much better Idea of the nature of Government
than your Court-bred Christians. They could tell us there was no
surer Characteristic to distinguish a King from a Tyrant, *than that
the former fought for the common Good, and the latter for his own
pleasure and Profit*".[16]

So much, then, for *Limitations for the Next Foreign Successor*
and the early 18th century Commonwealthman. To the Tory objec-
tion that "no prince would rule in such a kingdom", Toland replies
that the Elector of Saxony would accept an offer immediately,
should the *financial* considerations merit.[17] Toland's view of the
opposition in 1701 is interesting; they want the Pretender because
to resist him at a time when Louis XIV was supporting his claim
meant they would face oppression (1) should the Act of Settlement
not pass, or (2) were a French invasion to succeed.[18] This seemed the
more realistic view than that of suspecting all Tories of Jacobitism.
They must hedge their bets.

The theme of *Limitations* was a transmutation of the classical
republic (Harrington's and Aubrey's *rota*) into the Dutch model of
the Graecian. The Cromwellian notion, "republic", so bothersome at
this time because so impracticable, yet for all that necessarily
inherent in all Commonwealth utterances, becomes both clear and
practical when its classical original was realized to have been
antecedent to the Dutch Republic across the channel, and that the
Dutch Republic (model for "Great Britain", and currently England's
foremost ally for a Protestant Europe) was the present, nearly
perfect realization of the "Commonwealth Idea".[19] Classical *philosophy* had always been the club ideology, and Cicero its patron saint,
but the realistic path to the ideal was now through Holland, the
future "Great Britain", and their conjunction within the ever-
burgeoning Protestant Reformation of Christianity throughout
Europe.

The Death of King William

1701 was a wild year in the country, and in parliament, culminating in inevitable reversals of fortune attending the unexpected death of the King. The invitation to the House of Hanover, the impeachments, recognition of the Pretender by Louis XIV, the signing of the Grand Alliance, dissolution of the fourth parliament of William III, and the election of a fifth parliament all tumbled one upon the other. Toland had written his paeon to the Act of Settlement in *Anglia Libera* and received thereby a Court appointment to Hanover. He had been presented to the King in October at Loo, in Holland. Then, speeding back to England, he had informed the Whig managers well ahead of time that a dissolution was pending, enabling their runners to galvanize the constituencies before those of the unsuspecting Tory opposition. This activity or "leak" was not in the Old Whig interest, as before, but in that of the "apostates"! Whether for motives of self-interest or whatever else, Toland had foreseen the demise of Harley's coalition and, with that, the plummeting of Commonwealth influence. In company with Shaftesbury, he concluded that Whig solidarity was now more in order, after the Act of Settlement, than a plethora of splinter groups. It was a decision that looked perilously like "trimming". The once fiery idealist seemed to not a few now as one more ambitious main-chancer among the very many.[20] His behavior was at the least "paradoxical".

Paradoxes of State, written for Shaftesbury in 1701–2, appropriately presaged certain alarms felt among radical and Old Whigs that the Protestant Succession, recently a seeming fact of political life, was suddenly, perhaps, a chimera. The alarm had been sounded due to an altogether abrupt, sanguine resurgence of the Tory Party. Letters to St. Germain, the discovery of three Tory M.P.s at dinner with the French ambassador,[21] the sudden, angry rising of Convocation, and nagging suspicions that Louis XIV meant to honor his recognition of the Pretender by an invasion all tended to electrify disparate seething, rightest elements, drawing the Tory leadership apart, snarling, from the moderates of Harley's wrecked coalition. That coalition had after all accomplished its business, the passing of the Act of Settlement; but it was now useless. Moreover, as was known, the Princess Anne favored "the Convocation movement" as much as she disfavored the "protestant" Hanoverians. In brief, there was a vast trimming to the right among the majority of politicians in a realistic "adjustment" to these factors.

Fear, blatant and unalloyed, played a great part in the hardening of party lines. Many Tories had never expected a warlike posture on the part of Louis XIV so soon after Ryswick and the two Partition Treaties. Rather than risk war, many, it appears, were willing to reconsider an "honorable peace" even if it meant the Pretender! The time for discussing such a peace, necessarily discreetly, was before the embarrassment of Anne's coronation, not after. It was concluded the three Tories at dinner with the French Ambassador had been negotiating just this element of fine and adjustable timing, a preliminary to the real thing.

Conversely, war had now become a political necessity for the Whigs who had no means of covering their tracks should the Pretender invade and win. Partisans of the left, especially, were as adamant as were Jacobites on the right. Their survival had ever depended upon the success of the Protestant Succession. Of these extremists, Toland and Shaftesbury, each of whom had established connections in Holland in case of exile, were currently prominent. Their points-of-view during this crisis were the substance of *Paradoxes of State*.

The language for a Tory "peace"—later the so-called "Peace without Spain", during Bolingbroke's regime—is seeded firmly in this early manifesto.[22] The need to rally all Whig forces to the cause, making certain fundamental points clear, and to subordinate past differences to the present danger constituted the thrust of this latest diatribe. England must now follow through on her commitments to her Allies, and not jettison the Grand Alliance before its first encounter with the French. War fever will surely overmaster war fear. This, indeed, was the issue behind the "wild" electioneering of 1701. It was the spectre of war.

Past differences among certain of the Whigs had given their foes of the new day considerable political capital to spend. They hastened to deepen the Old Whig-Modern Whig fissure of the "coalition". The first heading in *Paradoxes* therefore "heals" this primal difference or historic rift, stating "*That the particular Interests of the Court and Country, of Prerogative and Privilege, of the King and People, may be and at this Time are actually the same*". In context this was a belated attempt to minimize the vicious attack upon the Junto unleashed by the Old Whigs in 1697.

Another section, the third, in *Paradoxes* attacks a second variation of this same division: "...the most inveterate enemies to civil liberty are those who would now act the part of Common-wealthmen...as contend for the...Presbyters against the Episcopal and Metropolitical Authority of the Church". The issue here is and will become complex, and it is better explained later in connection with Toland's *Memorial of the State* (1705). In 1701 and early 1702 it seemed simply one division amongst several that needed to be "healed". Certain of the more radical Commonwealthmen, diehard champions of religious freedom who were unwilling to submit Dissent even to the moderate Latitude Men of the Low Church, gave credence, by the virulence of their opinions, to very loud Tory rejoinders concerning "the Church in Danger". This platform, soon to dominate the horizon, re-enforced the Tory right in its anxieties for an immediate "peace", and provided a blessed secondary issue with which they might mask their fears of Louis XIV, while yet underlining the undoubted dangers for the High Church inherent in the Protestant Succession.

The *positive* message of *Paradoxes of State* was in Part V: "*That the Spirit of those, who, in the present circumstances of the Nation and of Europe, would declare for a Peace and against a War, is in Reality a Spirit of Sedition...as must end in...the Establishment of a French Government in England*". The implication, of course, was that to get the Pretender the Tories must accept both French and Roman Catholic power into the bargain.

The most far-reaching principle established in *Paradoxes of State* pertained to the Spanish Succession. This most crucial element of the Williamite "balance of Europe" diplomacy trumpeted in *Anglia Libera* seemed ever remote to most Tories, more in the national interests of Holland and the Austrian Empire than of England herself. Tory nationalism subconsciously opposed Whig internationalism in a deep, suspicious and lasting undercurrent throughout the entire Revolution Settlement until the fact of the Supremacy, later, gave ministers such as Stanhope and the younger Sunderland a free hand to inextricably commit British policy abroad. Toland and Shaftesbury (Sections VII and VIII) write that securing the Spanish Succession to Austria is in the interest of Holland and England "*as principals*", not merely as seconds.[23] Here Whig thought remained directed outward by the Commonwealth apologists toward a united, Protestant Europe; an idea ephemeral as yet to the landed Tory intellect. Whig concern for a network of alliances in Europe (as in its present concern to establish the British Empire) had become, however, a subtle force in politics. With William III Whig thinking, spurred largely by the London merchants, turned forever outgoing. The average Tory, by comparison, dug in his heels.[24]

The King's death a sudden reality, Whigs desperately trimmed to gain what ground they could before Princess Anne's accession to the Throne. Having secured the war's outbreak by a popular victory at the polling places in December, 1701, they tried one more tactical maneuver in the few days remaining. Toland's passionate, dubious and half-baked contribution to this last Williamite foray in the unending battle for a Protestant Succession was his disastrous *Reasons for Addressing his Majesty to invite into England their Highnesses the Electress Dowager and the Electoral Prince of Hanover...and...Reasons for Attainting the Pretended Prince of Wales*. Written and supposedly screened at Hanover, this piece appeared early in 1702 simultaneously in London and in Hamburg, much to the chagrin of Electress Sophia and of Leibniz, who at once attempted to suppress it.[25] Another theme emerges as a precedent here; *naturalizing* the Hanoverians and inviting them into the country to ensure a speedy transference of power after Anne's death. Anne herself naturally deplored this exigency, and, later, Whigs and Tories alike employed the threat of an "invitation" in parliamentary debates to further extort party support from the unfortunate Queen.[26] The "reasons for attainting the Pretender" were a timely adjunct to the Abjuration Bill (in preparation for William III's signature, and signed by him the day before his death, March 7, 1701–2). He died March 8, 1701–2. James Edward Stuart, the Pretender, was duly attainted July 2, 1702.

One paragraph in *Reasons for Addressing his Majesty* drew fire from watchful, militant Tory writers, and shows how unready the manuscript was for the German printer:

> These Jacobites have been so restless in their attempts...that they have at last brought over her Highness to their side, and she will not now be content with the Electress coming to reside in England. For you know, ladies' ambition sores (sic) high,

as they are jealous of nothing more than their place,
so no disputes are more warmly managed or re-
sented than those which happen on the score of
place or precedence...But I who am, tho I say it, a
great healer of divisions in both Church and State,
have I think pretty well pacify'd her [Anne] with an
assurance, that their dignities are so different, and
their ranks so well adjusted, and all by my conduct
alone, that there can possibly happen no disputes
between them on that head...I have been told indeed,
that I might with more decency and equal success
have addressed her Highness with reasons more
suitable to her dignity and character...But hang all
ceremonies, I was born in the bosom of a church that
has surfeited me with 'em, and made me hate 'em
ever since. They are quite mistaken who imagine I
mind persons; I have been more than once baffled in
politics and religion too, and want therefore [to be]
resolved now to make sure of my point by the irresist-
ible force of visible self-interest, which, they say,
never lies; *and has given me such success in the
present debate*, as makes it unnecessary for me to
insist any long on this head...[27]

This corrupt, perhaps even semi-drunken passage is revealing for
students of Toland, not only because it did him no good at home nor
abroad in 1702, but moreso in that it reveals the man's often
neurotically inflated opinion of himself, and of his self-appointed
role amidst the onrush of Augustan politics. He believes he is "a
great healer of divisions in both Church and State"! This conception, "healing", as we shall see, is one of three predominant terms
within Pantheism, his system, and a key to his future ethico/
political writings. Toland had a profoundly dialectical conception of
reasoning—the *locus* for it is in *Christianity Not Mysterious*[28]—and
long before Hegel or Marx he was convinced that conflict in human
affairs presupposed an underlying unity or *ratio positio* which,
when revealed to the contenders, must bring them back into
harmony. A rationalist and an idealist, Toland dogmatically applied
his infallible rule after consulting the facts on either side. A

tendency toward unity or commonweal had seemed to him "natural" in his formative years, and all divisions "unnatural", as the case had been centuries ago for his master Cicero.[29]

King William's unexpected death realized vividly the worst of existing Whig fears. If that side had committed the nation to the War of the Spanish Succession and to attainting the Pretender, the Queen's speech from the Throne on 25, May, 1702, effectively inaugurated a new and vigorous Tory counter-policy at home. Promising to defend the Act of Toleration, she concluded: "My own principles must always keep me entirely firm to the interests and religion of the Church of England, and will incline me to countenance those who have the truest zeal to support it".[30] With those patriotic, xenophobic words the Tories entered marching into the promised land, and even the most powerful Whigs considered themselves banished from it. A few extremists, Toland among them, left the country as fast as their legs could carry them.

Vindicius Liberius

The emergence of Atterbury's and Nottingham's "Convocation Movement" was, for Queen Anne's and later George I's reigns, the principle domestic theme.[31] The War of the Spanish Succession and its attending circumstances have somehow obscured this tremendous fact, and concentration upon the war has distorted our historical perspective. Tory domestic policy, the peace of 1710–1714, the Sacheverell Affair, the landslide of 1711, and the Fifteen are contextually all part of the "Convocation Movement", not the other way about. War, especially abroad and involving mercenaries, was endemic anyway. For Toland, the new clericalism unleashed by the Queen's Speech marked a grave turning point, and wrenched his thinking away from a certain naivete forward toward a now more pervasive mood of irony, maturity and disillusionment. Alienated from 1702 to 1704, his fatuous dreams for a Protestant Commonwealth rudely undermined by a clerical reaction of near medieval proportions, his view darkened in hue akin to that of the European anti-clericals surrounding Bayle and other Holland exiles. So shaken from his former confidence did re-emergence of this Tory virulence leave him, that his ruminations later on the continent produced in a kind of rebuttal the vitriolic first "letter" to Serena (1704). In this piece, clericalism stands for "the origin and force of prejudice", a cultural phenomenon of "unnatural" and world-historic proportions. In 1709 this first "letter" is still "de clef a tous mes autres ouvrages".[32] The reign of William III had become, with the passage of time, the halcyon days of Whig history, now vanished. The people of England, who had seemed so enlightened for a time, had now relapsed into a xenophobic reaction, engineered and led by the "priests".

At first, Toland thought he might withstand events, even challenge them, and remain at home in England. During the summer, 1702, in the months immediately following the Queen's Speech, he and the Scots Bishop Gilbert Burnet had been singled out for prosecution by Convocation's Lower House: Toland as the foremost living example of an "atheist",[33] Burnet as the now pre-eminent Latitude man. In Toland's case, it was *Christianity Not Mysterious* which had offended, though he tells us that many of his accusers mentioned his Commonwealth Club connections as well,[34] intimating that "atheism" and "Commonwealth" went hand in glove. (Perhaps he brought prosecution on himself by the invidious comparison, in *Limitations for the Next Foreign Successor*, between Plato, Aristotle, as opposed to certain "Court-bred Christians" little less than a year before?)

Toland and his printer hastily republished *Christianity Not Mysterious*, with the *Apology*, then brought out the lengthy *Vindicius Liberius*, his "defence". Subtitled "a Justification of Whigs and Commonwealthmen against the Misrepresentations of all their Opposers", the text of *Vindicius Liberius* is less interesting than the circumstances surrounding its publication. The government had set out this time to destroy its author. Toland rejected the charge of "atheism", claiming again that *Christianity Not Mysterious* had been written to defend the religion, never to attack it.[35] He admitted his Commonwealth connections, but defined the term generally, following Cicero on the "commonweal", and restating the Old Whig case for popular sovereignty.[36] A great part of the text was the printing of allegedly withheld evidence; letters for the most part from himself to Hooper, Prolocutor of the Special Committee of Investigation. The implication was heavily weighted that Convocation had been practicing, in his case, the nefarious, hypocritical tricks common to the history of all "priestcraft".[37]

The important element in this somewhat unfair confrontation had to do with the right to an individual to speak out in print on religious matters. With Burnet, of course, the matter was different, for Burnet, a member of the House of Lords, was under censure from his peers in orders. Toland was a mere layman, a "free-thinker".[38] His, it appears, was to be the test case in Convocation's latest attempt to free itself from the hated 25 Henry VIII, cap. 19; the infamous Act of Submission which took away Convocation's legal right to act equally as a second legislature of the realm.[39] Atterbury and Wake had been disputing over the wording of this opprobrious Act of the Tudors' since 1697, the latter altogether bravely defending the royal authority against attempted inroads by High Churchmen in what promised to be an intellectual fight to the finish between "tradition" *versus* "latitude". Convocation, against this historic background, held its breath and put two questions to the lawyers: (1) "Whether Convocation's giving an opinion concerning a book that is heretical, impious, and immoral, is contrary to any law?" and (2) "Whether the positions they had extracted out of *Christianity Not Mysterious* were such an opinion as is contrary to any law?"[40] The lawyers answered the first question in the affirmative, but the second in the negative. A compromise was immediately in order. In each case the "law" in question had been the Praemunire, 25 Henry VIII, the Act of Submission. These judgments by the lawyers (and certain precedents unwittingly set in 1689) temporarily derailed the Convocation Movement as such, and, while hardly legalizing "freethought", made it virtually impossible henceforward for the conviction of any "freethinker" on religious grounds! Had Toland been an "atheist", as claimed, he could no longer on this count be made out a criminal. This was an astonishing victory for John Milton and the free press. But the cost?

Perhaps Convocation anticipated the verdict in advance; the Praemunire was a well-worn subject by 1702. This is the more probable interpretation of the proceedings, which might yet have benefited Convocation, dramatizing the impudence of certain radicals, and proving, beyond doubt, that the Church was in danger. As for Burnet, he was vindicated from censure by his Latitudinarian friends in the Upper House, the ecclesiastical Lords. Still, the actions for blasphemy and censure had been publicly taken, and disunity within the Church had been cleverly presented to the electorate as an issue for the upcoming elections for seating Queen Anne's first parliament. A Tory landslide was in the cards, and, indeed, a splendid majority negating Whig gains the previous December was forthcoming. This triumphant electoral development encouraged the Queen to appoint a severe and reactionary ministry headed by the perfervid Nottingham and several other politically long-repressed High Churchmen. "No moderation" was its cry from the platform. Toland left the country followed by messengers with letters from Secretary of State Nottingham to the Courts of the Allies requesting that he be forbidden entry.[41] The Electress Sophia formally turned him away, but informally sent him on to Berlin where it was prearranged he should be received by "Serena", her daughter, Queen Sophie Charlotte of Brandenburg-Prussia.[42] The former Glasgow student was now, perhaps, for a brief moment, one of the most notorious men in the world. What, one must ask oneself, sustained him? Obviously, he had friends.

The Berlin Experience

Students of Toland often find themselves awash in paradoxes until the peculiar methodology of the Berlin period surfaces clearly and distinctly. This is his "esotericism", or "doctrine of double truth". It is crucial to his biography, as might be expected. It is interesting, also, however, for the intellectual history of the Augustan period, and for the Enlightenment.

Our source for this "method" (and the literary turning-point resulting in Toland's maturity in politics, theology and religion) is his book, *Letters to Serena* (1704), the Preface of which reveals that it was started at Berlin. Here, and for weeks after his arrival, Toland found himself hotly engaged in an extended *symposium*, in German and Latin, with several of the learned at Court,[43] not least of whom was the Queen Herself—"Serena"—who umpired the debates.

From the point-of-view of the resident intellectuals the upstart and fugitive Toland seems to have been a combination of the brave and the foolhardy, the brilliant and wrongheaded, a trifle mad, yet genuinely philosophical. He was particularly associated in the minds of Leibniz and the Berliners with Giordano Bruno, (whose *Spaccio della Bestia Trionfante* he had brought with him, to pass about among them) and with Bayle's crew of iconoclasts in Holland. Leibniz, who also wrote letters to "Serena" in 1702 (with with an over-heated reference to Toland in one instance) and had fixed upon Bayle as leader of the demonic anti-Christian circle threatening all modern Europe, at this moment set about opposing that writer's philosophical presuppositions with some of his own.[44] He considered all English philosophy—the empirical materialisms of Hobbes, Locke, and (as he thought) Toland—a theoretical support system to Bayle's researches into "ecclesiastical history", and, for this reason, he himself defended the notion of a supra-material "substance" or "spirit" in philosophy as the crucial foundation for the official Christian theology of the German Court. Leibniz had the high ground.

Bayle and Spinoza—perhaps Bruno as well[45]—were subjects for discussion in the crucible of cross-examination which now forged Toland's mature point-of-view. J.P. Erman's *Memoirs*, chief account that we have of the Berlin "*symposium*", tells us that Toland stood in great part alone against the others, who were led by one Isaac de Beausobre, a man who kept ideological company with the great and influential Leibniz. The first three "letters" to Serena will later record Toland's profoundest views regarding "ecclesiastical history", featuring terms such as "superstition", "prejudice", and "custom"; epithets common to Bayle and his circle. The final "letters" refute Spinoza's ethical cosmology in a way as partially to adopt it, adding to it conclusions from the ancient Heraclitean tradition of dynamism common to Bruno and the Cambridge Platonists. In each case, whether in the contexts of history or of cosmos, Toland by now seemed to have completely rejected whatever remained of his tenuously held, neo-scholastic Christianity. This is the sign of his maturity, the sweeping and fundamental change emancipating his entire outlook. The consequences for his politics were of the first importance.

Of no less of importance, perhaps, were the consequences for the man personally. *Letters to Serena* was conceived if not written in exile, proverbially that most bitter of experiences in which the alienated creature takes recourse in the consolations and ruminations of his own mind. The fugitive who returned to England from Germany and Holland in 1704 was no longer the ideologue who had attacked clerical "mysteries" in 1696 and attended secret

Republican conclaves on the eve of the Act of Settlement. *Letters to Serena* was his coming to terms with certain eternal verities, a philosophical book, a thinking things through. Basic questions had been asked: What is history? What is cosmos? Indeed, What am I?

The answers are truly interesting. They begin a new career-chapter for our author; of theism in religion, of metamorphic naturalism in philosophy, of *Realpolitik* in Revolutionary Settlement affairs; in brief of Tolandian "Pantheism".[46]

What is history?, ask the first three "letters". The answer provides us with a further deeper insight into Bayle's and LeClerc's "commonwealth of learning" in Holland. In the first place, history is itself but a secondary phenomenon, of less importance than the platonic or the transhistorical. Toland's overview is set forth in the Preface to the first "letter"—"de clef a tous mes autres ouvrages" as he wrote in 1709[47]—and in one terse, challenging sentence: "Mankind is in all Ages the same; the same Artifices have been ever used to raise their Passions or to misguide their Zeal". History, it follows, is the record of a monstrous fraud perpetrated on the race of men, a fraud bound up in "custom" as opposed to "Knowledge, which is "the Ornament and Perfection of our Nature". The antipodes are "custom" and "knowledge".

All "prejudice" derives from the sediment of history. History is "The Origin and Force of Prejudice", to quote the very title of the first "letter". Nurses, servants, parents, schools, universities, sects, and priests pass on the various and debilitating "customs" of history unexamined, which after generations of such passings on become hard and thickly encrusted "prejudices". Gross "superstitions" thereby acquire the ring of truth. One single grossest superstition has corrupted human nature to its very heart; namely, the belief that the individual human "soul" is immortal. Letter two, "The History of the Soul's Immorality among the Heathen", ironically dubs the Egyptians those "Fountains of Learning to all the East" for creating both the institutions of personal immortality and its servitor priesthood. This most vitiating enterprise and lie—"immortality"—became gradually for all men save for the most intelligent the "Origin of Idolatry" ("letter" three) and commenced a tragic process of degeneration in human polity: "I believe", says Toland, "I may without much difficulty prove, that such as first entertained Designs against the Liberty of Mankind, were also the first

Depravers of their Reason". These "designers" and "depravers"—the priests—are now for the most part European and Christian. Some of them were at Berlin?

Toland's esoteric solution to answering the "problem of immortality" was a rediscovery of Heraclitean metamorphosis. It was, he says, originally the solution of the brilliant Pythagorean sect of philosophers, who investigated metamorphosis in private while in public giving lip service to the so-called "transmigration of souls".[48] Esotericism, practiced later by Socrates, Jesus, Plutarch, Cicero, and others, may be traced to this divine and classical source. Philosophers were ever naturalists in private, while necessarily cryptically defending themselves in public from the local priesthood.

Toland's biological world-view was created by him to house "metamorphosis". It is non-historical, since metamorphosis partakes of an eternal round. It is fundamentally—and *at once*—matter and motion, the two components. Metamorphic intelligence is divinely expressed in the permutations and combinations of self-moving matter in its round. The essential point is that there can be, in truth, no "personal" immortality nor no phenomenon called the "soul"; Christians and other priestly traditionalists who promise immortality are liars. There are no Augustinian dimensions of grace nor damnation, heaven nor hell; nature is all there is. This is the esoteric truth, the hidden, recondite message of philosophy. Exoterically, however, one must come to terms with those often mighty historical traditions of the vulgar, presently triumphant in the world under this or that form of *pseudos* and governmental hierarchy. Toland had himself recently come to terms with one such tradition in England, the "Anglican". Deeply embittered, he writes Serena that all vulgar traditionalism is "evil".[49] The philosopher must accept it, but, secretly, wage a never ending, Faustian war upon it.

In Berlin, then, Toland came to his overall outlook based on the final cause of his life, the war to destroy priestcraft, and to restore mankind to his nature, his liberty, his reason. He came also upon a certain set of tactics to follow within this grand strategy, especially that method separating the philosopher from the mere ideologist, the idealist from the practical politician.

In secret (in truth) Toland remains a forever a Commonwealthman, a platonist, a Ciceronian. In public, however, he will appear, also forever, a chameleon, supporting this position, then that. He will even join the contenders justifying personal immortality, promoting Christianity, Judaism or Mohammedanism, sometimes separately,[50] othertimes together.[51] The key to his basic sincerity, however, lies in his hatred of the belief in personal immortality, countered by his love for the larger premise of a naturalistic metamorphosis or round. This esoteric/exoteric divide will deepen as he grows older, and it receives its final restatement in his last major publication, the *Pantheisticon* (1720).

Our own way of avoiding the fearful mumbo-jumbo of esotericism is to state simply that from 1704 onward Toland had recognized the overriding importance of *degree* in his dealings with his fellows. While it was ever his intention to press the cause of the Revolution as far toward the Commonwealthman's utopia as possible, he no longer wished to incur governmental persecution for turning out extremist literature. *Christianity Not Mysterious*, *Clito* and *Limitations for the Next Foreign Successor* had been premature offerings to premature gods, and were now a thing of the past. A Pantheist, on the contrary, pondered the vicissitudes alone and in private, after the servants had been sent away.

Memorial of the State

Is it surprising, when we read *Letters to Serena*, to find Toland so soon reentering the field of English politics in 1705 mouthing once again the potent, quasi-priestly phrases of Latitudinarianism and Low Church? Events since 1702 had made this the most expedient way to get oneself heard.

After 1704 it was apparent that the Tory ministry under Nottingham and Rochester had been a terrible failure. Rochester was dismissed first, and by June Nottingham would also be gone, paving the way for a new government under a new Whig junto or "triumvirate"; Harley, Godolphin, and the great general, the Duke of Marlborough. As soon as his enemies had been removed from office, Toland made his way at a leisurely pace back to London, eager to attach himself, if possible, to the forces of "moderation" once more in the ascendent.[52] For a year, however, to his chagrin he found he was not wanted. Defoe was Harley's man now, and Toland's very name

remained opprobrious. Facing real poverty, Toland kept himself
alive promoting various literary projects, steadily importuning
Harley for a new commission. Finally, it came in form of an "answer"
to an influential Tory pamphlet, written by one James Drake,
entitled *Memorial to the Church of England* (1704) which, in antici-
pation of the 1705 elections, had ably set forth the Tory platform,
"the Church in danger" with clarity and force. Toland's job was to
formulate a counter-platform for the Whigs, attractive to a broad
section of the electorate, so as to siphon away the source of
undoubted Tory strength built up upon the Church issue since
1702.

The setbacks of 1702–1704 did little to discourage your ordinary Tory from maintaining his quasi-formal ties with Convocation.
Drake's *Memorial of the Church* asked for an even deeper commitment from managers and the electorate to "the Church in danger",
"no moderation" and "Monarchical Church Principles". Failure to
repeal the Occasional Conformity legislation and alarm over the
passage and ratification of the Scots Act of Security (1704) would, it
was felt, harden rather than soften Tory resolve. People's minds
must be diverted from the war, now at the apex of its popularity
following the great Marlborough's spectacular victory at Blenheim.
If possible, link the Whig cause guiltily with that of the Dissenters
and Scots Presbyterians, and, at the very best, with the more radical
causes of certain "freethinkers" and other enemies of the
Establishment. *Memorial of the Church* dramatized the current
situation as an either/or dilemma comprised, on the one hand, of
conspirators against Church and, on the other, defenders of Church.
Drake's planks read in essence as follows, (Tories to the right of the
column and Whigs to the left):

Whigs *versus* Tories and the Queen
Dissent *versus* Established Church
occasional conformity *versus* conformity
Low Church *versus* High Church
Lords *versus* Commons
Upper House *versus* Lower House
"moderation" *versus* "no moderation"
Scots' Act of Security *versus* Test Clause[53]

The unspoken target of this disingenuous policy remained nothing less than repeal of the Toleration Act of 1689, with tactical victories over occasional conformity and the Dissenter's schools set to pave the way.

The strong point in Drake's argument lay in his oversimply identifying all Whigs with the Dissenters. If the Whigs were to repudiate this in their rebuttal, the hard core of their voting strength would automatically be shaken. The weakness of it, however, lay in opposing the "Low Church" of the Latitude Whigs to the "Establishment". "Low Church" was as "established" under the Clarendon Code as "High Church". In these two areas, the one of strength and the other of weakness, Toland concentrated his counterpoised arguments in *Memorial of the State*.

Memorial of the State denied at once the long-assumed and intrinsic connection between Dissent and the Whig party, much to the Dissenters chagrin:[54]

> ...one prime Artiface of the *Conspirators*, is, To talk constantly of the Whigs, as if they were all *Dissenters*, when their main Body are Members of the *Church of England*; the distinction of *Whigs* and *Tories* being wholly Political, and relating only to Civil Affairs. The Whigs maintain, That all good *Governments* are (under God) originally from the Choice of the People, for whom, and by whom, they are *Establish'd*; and that no *Government* is good which does not *consist* of *Laws*, by which the *Magistrates* are restrain'd and regulated no less than the *Subjects*, for their common Happiness. This End of all Society, they think, may be compass'd by several Methods, Means, and Forms...[55]

It had been given to Toland, in this paragraph, to announce one of the major shifts in Whig theory and policy since formation of the party as far back as the Exclusion Crisis. The die was cast, and the Dissenters were set adrift, crippling the theoretical strength of Drake's new Tory position: namely, that too-easy identification linking Whigs with Chapel and Tories with Church. As one writer put it, "The most important factor in the ecclesiastical development of the first half of the eighteenth century [was] the conversion of the whig party into the situation of supporters of the position of the Established church".[56] The *locus* of this "conversion" appears to have been none other than Toland's 1705 *Memorial*.

Several massive building blocks in Whig theory had to be shifted from their moorings in the decision finally to repudiate Dissent. Most obviously, Whigs now felt relieved of any scruples they previously may have held regarding the Dissenters' political rights; that is, the old, even more remote ideal of a full "comprehension". What Dissenting support they were going to lose on this account they would lose immediately and cleanly, no longer halfheartedly promising to do battle for an antiquated, non-existent cause. The Test Act in particular was now as Whig a measure as it was Tory! Occasional Conformity would be strengthened quickly by the influx of a large number of half-baked Dissenters into the Low Church (Toland himself took the sacrament in 1706), who would find themselves loyal enough to the Whig cause to accept the new dispensation as a practical, judicious settlement of the religious question, yet not too injurious to their consciences. Diehards quite rightly considered themselves betrayed, and placed their hopes once more in the distant future.

In consequence of abandoning their onetime traditional religious anchor, the Whigs now reconciled themselves instead to the Commonwealth ideology of Harrington's "government of laws and not of men", and to the theory of popular sovereignty. This was secular and classical, and meant that Church and Chapel were for the Whig gentleman now but a national concern, an Erastian religion, and henceforward secondary in importance to all matters of "civil liberty". Toland argues, in Sections I and II of *Memorial of the State*, that the term "Church of England" in fact now means the Low Church alone, standing midway as it does between the two extremes of High Church and Dissent. This is "moderation" indeed! The Low Church—that of the Latitudinarians—had not scrupled to consider itself Erastian in the first place. In alienating Dissent from the mainstream of this national church, then, the Whigs had made radical the Tories' beloved High Church counterpoise as well. It remained to be seen, of course, in what manner the clergy itself would react to this sea-change. The bishops were largely Latitude Men, and could be counted upon. The Lower Clergy were in the main passionately opposed.[57] They had been used, and contemptuously, to separating "Low Church" from the Establishment for decades of usage and "custom". This was that weak point in Drake's *Memorial of the Church* which Toland now powerfully attacked. Now, if any were separated from the Establishment, the Lower Clergy themselves were. Their hopes were being narrowed quickly to the point where only a Sacheverell or a Bolingbroke might attempt to save them.

The "Commonwealth idea", on the other hand, had been accepted finally as the true basis of Whig political theory, but inextricably attached to Latitudinarian Christianity! This was the "Augustan" solution. Its ideal form would now have to be abandoned for the more moderate Whiggery of a conventional "limited monarchy". Henceforth the men at the Graecian were incorporated into the Good Old Cause as mere progressives. More and more their "Revolution" had settled into that middling pattern summed up in 1733 by Bishop Gibson as simply "Whig"; Gibson then said: "the distinguishing characters of a Whig for thirty years together" were contained in "the settled principle of maintaining the Protestant succession, the church establishment, and the Toleration".[58]

Memorial of the State was a ringing success at Court, even with the Queen. Toland wrote to Harley, 14 December, 1705:

> It is no small satisfaction to me, that the judgment of
> the Queen, the Parliament, and the Ministry, do so
> unanimously concur with the book which, under
> your protection, I have published for their service. As
> for anything in it not just according to your senti-
> ments, which perhaps may happen in a point or two,
> you will have the goodness to consider that I wanted
> the opportunity to consult you personally.[59]

The compromise Toland's book and Harley's policy effected between Dissent and High Church brought Whiggism officially into the Anglican fold. This united both major parties against the Scots Presbyterians, and at the same time it protected the Toleration Act, hence, protecting those same Presbyterians from reactionary zealots on the other side who had placed all their hopes upon the success of the Convocation Movement. Tension was eased preparatory to an Act of Union and to the advent of "Great Britain". No wonder Queen Anne was pleased. The doorway of occasional conformity was still ajar for any Scots who wanted future political rights more than a Calvinist purity of conscience.

For Toland, however, as we know, *Memorial of the State* was but a tactical maneuver in the dimension of proto-Bismarckian *Realpolitik*. He never ceased desiring the repeal of the Test Act and raising the Dissenters to full-fledged citizenship. His *State Anatomy of Great Britain* (1716) demands these rights for Dissent as if he had never heard of *Memorial of the State*. The religious settlement of 1705, so pleasing to Harley, Queen Anne, and later to Robert Walpole and Bishop Gibson was not for Toland, and the latter's resorting to Occasional Conformity himself in 1706 was an outrageous, calculated act, utterly "tactical" when considered with reference to his "pantheistic" outlook.

In January, 1705–6, Toland, riding high again, sent out a challenging circular entitled *A Letter Sent to some of the several denominations of Protestant Dissenters, demanding their opinion concerning Toleration*.[60] Denying that "toleration" meant either licentiousness or indifference in religion, Toland asked the Dissenters to "signify to me" whether (1) "you hold and approve an impartial Toleration in Religion...", (2) "Whether you think diverse Religions, or diversities in the same religion...to be consistent with good Government", and (3) "Whether you believe that not only all Compulsion in matters of mere Opinion is improper, useless, and unjust; but that depriving men of their native Advantages and excluding them on the score of such Differences from civil trusts, is a real Force or Punishment...according to the precept of *our* Savior, who injoins his followers, *to do unto others, what they would be done unto*?" All three questions were rhetorical, to be answered "yes". Their aim? Repeal of the Test Act! Obviously, though the party had jettisoned the Dissenters, Toland had not. Securing their civil liberties, in his view, was the next step to be taken in this never-ending, ever-progressive, ever-incendiary religious settlement. Knowing this, Defoe wrote in his *Review* that Toland was now "the most extreme for toleration".[61]

Pantheism

1705 marks the period of Toland's maturity; the crystalization of his thinking on Toleration and Civil Liberties within "Pantheism".

Indeed, the modern career of this word begins in 1705, the publication date of Toland's *Indifference in Disputes: A Letter from a Pantheist to an Orthodox Friend*. By 1705 the now middle-aged scholar from Ireland, Holland and Oxford had summed up and criticized his stock of ideas, motivations, "principles". From that year forward we date the two projects which, throughout the remainder of his life, will occupy his time; natural philosophy and biblical history. The Revolution—his vocation and the pedal point underlining all his acts and words—has split as it were into two; an intense Platonic idealism practised in secret, and an equally intense public involvement in political affairs. In affairs, Toland fluctuates between the moderate and progressive Whig positions, always in the van to support the War, the Protestant Succession, and, later, the Whig Supremacy. His idealism always shatters his Whiggism, however, never permitting achieving these goals to close the Revolution down, always treating them as preliminary steps along the way toward a more perfect "settlement". Though in no sense a democrat—*Anglia Libera* and *Vindicius Liberius* contain convincing denunciations of that brand of folly—Toland was now a republican progressive who thought of the Revolution as naturally, perpetually and infinitely pointed toward the classical utopia of his Ciceronian "Pantheists";[62] *viz.*, the "republic" or *cosmopolis*. He is disillusioned enough with England to pretend to accept the Augustan reality in place of the classical ideal, even as Cicero had himself accepted Rome as his own imperfect model, a "moving image of eternity". Realizing that the gains of the Revolution must end in distortion and imperfection, the Augustan philosopher struggles, in spite of mere actuality, for the "natural", the "real", the perfect. Classical morality demanded this proto-Faustian struggle, imperfect results to the contrary notwithstanding. In line with this, Toland's attitude, by 1705, had become disciplined against his former violent fluctuations of optimism and pessimism. Youthful optimism, personified in *Clito* (1700), was dead within him.

The above coming of age is graphically, even technically demonstrable as we peruse the structure of "Pantheism". That structure—a "methodology" with regard to politics—enables your Pantheist to gravitate at will between the ideal and the actual, all the while keeping a firm grip upon his own integrity. Whether the move he makes at this or that time is strategic or tactical, the *criterion* by which the action is taken remains constant; an indifferent, inner law of the mind.

There are three parts to Pantheism in this "exoteric", political frame of reference. They are, respectively, "healing", "diversity", and "indifference in disputes". They are never stated in this systematic way, save in oracular and adumbrated fashion. That they are implicit, however, is certain for the anyone who follows the course of his argument.

"Healing" was the Pantheist's quest for unity, resolving inessential differences or interests in order to heighten their ultimate harmony in context. We find this word—"healing"—explicit in *Reasons for Addressing his Majesty* (1702), when Toland boasts he is "tho I say it, a great healer of divisions on both Church and State". Indeed, the "healing" process had been central to all Toland's political utterances (save in specific anti-Catholic, anti-French, or anti-clerical instances) from *The Militia Reformed* to *Memorial of the State*. As *Memorial of the State* was his most recently successful effort, and contemporary to our story, let us examine it.

In Section I (of *Memorial of the State*) Toland asks, "Who is to be the judge?" between Dissent and High Church, the "dispute" raging in 1704. Scots Presbyterians are subsumed under the Dissenting "side", to further accentuate the dilemma. Both sides are intolerant of one another, it is assumed, with no ground for a coming together. There is, however, the Low Church. Its "latitude" is precisely geared to the difference between Anglican and Presbyterian forces in religion, and had been since the days of Chillingworth. Standing above the conflict throughout Civil War, Restoration, and the Glorious Revolution, it had always been "indifferently" congenial to both sides, whether Tory Church or Whig Chapel. Its theology, "natural religion", was classical and Christian at once, yet by no means lukewarm. It traditionally placed the well-being of the country before any faction, and the "religion of Protestants" before either Anglican or Presbyterian. It had proven Anglican enough to comprehend the Tory point-of-view, yet Arminian Calvinist enough to comprehend Presbyterian Whiggism. Its lone requirement for continuing in this umpire's position was the Toleration Act. Its very purpose being the presentation of this Act, it had become (Toland infers) a potentially Erastian Church, preaching for religious liberty as a reason of state:

> Now...it follows as clear as the sun, that the magis-
> trate taking care of the civil interests of the govern-
> ment, is to leave men to their own persuasion in
> matters of mere religion; and that admonitions and
> advice, persuasion, arguments, and examples, are
> the only efficacious spiritual arms, or just means of
> converting the erroneous. The question is not if
> men's *opinions* be true, or that their *ceremonies* the
> best, but if they be hurtful or not; and tis still less to
> be forced when reckoned *indifferent*...[63]

It was to this Erastian center that the clever Harley drove the Whig party in 1705. Toland, his writer, asks in effect why the opposition cannot forsake their radical wing for this center even as the Whigs have cut themselves off from their own left-leaning extremists. This was Pantheism when "healing".

"Diversity" would seem to overturn all arguments into paradox, when placed alongside "healing". It is a principle of separation rather than of unity. Yet Toland embraced "diversity" by 1705 in the profoundest sense. Immediately preceding his declaring for Low Church Erastianism in *Memorial of the State* we read the following remarkable passage: "...as men have different capacities, apprehensions, and opportunities, so they possibly cannot have but *different notions* of things...But a great variety of opinions is a certain sign of a free government..."[64] It is not enough to gain a spurious unity. Unity, once gained, must demonstrate a criterion of maximum richness. No differences at all, it would appear, will detract from any healthy society. All differences, not positively disruptive, are salutary. An instance of "diversity" in 1705 was Toland's own circulatory letter to the Dissenters.

Toland's second question to the Dissenters asks, "whether you think diverse Religions, or diversities in the same Religion...to be consistent with good Government?" The point was that, should the Dissenters answer "yes", then it is *eo ipso* unreasonable for their opposite number, the High Flyers, to answer "no". The High Flying argument, that the exclusiveness of Dissent had put "the Church in danger" must come crashing to the ground, and with it that desperate, reactionary Tory policy of 1702–1704.

Whether writing for unity or for diversity, there is a constant mean proportional to be maintained at the center, labeled "indifference in disputes". The Low Church is the only proper arbiter between Dissent and High Church in 1705 because, as with Harrington's immutable "law" governing vagaries of "men", it is "indifferent" to the interests of either side, a dialectical third balancing their "dispute". This "indifference" is hardly compromise or unconcern, but is rather simply fair and impartial to both sides insofar as each, independently, has a legitimate stance. "The mean", as Aristotle said, "is itself an extreme". Whiggism, moving from left to center in 1705 (with Harley and with "moderation"), had in fact embraced Toryism equally with Dissent by a process of denying both equally! In this solution Whiggism captured the mainstream of the electorate over the long run. True, the Whigs had nationalized religion in the process (turning Commonwealth theory quietly into a secular religion) but the prospects were now good for a full-fledged Erastianism, in counter-reaction to the repressive Anglicanism of 1702 to 1704, the religious crackdown which so conspicuously had failed.

The *locus* for "indifference in disputes", in 1705, then, is precisely *Indifference in Disputes: A Letter from a Pantheist to an Orthodox Friend*, published that year:

> I did further assert, as you may remember, that those could be found in the world (particularly the PANTHEISTS) who not only were, but also appeared unconcerned in all disputes, of which number I confess to be one. Their System of Philosophy I did in confidence communicate to you; and of this system you acknowledged such an indifference to be a necessary effect.[65]

Toland transfers "indifference" at this point from a social to a personal frame of reference, indicating that it is a structural to human nature as such, and, for that reason, perennially effective in politics:

> I wish you were grown better acquainted with that Indifference of Temper, which in me you seem so much to condemn; for Indifference of Opinion I neither approve, or believe to be possible. Yet the

> opinions of others cannot hurt your judgment, if you
> govern it by sound reason; their variety must delight
> your contemplation, their opposition will augment
> your knowledge, and their difficulty should abate
> your censure.[66]

In accordance with the Stoical physics in *Letters to Serena*, therefore, Toland revives the stoic moral "indifference" of temperament
through an essential reference to *coincidentia oppositorium*, Giordano Bruno's logical rule. The Pantheist does not merely suffer
indifferently; he participates and judges indifferently, gripped by a
moral passion far removed from "Indifference of Opinion".

When Pantheism—"healing", "diversity", and "indifference in
disputes"—is abruptly compared backward with *Christianity Not
Mysterious*, we see the change in Toland from his "Juvenile Thots"
to those of his maturity. Both are formulations of Natural Law, that
classical ethic emanating with great historic power from Plato's
Philebus 16a, then coursing down through Ciceronian Roman Law
by way of the later Stoic tradition within late Hellenistic philosophy.
The difference between the two formulations is that the earlier had
been articulated in a Christian frame, deriving from the Gnostic
Origen.[67] The latter is non-Christian and eclectic, deriving from the
secularist philosophy of the Commonwealth. *Christianity Not Mysterious* held that reason and the scriptures "agree", uniting *de facto*
in Natural Law, with Jesus as divine personification of the rule.
Pantheism elevates reason *above* scripture, denying any "agreement", and subordinating all scriptural claims, sects or persons to
a Stoical indifference of temper and law. Toland tacitly subordinated
scripture to reason, even as the Whig party had tacitly created its
Erastian church, in which law subordinated scripture to the concerns of the Commonweal.

We have this modernist change from the Christo-Stoic to
the Ciceronian-Stoic Natural Law carefully, cautiously worded in
Memorial of the State, in a passage seemingly deliberately obscure,
yet for all that clear enough and suitably important:

> As a judgment of God the Tories might justly suffer
> in King William's time under the bribed judges and
> perpetual parliaments, without knowledge of their

crimes, or advocates to plead their cause, for promoting those hardships formerly against others, without
considering another time how they might turn on
themselves. But such a spirit of partiality, arbitrari-
ness, and revenge, was strangely unbecoming any
Whigs (and detested indeed by the true Whigs) who
by their principles are patrons of the Liberty of
Mankind, and formerly struggled to obtain those
Laws, as being most genuine dictates of Nature.[68]

The basic comparison is between Tory "God" and Whig "Nature".
Christianity Not Mysterious, written "in King William's time", had
employed the language of the Tory "God" when defining Natural
Law. Not so Pantheism. It is completely "true Whig"; that is,
completely "natural". The picture drawn of the prisoner without
recourse to a writ of *habeus corpus* is the paradigm of the Tories'
"government of men", in which gaolers brutally enforce the monarchical will, God approving from on high. The Tory error was always
in allowing any *personality*, divine or other, to arbitrate. There is no
"indifference" in Toryism, neither in law nor in temperament. A
"Government of Laws", however, as Grotius, Pufendorf and even
Coke had maintained, is "natural" because indifferent both in
objective fact and in subjective temperament. Rationally established, "laws" cannot be enforced prejudicially. Moreover, they must
allow if not promote differences—"diversity"—or they are not laws in
which we place our confidence. Laws that are natural, say the "true
Whigs", are such as actively promote the "Liberty of Mankind" when
not merely passively arbitrating disputes.

At this point Toland's radical Whig "Pantheism" fairly collapses
into a more comprehensive systematic philosophy, that cosmological framework of the fourth and fifth "Letters to Serena". In the
Stoical manner, he has built his ethics and his politics upon his
physics. His logic—hidden save in *Christianity Not Mysterious*—is,
as in Platonism and Stoicism, fused with ethic; Natural Law propels
the individual by dialectic along "the upward and downward path";
up from Plato's cave, then back down into it.

In conclusion, we note two significant developments in Toland
by 1705: first, he had abjured idealism for meliorism and proto-
Bismarckian *Realpolitik*; second, he had forever separated the

classical from the biblical in his studies; in each case "exoteric" truths were subordinated to "esoteric" truths.

Compare the following on "despair", from *Indifference in Disputes*, (1705) to the excesses of *Clito* (1700):

> You, who no less expect than wish to see...different parties reconciled, must needs have a detestation for everything that widens their breaches or retards their union;...I, who despair of any uniformity in men's opinions or practices (which I hold to be impossible) must be pleased with examining the grounds of those notions, and springs of those actions, which though I cannot help or prevent, yet give me a further knowledge of human nature...[69]

Toland has admitted the necessity, within his purview, of a permanent dissension or disunity as well as of a permanent need for "healing"; of breaking up as well as of putting together. Moreover, "diversity" is as sacred a canon within Pantheism as is "unity". They are equal. Idealism is no longer Miltonian, but has been replaced by a more realistic interpretation of life, befitting practical involvement on the part of the Pantheist in the affairs of the marketplace and of the forum.

The rejection of bible allows the Pantheist to attempt to reconstruct in himself his own personification of the law, replacing the Christian tenet of personalist authoritarianism based on scripture. Pantheists are now free to think for themselves, they are "freethinkers". With its process of "healing", "diversifying", and of "indifference in disputes", Pantheism has become the very realization of "toleration", but altogether naturally and rationally. Under the aegis of this "system",[70] divined originally by Cicero from out of various Platonic and Stoic texts, then reshaped by Toland in his own time, true Whigs will be closer bound to *cosmos* than ever before. The universal *polis*, binding stars, men, vegetation, gods, and earth into one process is now to a degree more harmonious than it was.[71] *Cosmos* is reflected in the *cosmopolis*, its "moving image".

The motive for these changes, whether the language is philosophical or ideological, is an ever deepening anti-clericalism, brought about by the conviction that, were it not for the priests, human reason would never originally have permitted any "pre-judicium" of its will.[72] Toland opposed scripture because scripture demands blind obedience, as if the truth had been pre-judged. Reason, contrariwise, begins ever anew, a trans-historical, constant, impartial authority. Toland subjects scripture to reason, therefore, as the only means whereby the human mind will free itself from its historic bonds of prejudice. In the ideological language of the English Revolution this—reason's primacy over scriptural authority—was the veriest weapon for attacking the priestly, reactionary forces of Convocation. In the philosophical terms of *Letters to Serena*, however, the primacy of reason signifies man's now resurgent hope for regeneration after centuries of clerical darkness. The English Revolution was but an instance of the philosopher's never-ending struggle against hierarchy. Scripture, however well-intended when first composed, is inherently prejudicial. Christian scripture (the Gospels for example) is hardly an exception. It is in fact the paradigm of deceit.

The role of the Pantheist, it follows, is to subject prejudice to reason, the *materia secunda* of history to the *materia prima* of the eternal, the "exoteric" to the "esoteric". These are the two dimensions of reality, as in the Platonic tradition. The rational or ideal is at war with the customary and the "real". A Pantheist is one who insists the latter never must rule. In his despair that humankind will ever achieve the regeneration of its reason, the Pantheist strives, nevertheless, to elevate the lower nearer and nearer to the higher order. He plunges into the maelstrom of politics, even as the philosopher plunges down into the darkness of Plato's cave, to strive there for the regeneration of other men. He is a philosopher when alone; but in the rough and tumble of politics, in the *cosmopolis*, he struggles mightily, ceaselessly, but in vain.

CHAPTER III

NOTES

1. Toland, *Christianity Not Mysterious*, p. 176.

2. Toland, *Limitations for the Next Foreign Successor*, 1701, p. 14.

3. Toland, *Oceana* edition Preface.

4. Toland, *Limitations for the Next Foreign Successor*, pp. 30–31.

5. Toland, *The State Anatomy of Great Britain*, pp. 8–9.

6. Toland's introduction to his edition of *Letters from the Earl of Shaftesbury to Robert Molesworth, Esq.*, 1721, pp. vii-viii, cites Shaftesbury, the leading Commonwealthman, was rival to Halifax before 1702.

7. One provision suggested by the Commonwealthmen which passed was a place clause, forbidding Crown placemen to sit in Commons. It was repealed in the Regency Act; also the clause transferring all ministerial business to Privy Council. G.M. Trevelyan, *Ramillies*, pp. 94–97.

8. Toland, *The Danger of Mercenary Parliaments*, introduction, 1722 edition. Also Caroline Robbins, *The Eighteenth Century Commonwealthman*, pp. 182–183.

9. Charles Davenant, *The True Picture of a Modern Whig*, 1701, pp. 69–70. Toland, presented to William III at Loo by Lord Macclesfield in October, 1701, is herein described as quickly crossing

the channel to inform the Whigs of an impending dissolution. Davenant claims this gave Whig managers at home a headstart in the 1701 December elections.

10. The text for all "limitations" is *Limitations for the Next Foreign Successor*, pp. 11–13.

11. *Ibid.*, p. 24

12. Toland, *Limitations for the Next Foreign Successor*, p. 24.

13. *Ibid.*, pp. 24–26.

14. *Ibid.*, p. 27.

15. *Ibid.*, pp. 27–28.

16. *Ibid.*, p. 29.

17. *Ibid.*, pp. 30–31.

18. *Ibid.*, p. 32.

19. *Ibid.*, pp. 26–27, 32–33.

20. Anonymous, *The Old and Modern Whig Truly Represented*, 1702, pp. 17–19. Toland is "the only Republican and Socinian at Court" and "the tool of party and no party". Toland's independence involved him often in misunderstandings of this kind: see Toland to Shaftesbury, 22 October, 1705 (P.R.O. Shaftesbury, G.D. 24, bundle 20, 105) in which the Graecian politicians turned on him for a "Tory", because persisting in associating with Harley!

21. Davenant, Hammond, and Tredenham. This seeming conspiracy mushroomed into the major "issue" of the 1701 elections.

22. Toland, *Paradoxes of State*, 1702, Part V.

23. *Ibid.*, VII. VIII.

24. Toland, *The State Anatomy of Great Britain*, 1716. esp. Part X. Reflecting on the past, Toland was himself one of the major sources for recognizing this basic tension between the two parties. The first measures of the Supremacy after 1715 were to return to certain policies of William III.

25. Adolphus Ward, *The Electress Sophia and the Hanovian Succession*, London, 1909, p. 367. Also Waltraut Fricke, "Leibniz und die englische Sukzession des Hauses Hannover". *Quellen und Darstellungen Zur Geschichte Niedersachsens*, Band 56, Hildesheim, 1957, pp. 36–37.

26. G.M. Trevelyan, *Ramillies*, pp. 91–93.

27. The reprinting of this explosive paragraph in Arthur Annesley's *An Answer to Mr. Toland's Reasons for Addressing his Majesty*, 1702, increased Tory detestation of Toland to the point where, failing conviction by Convocation, the Whig-controlled House of Lords forced him into exile rather than risk his defence.

28. Toland, *Christianity Not Mysterious*, pp. 12–13.

29. Cicero, *On the Commonwealth, passim*. Toland's Pantheism later modified this, realizing possibilities for "diversity" in dialectic as well as for "unity".

30. William Cobbett, *Parliamentary History of England*, Speech of 25 May, 1702, (quoted in Feiling, *History of the Tory Party, 1640-1714*, p. 362).

31. G.M. Trevelyan's *England Under Queen Anne* creates the impression that the war and not Church was the proper theme. This is misleading, especially during the early years of Anne's reign. Feiling states: "The question of the war was only to come to a head much later, when the Blenheim laurels had been tarnished by Malplaquet..."; *History of the Tory Party, 1640-1714*, p. 368.

32. Toland, British Museum Additional Manuscripts, Add. Mss. 4465, f. 7; quoted in F.H. Heinemann, "John Toland and the Age of Reason", pp. 42–43.

33. Toland, *Vindicius Liberius*, 1702, p. 37.

34. *Ibid.*, p. 147 f.

35. *Ibid.*, pp. 18–19.

36. *Ibid.*, pp. 127–128.

37. *Vindicius Liberius* was written in a spirit of outrageous irony, as in the following reference to the *Amyntor* dispute with the High Churchman Blackall in 1699 (p. 20): "as for *Amyntor*, everybody knows how Mr. Blackall drew me into writing it, when no such purpose had ever entered my head before. This book consists of matters of *Fact*, and some *Observations* on them. The Facts are all or most of them collected out of the *Fathers* of the *Church*..."

38. Toland was the archetypal "freethinker"; the term emerged first in connection with *Vindicius Liberius*, usually in company with "atheist". Addison's *The Drummer*, 1715, Act. I, contains the line, "Atheist is an old-fashioned word, I'm a Freethinker, child".

39. Norman Sykes, *Church and State in England in the XVIIIth Century*, pp. 297–310.

40. Reprinted by Andrew Kippis, article "Janus Junius Toland", *Biographia Brittanica*, Vol. VI, p. 3970 n.S.

41. Toland, *Miscellaneous Works*, Vol. II, p. 345. Also Adolphus Ward, *The Electress Sophia and the Hanoverian Succession*, pp. 367–368.

42. For Toland's general comings and goings in Germany prior to 1707 see F.H. Heinemann, "Toland and Leibniz", *Philosophical Review*, XIV, number 5, 1945. esp. pp. 439-441. See Adolphus Ward, *The Electress Sophia and the Hanoverian Succession*, p. 336. Robert E. Sullivan's, "John Toland, a portrait", the first chapter of his *John Toland and the Deist Controversy*, (Harvard University Press, 1982) is at present the last word on the details.

43. J.P. Erman, *Memoirs*, pp. 198–211. This account is the main source for what we know of Toland's visit to Berlin in 1702.

44. G.W.F. Leibniz, *Philosophical Letters and Papers*, edited Leroy E. Loemker, Vol. II, Chicago, 1956, pp. 888–898. Also pp. 899–910. These two letters to Sophie Charlotte are an admirable summation of Leibniz' basic principles. They support the Christian religion.

45. See Arthur D. Imerti, *Expulsion of the Triumphant Beast*, "Introduction", Rutgers, 1964, *passim*, for the place of the Nolan in 17th and early 18th century thought. Toland was indebted to Bruno especially in the areas of logic and method.

46. "Pantheism", the tradition in philosophy today associated in the main with Spinoza, attacked Christianity, identifying God with extension and matter in contradistinction to the transcendence of the Divine within the Augustinian frame of reference. A respectable philosophical position, it was "atheism" to most Christians of the time. The term "pantheism" is modern, introduced into the language by Toland in 1705; publication date of his *Letter from a Pantheist to an Orthodox Friend*. Toland writes Leibniz about Bruno's role in "pantheism" in 1709, and Benoit uses the term against Toland in 1712. See the *Oxford English Dictionary*, article "Pantheism"; also Andrew Kippis, "Janus Junius Toland", *Biographia Britannica*, pp. 3975–3976, n.S. A very important contribution in this essential context has been made by Arthur D. Imerti, whose introduction and Notes to his translation of Bruno's *Spaccio*, (entitled *The Expulsion of the Triumphant Beast*, New Brunswick, N.J., 1964) links Toland's secret society, the "Pantheisticon", directly to the Florentine Academy by way of Raleigh and Hatton's discussion-group that welcomed Bruno into England the 1580s. A paper from the Florentine Academy, Davanzanti Bostichi's *A Discourse on Coins*, had been translated from the Italian by Toland prior to his publication of *Christianity not Mysterious* (1696).

47. Toland to Baron Hohendorf, British Museum, Add. MSS. 4465, f. 7; (quoted in F.H. Heinemann, "John Toland and the Age of Reason", p. 42).

48. Toland "The History of the Soul's Immortality among the Heathen", *Letters to Serena*, 1704, pp. 57–58.

49. *Ibid.*, "The Origin of Idolatry, and Reasons of Heathenism", p. 100 ff.

50. As in *Christianity Not Mysterious* and *Reasons for Naturalizing the Jews in England* (1713).

51. Toland, *Nazarenus*, 1718, *passim*.

52. A report to Harley dated 5 July, 1704, states: "They say John Toland is in England and hard at work with his pen". *Historical Manuscripts Commission Report, Portland*, IV, p. 98.

53. James Drake, *Memorial of the Church of England*, 1704. Another edition following the Sacheverell Trial, 1711, *passim*.

54. Two anonymous answers to *Memorial of the State* quickly registered a reaction: they were (1) *A Letter to the Author of the Memorial of the State*, 1705, and *Remarks on the Letter to the Author of the State-Memorial*. The latter is believed penned by Thomas Raulins to whom, earlier, Toland dedicated his *Life of Milton*.

55. Toland, *Memorial of the State*, p. 76.

56. Norman Sykes, *Church and State in England in the XVIIIth Century*, p. 34.

57. Toland's *State Anatomy of Great Britain*, 1716, states in retrospect that "inferior clergy" and "peasants" made up the High Church forces. Part I, pp. 6–8.

58. Quoted by Norman Sykes, *Church and State in England in the XVIIIth Century*, p. 33. Gibson was by this time Walpole's second in command, in full charge of the *ecclesia*.

59. Toland, *Miscellaneous Works*, pp. 354–355.

60. Reprinted in *The Second Part of the State Anatomy of Great Britain*, 1717.

61. Daniel Defoe, *Review*, VI, 410b.

62. Toland, *Pantheisticon*, Introduction.

63. Toland, *Memorial of the State*, p. 47.

64. *Ibid.*, p. 44.

65. Toland, *Indifference in Disputes: A Letter from a Pantheist to an Orthodox Friend*, 1705, p. 7.

66. *Ibid.*

67. Toland, *Christianity Not Mysterious*, Section III, Chapter III, p. 118.

68. John Toland, *Memorial of the State*, p. 80.

69. Toland, *Indifference in Disputes: A Letter from a Pantheist to an Orthodox Friend*, p. 5.

70. Toland, *Second Part of the State Anatomy of Great Britain*, p. 47; "Among other views it was my intention, to reduce the doctrine of Toleration to a clear and positive System". This in reference to his circular letter to the Dissenters, January, 1705–6.

71. Toland's fourth and fifth letters to "Serena" abound with references to metamorphosis, in which politics is but a category of *cosmos*.

72. See Toland, the first letter to "Serena", entitled "On the Origin and Force of Prejudice", 1704.

CHAPTER IV

SUCCESSION AND ENLIGHTENMENT

The Two Strands

Toland's dialectic of double truth—"esoteric" and "exoteric"—pre-disposed him to separate history and ideology from philosophy from 1705 until his death in 1722. His writings reflected this fissure sometimes more clearly than at others: the separation was particularly glaring during the protracted crisis for the Protestant Succession, 1710–1714.

The Succession had become the linch-pin both for the Toleration and for Civil Liberties; a restoration of the Stuarts would have been inimical to both. The unfortunate combination of Queen Anne's physical decline coupled with another virulent resurgence of the Tory right under Harley and St. John after 1710 spurred Toland to concentrate his ire and best literary energies on the ideological conflict defining the British-French negotiations leading forward to the signing of the Peace of Utrecht. For this reason, one has to treat the Succession almost as a topic unto itself in this penultimate flourish of Toland's biography.

At the same time, sub-dominantly, Toland stole weeks here and months there to deepen his theoretical and philosophical explorations into western history and polity. For us, his conclusions sometimes relate all-too-easily to the British situation, but at others they transcend it, reflecting more his interests in upcoming developments pertaining to the 18th century Enlightenment. Certain of his writings urged for a general naturalization, for example, bringing pressure to bear on Queen Anne's government, hence, indirectly, impinging upon events in the seemingly unending crisis of the Succession. Tory hatred and fear of certain non-Anglican minorities, fired by Sacheverell and by Convocation, tilted against naturalization and encouraged Jacobitism at one and the same time. To a lesser extent, Toland's "Freethought" connections prior to 1714 were, if radically, part of a general Whig distrust of High Church and consistent with traditional Whig support for minorities' rights. The topics of naturalization and of Freethought are large, of course, and cannot be explained in terms of the Protestant Succession alone. On their deeper side, they would represent an undercurrent within Pantheism and within the Toleration movement for over a hundred years. Toland's story is therefore binary but not Machiavellian; with England as context the Protestant Succession is dominant, whereas, sub-dominantly, the European Enlightenment hovers nimbus-like in the background. There was no separating England from the continent in overall strategy; a Protestant Europe, once the Hanoverian Elector succeeded in England, was suddenly a realistic possibility. In tactics, however, fragmentation remained the order of the day: a Protestant Europe was absurd without Hanover succeeding to the British Throne, redirecting arms and diplomacy toward the old Williamite "Balance of Europe" policy, and engaging British commerce once again in the thick of European affairs.

In brief, the Succession issue dominated decision making in the foreground from 1706 through 1714, especially subsequent to the reversal of Harley's political fortunes in 1710. Other considerations, of more lasting interest to students of Toland's personal or intellectual development, were shoved by sheer weight of circumstances into the background and would not re-surface until the Whig Supremacy rested secure. The ideological battle had to be won first. After that certain long-range philosophical battles, no less important, would remain to be fought. Since Machiavelli's *The Prince*, "double truth" was hardly new. Toland's idealistic interpretation of it, however, stood the Florentine upon his head.

Toland and Harley

In the period of the Revolution Settlement, theoreticians of the day were also men of action. The elder Halifax was a cabinet minister, Locke and Newton were involved respectively in the Bank and at the Mint, Shaftesbury had been a parliamentarian before his illnesses,

Defoe and Swift were agents, secretaries or pamphleteers. Toland was no exception, and his intermittently close relationship with Harley forms the indispensable background against which we must assay his furious political writing prior to 1714, the year of Queen Anne's death. It was a relationship seldom disconnected from Toland's contribution to the Settlement's outcome, for, as we have seen, Pantheism had been forged in the twin crucibles of exile abroad and strife at home. Toland's thought was historically founded, deriving its "principles" from his observations of events. It was imminent and involved; never removed nor abstract. Pantheism, metaphysical in philosophy and theoretical in theology, was practical in politics, a near revolutionary device.

There appears to have been a deepening sense of distrust between Toland and Harley from the Act of Settlement period onward, resulting finally in rupture and disavowal. Harley wrote to Lord Raby in 1707 that he sometimes admitted Toland into his company because he had "read much",[1] and Toland wrote Harley at one point about "arcana literaria" with which he hoped to "divert your leisure hours".[2] This pointed to a genuine, non-political bond between them within the Commonwealth of Learning. Their more important ground for mutual self-interest lay, however, in their desire to realize the ongoing constitutional reforms described in *Anglia Libera* and in *Memorial of the State*, and their overall concern for the Protestant Succession. To help secure the Succession, Toland sought and obtained employment under Harley as a spy in the courts of the Grand Alliance more than once, particularly at Hanover. When Harley commenced to veer slowly rightward after his appointment as Chancellor of the Exchequer, in 1710, forsaking all but the most moderate Whigs and Hanoverians, these shared points of interest gradually threatened to evaporate.

Significance of the Protestant Succession

In the grand context of the Glorious Revolution (1688–1714), the Protestant Succession meant an end to the darkness of Catholic hegemony in Europe and the simultaneous rising of the sun of neo-classicism upon a new Golden Age, the so-called Augustan Period. Contained in this contextual event were subsidiary "revolutions" in more partial areas of constitution, trade, religion, foreign relations, education, social relations, professional careers, political party; the entire spectrum of early modern life. As the crisis itself drew nigh, a sword of Damocles hanging over the old ways with every passing hour in the life of Queen Anne, tension mounted to the crackling point in the lives of the British people, and lines were drawn setting prerogative against constitution, land-holders against town merchants, High Church against Low Church and Dissenters, French power against the Balance of Europe, Ancients against Moderns, family scions against *nouveau riche*, nobility against a new race of lawyers, merchants, and professional soldiers, and Whigs against Tories. What had commenced as a political revolution now permeated the entire culture. Toland's writings were couched more and more in violent contrasts as the great event approached. The vehemence and single-mindedness with which he states them, and the several areas in which he saw the morality of the struggle reflected, tell us to no small degree how deeply he had delved into western history and how widely by this time he had traveled and read. His desperation to help secure the Protestant Succession is explained when we realized that, a very radical Whig, he foresaw the absolute ruination of his own fortunes attending any failure to bring in the House of Hanover.

Toland's Vocation

To radicals such as Toland and John Tutchin, the Good Old Cause and the Revolution were by now their way of life, not merely convenient props for hammering out a living. As often happens in times of upheaval, certain figures emerge who consider themselves committed to destroy the old order, as, indeed, others emerge determined to oppose them. Much of Toland's arrogance—distasteful to Locke and others—is explained if we connect his enthusiasm for the Revolution with an apparent sense of personal destiny to serve it. As one writer put it, "the world has but little toleration for men who show a consciousness of their own greatness...He [Toland] may have been vain, perhaps he was impolitic, certainly he was unfortunate; but he was one of the world's great men".[3] Upon putting Toland down, however, it is hard to avoid the conclusion that this alleged greatness hinged upon his dedication to one single idea rather than on those extraordinary gifts such as had created a Newton, a Leibniz, or even a Locke. Nothing is more demonstrable in Toland at this time than his all-consuming drive for the Succession. In this sense, not Harley but the Hanoverian Sophie Charlotte of Brandenburg-Prussia—"Serena"—had been his ultimate patron.[4]

That the dilemma of the Protestant Succession (the other horn being a conspiracy with Catholic France) was Pantheism's spur is clear when we compare those many books and pamphlets beginning with *Anglia Libera* (1702) through the *Art of Restoring* (1714): they were *Reasons for Addressing His Majesty* (1702), *A Phillipic Oration* (1707), *Gallus Aretalogus* (1709), *Reflections on Dr. Sacheverell's Sermon* (1710), *The Judgment of King James the First* (1710), *The High Church Displayed* (1711), *Her Majesty's reasons for creating the Electoral Prince of Hanover a Peer* (1712), *A Letter Against Popery* (1712), the attributed *Appeal to the Honest People* (1712), *Dunkirk or Dover* (1713), *A Collection of Letters* (1714), *The Funeral Elegy and Character of the late Princess* (1714), *The Reasons and necessity of the Duke of Cambridge coming to, and residing in Great Britain* (1714), and *The Grand Mystery laid open* (1714): these were all writings or editions for which the Succession offered the underlying theme. Many letters also reflected it, as for example the following (to Harley, December, 1711):

> ...Instead then of your Priors and your Swifts, you ought to dispatch me privately this minute to Hanover; where you'll find me as secret, as I hope to be successful. In my judgment it imports you not a little, were it but for the Queen's service, to clear up some things there...I need say no more but that as my interest is inseparable from that family, so none upon earth wishes better to your particular person.[5]

Or earlier, that same month:

> I am ignorant...whom you meant by my particular friends that are against the peace; but of this I am sure that all my acquaintance are unanimous in their sentiments. Particular friends in this case have I none, but the house of Hanover; and though a good

> peace be a good thing, we are persuaded no peace
> can be good for their interest at this time; and much
> less any peace that gives up Spain and the Indies to
> a Prince of the House of Bourbon...[6]

Even the Sacheverell affair seemed to him purely and simply yet another desperate attack on the Hanoverian Succession (as in the following to Leibniz): "...And the articles since exhibited against that Incendiary [Sacheverell] by the Commons show...that I nowhere stretched his meaning; and that his principal view has been the defeating of the House of Hanover".[7]

Toland's truly heroic work for the cause from 1705 through 1714 is not at all well known; having failed to gain his living from Godolphin or Harley under the "triumvirate"—Marlborough disliked him[8]— and despite of the fact that he had taken the sacrament in 1706 and had been promised this and that, he once more requested service as an agent under Harley to gather intelligence abroad. This was granted, at long last, to the extent apparent in the following (from Lord Raby in Hanover to Harley, November, 1707):

> ...I cannot help acquainting you that Mr. Toland
> since returned from Vienna has been pleased to brag
> to one in a high post here of your great kindness to
> him, which he says goes so far that you writ him word
> of the little note I sent formerly about him, and what
> answer you sent me, adding that, could I think you
> would tell me the secret commission you have given
> him to inspect and inform himself of the behavior of
> all her Majesty's ministers abroad and how they were
> looked upon in the several courts where they are, I
> should be very sorry my character was to be given by
> him who is so very ignorant of all that passes here
> and seems to me to have but a very superficial
> knowledge of anything that passes in other Courts,
> even in that of Dusseldorf for all that he has written
> a book to vindicate that Elector's proceedings...[9]

From spring, 1707, until Harley's dismissal in 1708, and probably beyond (for Harley was sure of his lasting influence with the Queen

after 1708), Toland drew on Harley as the latter's agent, but
unrecognized by any official preferment from either the Lord Treasurer or Secretary of State.[10] Residency in Holland during 1709–10
kept Toland in close proximity to the attempted peace negotiations
and to the war, and, though access to the secret service money was
by this time no longer a possibility, as it was when Harley had been
Secretary of State, it remains likely that the latter then supported
Toland privately, along with Defoe, Prior and others. Toland's letters
of the period do not show him altogether short of funds, and Harley
was anything but inactive during 1708–10. Toland's description of
this curious employment appears in a *Memorial* to Harley, December 17, 1711:

> ...I laid an honester scheme of serving my country,
> your Lordship, and myself: for seeing it was neither
> convenient for you, nor a thing at all desired by me,
> that I should appear in any public post, I sincerely
> proposed (as occasions should offer) to communi-
> cate to your Lordship my observations on the temper
> of the ministry, the disposition of people, the condi-
> tions of our enemies or allies abroad...which advice
> you were to follow in whole, or in part, or not at
> all...All wise Ministers have ever had such private
> monitors.[11]

That this arrangement was not merely financial we discern from
certain statements prefixed: "...My management abroad, my behavior at home, what I whispered in private, and what I printed to the
world, all speak the same language, all tend to the same end", for
which Toland says he was "constantly refusing the most tempting
offers, and often when I had not many guineas left for superfluous
expense". However, "without direct answers to my proposals, how
could I know whether what I did here....helped my friends elsewhere, or betrayed them contrary to my intentions? And accordingly, I have for some time [since 1708?] been very cautious and
reserved..." Harley having been out of power for two years, Toland
had suddenly grown wary: "My impenetrable negotiation at Vienna
(hid under the pretence of curiosity) was not only applauded by the
Prince that employed me [Eugene of Savoy, a known patron in

1709?], but also proportionably rewarded". Finally, "as for the
principles on which we are both to act,.....the general ones which
with me are unalterable and indispensable, are Civil Liberty, Religious Toleration, and the Protestant Succession. These are my
conditions *sine qua non*: and he that will not agree with me on this
foot, must never employ me nor ever trust me". Also, "Sooner than
recreantly espouse Prerogative, Persecution, or the Pretender, let
me be utterly discarded".[12] Here, then, is an unequivocal statement
of Toland's commitment to the Revolution, the strategy underpinning the variety of his tactics. It was also a personal challenge to
Harley. Indirectly, from Hanover, we might inquire?

Harley's Latter-day Trimming

Though anyone may rightly desist from hurling the epithet "Jacobite"
at Robert Harley in view of his ever more desperate contending with
St. John inside the ministry from 1712–14, there is little doubt that
his permitting the situation to drift toward the Stuart side in a haze
of alcohol and despondency was, in the end, a form of complicity by
default.[13] Toland's outrage at this sail-trimming, expressed in *The
Art of Restoring*, had been prefigured as early as his *Memorial* dated
December 17, 1711, revealing Harley's greatest miscalculation as a
politician, and the central reason for the severity of his rejection by
George I after 1714:

> ...Having expressed myself so copiously, My Lord,
> upon Liberty and Toleration, I may be the shorter
> upon our third principle of the House of Hanover,
> from which the other two are inseparable. Liberty
> and Property, Toleration and Union, have occa-
> sioned that Succession. On these it is founded, by
> these it must be maintained against all opposition.
> And, as a sure earnest of a glorious future prospect,
> these are the domestic hereditary principles of that
> House: for, whatever our fools or knaves may prate of
> arbitrary power there, the inhabitants are Syncretists
> by profession (that is German Occasional Conform-
> ists) and never were there subjects on earth better

> used, or more content; the Barons having an appeal
> from the Prince to a higher court, tho' they never
> have occasion given them to make use of this right.
> Your Lordship appeared for this cause as early as
> any, and if to the same you are not still as firm as any,
> what a wretched politician am I? how greatly misled
> myself? and how great a misleader of others, espe-
> cially of that illustrious family?[14]

Toland's fear that his support for Harley while he resided in Hanover
might backfire should the latter turn his coat was all-too-quickly
realized; he had indeed, after all these years, staked the wrong
horse. More abhorrent than "Tory" in that Court became the name
"Harley" after 1712. Toland incurred his share of guilt by association with "Robin the Trickster". *The Art of Restoring* was a belated
attempt to disengage himself from the fact of Harley's patronage over
the years previous to Queen Anne's death.

Harley's strange defection meant not only ruination for Toland
and others; it was a terrible threat to the Revolution overall, to that
"Liberty and Property, Toleration and Union" which "have occasioned that Succession". As the threat emanated from a man now
"Prime Minister" under Queen Anne, could it be taken lightly?
Toland, giving voice to his mounting apprehension that Harley had
begun to waver, writes:

> This, I cannot forbear telling you, is the place [Ha-
> nover] in which your enemies now attack you with
> utmost vigor, and, from certain odd circumstances,
> they persist in their accusation with the most san-
> guine hopes of success. It is here therefore that I
> daily exert my greatest efforts in your defence, and
> where I have a better right to be credited than any of
> your new friends. To this House, in a word, I am
> wholly devoted out of inclination and principle. I
> have no other interest than this, which I take to be
> the common interest of us all.[15]

How ironical that Hanover's dramatic success in 1714—the realization of Toland's lifetime ambition for Britain and for Europe—had

necessarily come to mean the peril of his own rejection at the moment of victory, despite his many years' writing, scheming, even spying for the cause. This personal disaster was the price he had to pay for furthering "Liberty and Property, Toleration and Union" in company with Robert Harley, now raised to the peerage as Earl of Oxford.

An Attempt at Coalition

Outbreak of war in 1702 and the emergence thereafter of a "French interest in England" logically extended the meaning of Toland's motto—"religious toleration and civil liberty!"—to including "the Protestant Succession". Its triumph in 1714 would mean virtual ratification for the Toleration and for Civil Liberty, not to mention final Union with Presbyterian Scotland. Even as the Whigs would reign for forty two years, they might just as easily have been ruined had a Restoration of the Stuarts taken place. It was either/or for both sides. The spectre of impending catastrophe spurred Toland and the Whigs with increasing violence during the last years of Anne. Drawing an analogy between the crash of William III's Junto in 1701 and the fall of that same cabinet structure in 1710, we easily see why the re-emergence of Harley in 1710 misled many Whigs along the path toward hope and not despair. Had not Harley's approach always been coalition and reconciliation rather than party? Would he not do the same now, joining Whig and Tory despite the fact that the last Junto had discarded him in 1708? It was a snare and a delusion that gripped many, Toland among them. True, the situation had changed: the "new country party" of 1698–1701 had bitterly opposed kingly power, whereas the 1710 ministry, contrariwise, was discreetly amenable to Queen Anne and her "newly discovered desires" for a peace with Louis XIV. And the "Old Whigs" of 1697–1701 had been, since 1705, one with the "Modern Whigs" for a "Latitude in religion" and for crushing the "French interest"; any coalition in 1710 would have to be based on some new, undiscovered commonality, altogether different from that which had joined the Old Whigs and Tory squires in 1697.

Lines of policy broke down over two conflicts, one domestic, the other foreign. Domestically, Convocation's attack on the Toleration was now at its most virulent and perfervid due to its active role in the Sacheverell Affair, and the division was razor sharp between those opposed to Occasional Conformity, Dissenting Schools and the constitution, and those who were for them.[16] In foreign policy Tories now openly clamored for a negotiated peace and Whigs, equally openly, for military victory. Harleian precedents pointed to his opposing Tory extremism despite a massive Tory sweep in the 1710 elections. That minister had never sided before with the High Church. He had labored assiduously for war while a member of the "triumvirate", even while putting up with the great Marlborough's open contempt for him. Coalition was surely again possible with this inveterate mediator running the proceedings.

Declaring that "particular friends in this case have I none, but the House of Hanover", John Toland became the not very "secret" spokesman for a coalition. In *A Memorial For The Most Honorable Earl of****Containing A Scheme of Coalition*,[17] written sometime during 1711, "the heats about Sacheverell being quite allayed", Toland claims he now writes to Harley for "the moderate Whigs and the moderate Tories" who are "the true friends of the Country". Among these "a person of undoubted credit among the Whigs" had proposed a scheme to Harley, which Toland has now transcribed: (1) Godolphin and Sunderland being left "for some small time unemployed by consent", other Whigs should balance in number Bolingbroke and his ministry Tories, Harley remaining Treasurer "as a security whereof the balance of the Parliament should be put into your [Harley's] hands"; (2) the fourth parliament of Anne must be dissolved after a year's service [as with William III's fifth parliament in 1701], ensuring a new Whig majority by virtue of the recently passed Qualifying Act of 1710; (3) a propaganda campaign would be unleashed with "pretexts for the dissolution", especially since "the money'd people will never trust this Parliament", even if most landed gentry might; and finally (4) "A certain number of moderate Tories [would be] named, in conjunction with whom the Whigs were willing to act".

Toland refused at first to deliver this over to Harley, complaining the dissolution pretexts were too weak. He felt the timing wrong, and that only a master pretext touching "High Church projects against the Dissenters", or parliament's "falling into heats about the Peace" would serve to "beget a better disposition in the electors".

With that keen sense of timing which seldom failed him when it came to publicity, sharpened to a hair after years of experienced battling, he determined that only basic issues would serve, whether domestic or foreign. Moreover, "The proper time", he advised his Whig patron, "would be after this [fourth] parliament should grant the year's charge", and finish with its first agenda. The appeal once again is for "moderation", as in 1704 and 1705. During those terrible years the thrusts of Nottingham's Tory militants had all but been successfully parried. Why not revive "moderation" under its perennial champion, Robert Harley, and likewise turn aside this second assault in 1711? Harley knew the answer. These same people had betrayed him in 1707 when, after having pushed "moderation" through in the 1705 elections, they had abused their then-recovered power to re-elevate the Junto, turning their savior out in 1708. Was it any wonder "the trickster" would not take the bait scarcely three years after this humiliating debacle?[18] Harley ordinarily insisted upon short memories and very high boiling-points in his dealings with others, but three years had not softened his anger toward the Whig Junto, which had itself fallen the year previously, in 1710. Besides, his personal hatred for Marlborough now equalled the latter's for him,—a battle of giants would now take place over the war.

The Attack on the Lords

If yet blind to the fact that his great patron had turned his coat (or pretending to be blind to better inform Hanover) Toland continued to draw on Harley as late as the spring, 1711. Suddenly, he was summarily dropped for Swift, Prior, and Defoe.[19] Yet he dared not renounce Harley, now Earl of Oxford, for two years more. In a neurotic pattern of frustration, threats, cajolery, and sometimes avowed disbelief, Toland turned out letter after letter, pamphlet after pamphlet, attacking Harleian policies without associating them by name with their undoubted author.

The truth was that Toland's Commonwealthman's position on the political spectrum had no influence after Harley crossed the line and had moved to the right. Ever since 1697, the date of the emergence of the "new country party", the fortunes of "Commonwealth" had depended on the possibility of a third party existing in the middle astride the differences between Junto Whiggism and High Church Toryism. "When Whigs and Tories join", echoed *Clito*, the Miltonic poem of 1701. Unable to *admit* the demise of this third party of the center, Toland carried on in the delusion that Harley, its sometime leader, would return to his senses. After all, "moderation" and Old Whiggism had been accounted submerged before, first in 1702, later in 1708. Fighting the battle for his existence, alone and in poverty, Toland stayed fast at his writing table, circulating intermittently among the London coffeehouses and political clubs, trying to keep the commonwealth strategy alive by concentrating on the great tactical maneuver of the Protestant Succession. Little did he or anyone else realize that Harley's abdication of the center in 1710–1714 had created the precise conditions for that "two-party system" of majority and opposition later to become enshrined throughout the Whig Supremacy, 1714–1760. "The art of governing by parties" was but a few years distant from becoming the art of governing as such; the era of Walpole was just around the corner. It is easy for us to envision now what seemed quite improbable during the last years of Queen Anne, however.

At this point it is well to introduce certain massive changes in prerogative and majority rule which overnight occurred in the course of the "peace" legislation leading forward to Utrecht. In January, 1716, John wrote, "...the deadliest blow which was ever struck at the vitals of Parliament, has been the creating *a whole dozen of Peers* in one day, by the late Queen, while a most material question was depending in the upper House".[20] The date of this astounding event had been New Years Day, 1711–12, just after the second meeting of the fourth parliament, and after Harley, now Oxford, had rejected the Whig-Tory coalition scheme proposed by Toland in his most recent *Memorial*. Though *The Art of Restoring* was not penned until 1714, two years after this creating of the twelve peers, there seems little doubt upon hindsight that, for Toland, that this event was the straw that broke the camel's back. No more would our befuddled agent entreat his master for money or favor. No more would the "trickster" serve in either the strategy or tactics of Commonwealth.

The crisis which broke Whig power in 1712 has been well recorded, down to its constitutional overtones.[21] Upon overriding the Dissenters and passing an Occasional Conformity Bill to assuage Nottingham's moderate Tory following, the Whigs in the Lords enlisted the latter's Whimsicals and braced themselves to overthrow Bolingbroke's Peace without Spain, sent up from the Commons. Only in this manner might they checkmate the Pope and Louis XIV so as to secure the Hanoverian Succession. Harley would fall as a consequence, for a ministry in those days was measured not so much by its majority in Commons as by its control over the Lords. All Tory ministries since 1688 had foundered on this Whig rock. The government seemed paralysed as Oxford, Bolingbroke and the Queen closeted themselves. The creation of the peers climaxed the most exciting session in years, reversing a complete disaster into a complete *coup*. Now it was the Whigs who were in despair, for they had lost all, apparently, with the re-setting of this precedent. The Lords mortally weakened, the government now worked round that body employing the prerogative in unison with its Commons majority. Convocation appeared avenged. The Whigs of the Supremacy later adopted this same governing pattern, refusing after 1714 to relinquish the constitutional weapon wielded so successfully against them by their enemies two years before. The irony here was a savage one. A massive step toward the two-party system had inadvertently been taken. Toland was wrong when he thought the creation of the peers had weakened parliament. Ultimately, as we know today, parliament had been strengthened immeasurably in its fundamental structure; "the art of governing by parties" had been rendered manageable. In his fear of the prerogative, Toland had been blinded to the future. In 1712, however, the passing of the Peace without Spain boded the present danger to the Protestant Succession, for Bolingbroke's radical right wing was finally in position to exercise itself. Harley, fighting for control of the majority, reluctantly supported his sworn inter-party enemy rather than return to the flatulence of "moderation". He was now either in league with the Stuarts for the first time in his life, or isolated from all save the fast failing Queen. Did this mean that he had, with Bolingbroke, forsaken the Protestant Succession? For the time being, it was impossible to tell, and Toland, unsure, held his fire.

The plethora of pamphlets from 1712 through 1714 demonstrated Toland's new proximity to his Whig patrons following Harley's triumph at the New Year. Bolingbroke, to silence animadversions to Swift's *Conduct of the Allies* and Arbuthnot's *The History of John Bull,* passed a Stamp Tax at the rate of a penny a sheet on newspapers and pamphlets in *lieu* of any possible censorship legislation.[22] Many printers went to the wall or were forced to double their prices. The Whigs chose certain of their more effective writers for subsidization, Toland being one, then clubbed together to pay them. Toland, surprisingly, was not yet isolated in company with his former patron. As in 1701, his agile positioning had proven itself to have been sufficiently Whig, especially in his zeal against France, to merit him a place in the ranks during the dark days from 1712 to 1714.

The Campaign Against France

Toland's writings against France after *Paradoxes of State* (1702) merit a word unto themselves, so amplified had his Gallophobia become during the reign of Queen Anne. This might appear superfluous—the Pretender resided in France—had not the war become a tremendous ideological force in the deepening strains of both Whig and Tory thought. Toland continually appears to have worried over all the details of the struggle. In large measure this reflected a general Whig mentality which, by 1712, considered the "Peace without Spain" no less than defeat in a war begun a decade before over the Spanish succession, and moreover, the final degradation of that "balance of Europe" policy extolled in *Anglia Libera.* Toland now raised his voice for the "war party", opposed to the "peace party", in much the same manner as, from 1697 to 1701, he had campaigned for the "country" against the "town".

The Art of Governing by Parties had won Toland not a few adherents among even Modern Whigs in late 1701, especially for its anti-French polemic; likewise his Preface to Matthieu Schiner's *A Phillipick Oration to incite the English against the French: But especially to prevent the treating of a Peace with them too soon after they are beaten...* saved his status among them years later. This piece, written by Schiner in 1514 (handed over to Toland by Harley in Latin manuscript) was printed in English first in 1707, then again in the Latin two years later, when Toland was residing near to Marlborough's camp in Holland.[23] Ironically, it had been dedicated to Queen Anne, who in those days officially favored the war. "If human nature were not ever the same", the Preface begins, "it would be to no purpose to read antient history, wherein we converse with the dead, and learn how to deal with the living". It was Queen Anne's mission to fight Louis XIV as Henry VIII had been destined to contend with Francis I. The traditional rivalry between England and France had become a recurrent death-struggle, despite Anne Stuart's gallic lineage and the French King's commitment to that lineage.

Catholic France, for Toland, was black to white, the evil opposed to all that was good in Europe, the perennial opposite number. Its policy, *contra* the "balance of Europe", was monarchical, not only at home, but abroad. Thus: "...it shall no longer be at the pleasure of one Prince to disturb the repose and endanger the liberty of this part of the world". "The pleasure of one Prince" stood for the *persona* of France in international politics. Control of Spain by France ensured a prolongation of this medieval policy, as did neutralization of the Low Countries and expansion to the Rhine. Toland's neo-Williamite conditions for a peace were deliberately absurd: there must be "Tribute due to us from France...(as well as more favorable conditions for trade...) with a round sum for arrears since the death of Henry the Eighth"! The *Phillipick Oration* was but a quasi-serious proposal—based on Schiner's century-old argument—that France must acknowledge war-guilt for two hundred years of aggression against the Allies, then pay for it in money! The War of the Spanish Succession was no war among many, but a vast culmination. The alternative to peace would be simple annihilation, accomplished by Marlborough—that "phoenix"—the Scourge of God. The purpose of reprinting Schiner's splenetic piece was to provide a re-written military history in some sense consistent with England's now new and almost triumphant constitutional history.

The "proof" Toland sets forth to most vividly contrast these two warring titans of Europe was one of political economy. There is, he says, no "public credit" in France. This phrase—"public credit"— figured ever larger in the literature of the Revolutionary Settlement. One of its various meanings is made clear thusly: "...what native Frenchman...would be such a fool as to put his money in any public fund at home, for either security or improvement: all engagements of that kind have been so frequently violated, with so many bankers broken and undone, to the no less scandal than detriment of the court". For this reason, "France cannot pay her troops". The "public credit" of *Anglia Libera*, on the other hand, was and is the central business of parliament, backed by the affluent banks and merchants of the City of London.

The once militant Harley had come to change his mind (and the mind of the Queen) a few years after publication of *A Phillipick Oration*; but their creature could not now follow their lead. Witness *Dunkirk or Dover, Or The Queen's Honour, The Nation's Safety, The Liberties of Europe, And the Peace of the World, All at Stake till that Fort and Port be totally demolished by the French* (1713). Here, at the moment when the negotiations at Utrecht were drawing to a cloture, Toland states flatly that "England and France are irreconcileable", the official Whig position. One might as well reconcile "Papism and Protestantism". Everything had come down to the wire. The ninth article of the Peace of Utrecht, not yet made public (Toland says), concerned the channel ports of Dunkirk and Dover. Anne had been given Dunkirk by the French on July 8th, 1712. This, Toland warns, is hardly enough. The port—a nest of pirates from which the Pretender had launched an abortive invasion of Scotland in 1708— must (1) be razed, (2) its harbor filled, (3) its moles and sluices levelled for cleaning (4) no more than five months after the signing of the Peace, and (5) at Louis XIV's expense. Why these precautions with the port now in English hands? To prevent evil ministers in England from "selling it again to the French"!

The Art of Restoring

Dunkirk or Dover opened a two-year campaign of innuendo against the most powerful minister in the land, a bearer of the White Staff and Toland's former patron. "All our calamities", it states, "proceed from the weakness or viciousness of our ministers". More particular than this general condemnation was the monstrous allegation (true regarding Bolingbroke) that the reason the present ministry had not razed Dunkirk had been, in a certain sense, to present the French with Dover; that is, to likewise present the Pretender with a springboard, after Anne's death, for another invasion of England patterned after 1708! This was the distinct possibility of the times the Whig side feared most. If successful, it would demolish their side. For some years the Pretender had been offered the Throne would he submit to Canterbury.[24] Bolingbroke, heady with power, was apparently willing to unleash a second civil war to effect this counter-revolution; and an invasion would be necessary to secure another Restoration. To scotch this, Toland wrote his piece urging an immediate, provisional residence in England for the Duke of Cambridge, the future George II.[25] With a Tory ministry, a Tory majority in Commons, the Lords crippled, the Stuart Queen dying, all Whigs concluded rightly that their backs were to the wall. The line between "freedom of the press" and "sedition" grew perilously thin. England desired an end to the war, but did it want as the price of peace a Restoration? Would the Regency Act—the machinery of the Act of Settlement—hold or face repeal? This was the burning question in all quarters. The Whig press dinned it from the house-tops; it was ferociously suppressed by the ministry and at Court.

If "all our calamities proceed from the weakness or viciousness of our ministers", then Harley's role had been one of regressive weakness in the face of Bolingbroke's progressively desperate sanguinity. Harley in 1714 operated daily in a haze of alcohol, allowing himself to be dragged blindly to the right, nearer and nearer to Jacobitism, a truly paralytic politician. Having resigned the center and cast in his lot, he could no longer retrace his steps. His agony was now complete. All Whigs turned on "the trickster", as earlier the equally shameless Tory press had turned on great Marlborough. It was all part of a non-shooting civil war raging in the press to incite public opinion. Marlborough soon fled to Holland, opening negotiations with Hanover, proposing to lead in a Protestant army should a second war for the Succession commence in England. Perhaps this was what tipped the scales.

The Whig attack on Harley was led by John Toland, who managed somehow to publish for the Succession throughout the crisis. He was not driven underground until after *The Art of Restoring*[26] (1714), an explosive pamphlet which sold fourteen editions in one month. Posterior to this blast had surfaced his *Collection of Letters Written by His Excellency General George Monk, Afterwards Duke of Abermarle, Relating to the Restoration of the Royal Family*, also in 1714. In the Introduction to *A Collection of Letters*, the infamous "Monk" is clearly identified with "Sir Roger", Harley's pseudonym. The complete title to *The Art of Restoring* was spun out as *the Piety and Probity of General Monk in bringing about The Last*

Restoration, Evidenced from his own Authentick Letters: With a Just Account of Sir Roger, who runs the Parallel as far as he can. The literary device of alluding to Monck's letters was a means for circumventing prosecution for libel as well as a delicious conceit for avid Whig readers. (The gratuitous misspelling of Monck's name in favor of the monastical version no doubt added salt to the wound.)

The first page of the Preface to *The Art of Restoring* stated flatly that "Sir Roger" was no longer to be considered an Hanoverian, by which it was left to the reader to conclude that he now favored "restoring" the House of Stuart. This, in conjunction with the author's assertion that "I know him so intimately", became the pamphlet's vogue. Any who threw dirt on Marlborough were remote or known enemies, but Toland had long been recognized a Harleian lieutenant by Whigs and Tories alike. This intimacy of acquaintance highlighted and verified Toland's subsequent accusations, which were fulsome and acid.

Toland's "revelations" calculated to expose and humiliate Harley might be reduced to three: that his "handful of Jacobites" had become "most alarming"; that he had broken faith with "the Protestant Dissenters" by supporting the Occasional Conformity and Schism Acts; that his need for money had enabled the French to bribe him for a peace. This last (Toland claimed Harley had barely five hundred pounds *per annum* of his own) fairly answered the incessant Tory accusations of corruption against Marlborough? The conclusion of the Introduction to *The Art of Restoring* is eloquent proof of the tortuous polarity of English politics in 1714:

> ...he's the best Englishman, who's the heartiest against France. Whig and Tory, High and Low Church, will often deceive you, some of these being worse, as others are better, than the Maxims of their Party would make them: but the now-mentioned rule is ever infallible...so he's in earnest (and he only) who is against Enlarging the French *Territories*, or Advantaging their *Commerce*.[27]

For students of Toland this is revealing, not merely another polemic. His courage, attacking Harley on matters of principle, was superb. On domestic issues, it is implied that there was now, finally, a working dialogue between the two parties, for "some are worse" and "some are better" than "the Maxims of their party". Toland has accepted the dreadful antagonism between Whig and Tory as politics rather than the continuation of "civil war". Threats of French domination had made him a "moderate" on the foremost domestic issue of the day. All "whimsical" Hanoverian Tories were now his friends, especially the eccentric adherents of Nottingham.[28] It was the right wing only that now continued alienated, the "French interest". Harley for all intents and purposes was now a Jacobite, and Toland, associated with him, made haste to disown him.[29] 1714 was the year of decision for all Englishmen: Stuarts or Hanoverians. Had Toland not declared himself publicly against his former champion, he would have remained suspect. As it transpired, Toland had been to some extent indelibly branded. But *The Art of Restoring* saved him from the fate of Fiddes, Swift, Defoe and others who had not renounced their chief in time. *The Art of Restoring* and *A Collection of Letters* were part of what Feiling has described as "the furious agitation raging in the press, the coffeehouses, and the provinces, over the dangers to trade and dynasty" accompanying "the long postponement of Parliament till February 1714". The cause of this postponement was the protracted negotiation over the "Asiento", or commercial treaty of the Peace. Toland concludes his Introduction to *A Collection of Letters*: "the Bill of Commerce is not yet passed, as I hope it never will be". By this he argues not so much with the Bill's terms as with the final agreement between England and France on Spanish trade rights the Bill came to represent, and dangers inherent in that agreement for the Protestant Succession.

Poring over the Peace Proclamation drafted by Harley, then alluding once more to the Treasurer's incessant drinking, Toland drew attention to Harley's alleged "twice deferring" to the "Most Catholick" King of Spain. This was hardly protocol, but "a perfect novelty", and, therefore, no doubt dangerous. And why, he asks, are Geneva (Protestant) and Danzig (Catholic) compared in apposite columns in the Proclamation's text, the one column in English, the other in Latin? Is this a mistake, only an attempt to confuse, or was it deliberate? Harley must be watched, for he possesses "the Art of Restoring Credit by lowering the Stocks, the Art of making the North Sea pass for the South Sea,[30] the Art of making War on Inland Potentates without Land Forces". The Lord Treasurer's legendary capacity for "mediation" had now become his capacity for playing both ends against the middle. Toland, finally, had joined the ranks of those who feared and distrusted Lord Oxford. Like "Monk", with whom Oxford is identified, it was the latter's intent to "restore" the Stuarts: "Monk" had "projected the Restoration early in Scotland [as Toland's letters purported to prove] *and was not carried into it by the Stream in England, as the only good thing he either could do, or could not avoid*". In order to ensure Oxford's downfall should the Hanoverians succeed, therefore, *A Collection of Letters* insisted before the fact that being "carried into" a Restoration shall never merit credence. Harley would not plead helplessness nor wriggle out this time! He was committed. Would he one day stand impeached?

Toland never would have been able to remain in England to attack the august Lord Treasurer were he not supported by "some of the most considerable men in the Nation and City". As it happened, he was driven underground, and faced exile once again. Suspicion still divorced him from many, and the financial rewards for his writings hardly measured up to his efforts for the cause. Might not he still be in league with Harley, merely pretending to attack him? What proof existed that he had "utterly renounced" Harley's friendship "upon certain (as he thought) ambiguous words he let drop about the House of Hanover";[31] words allegedly let drop a full two years before *The Art of Restoring* saw the light of day? As there was now little that, prior to Queen Anne's decease, Toland might do for the Protestant Succession, he retired to the country. The Electress Sophia had died in 1713, reducing his chances from that quarter. "Lord!", he wrote ruefully to a friend while in hiding, "how near was my old Woman being a Queen! and your humble servant to being at his ease"! But "All is not over yet, and some symptoms are promising enough".

Political Significance of the War

The deep division characterized by "Whig" and "Tory" emerges more clearly after we have gazed upon it through the prism of Toland's writings. There is a first stage of development: to these nostalgic beginnings belong the Editions and Miltonic writings of the late 1690s, Holles' *Memoirs*, Sidney's *Discourses*, Harrington's *Oceana*, the *Life of Milton* and *Amyntor*. A second stage reflects the Whig crisis of 1697, resolved in the Act of Settlement. Finally, a third stage divided the two factions over Church, the war, and the "Peace without Spain". Throughout each of these agonies the governmental machinery, buffeted severely, managed to adjust itself and to survive. Civil war—that 17th century spectre—was always narrowly but skillfully averted at the last second by parliamentary actions of one sort or another.

It was the third crisis—the war with France—which forged the so-called two-party system. Violence had been rife from 1702 through 1716, especially during election years. Governments rose and fell with rapidity. Heroes the like of Marlborough were elevated to mythical heights then vilified and laid low. Waves of emotion periodically swept the country, whipped up by the partisan press. Allegiances were exchanged. Yet in every instance the bitter dialogue between the parties continued apace on until a *modus vivendi* was in some manner reached. By 1714 this "working arrangement" had assumed the proportions of a political habit encrusted with legal precedent consistent with parliamentary and constitutional norms. The idea of a third party had of course been experimented with, but it had failed. Nottingham's "whimsicals" were ineffective save as a power to tip the scales when it came to forging a majority coalition. The electoral "civil war", earlier deplored by our author, had, slowly, of necessity, been institutionalized. The running struggle between the majority and its minority "opposition" assumed the permanence of a method on the various existing levels of government; judicial, administrative, legislative. This now systematic struggle could no longer be ignored, denied nor averted. It had been built into the day to day structure of the Revolution Settlement.

Toland's personal battle with Harley, though but a footnote to the history of Queen Anne's reign, sheds a certain light on the Settlement, pinpointing the fate of the Harleian and Commonwealth positions as both were swept away amid the 1714 partisan tidal-wave. Toland had earlier found himself forced into the Whig camp in company with the Junto, whilst Harley was insensibly propelled by the Peace into the Tory camp. The War of the Spanish Succession (which might easily have been called the War of the Protestant Succession) admitted no compromising when it came down to basic issues. To be sure, Harley tried to keep one foot on either side until the end, but this resulted merely in his alienation from either. With Harley suddenly dismissed and the Queen dying, the government was for two days in Bolingbroke's hands, precipitating the severest crisis. Had the Queen lived but a few hours longer, it would have been even more unimaginable, with Jacobites placed into he next ministry and the army purged. This would have whipped Whig and Whimsical opposition to the sticking point. But the law and parliamentary sovereignty, as it happened, were not tested. The Stuarts were finished.

Not until 1716–17 did Toland make explicit his grudging realization that "coalition" had given way finally to an uneasy balance between the two parties in Britain. In the *State Anatomy of Great Britain* (1716), he summed it all up. Yet signs we derive from his writings during the crisis of the Succession itself point to his gradual realization of the new order of things, and to a profound resignation concerning the extinction of "Commonwealth", save in its weakest, most modified form. The two-party structure belatedly had dawned upon him, eliciting his crucial admission that "some are worse" and "some are better" than the "Maxims of their party". This marked an end and a beginning in his political thought. Once opposed absolutely to "the art of governing by parties", we will watch him embrace it in *The State Anatomy* as the emerging political reality of the Revolution Settlement.

The Enlightenment Undercurrent

Admidst the terrible struggle encompassing the Protestant Succession, Toland's long-range contributions to the Enlightenment were almost imperceptibly developing. In accordance with the intensity of the political struggle, the pantheistic philosophy had remained necessarily sub-dominant, but certain ideas continued to develop pertaining to the onrushing eighteenth century for which Toland was to some extent, if not in the main responsible. By 1713, at the height of the Succession controversy, a school of so-called "free-thinkers" had finally been recognized in England, typified in the persons of Toland and Anthony Collins, whose *Discourse of Free-thinking* had been published that very year. Toland's libertarianism had likewise taken on palpably concrete form in his renewed campaign for a general naturalization after 1705. Tied in with these themes was his apparent Unitarianism, defined by his, Collins', and others' admiration for the monotheisms of the ancient Hebrews and the eighth century Mohammedans.

To maintain that "freethought", "naturalization", and "Unitarianism" were unconnected with the Succession and its problems would be unhistorical; Tory xenophobia and Convocation were inimical both to Hanover and to these new ideas in one and the same breath. As "doctrines" rather than actual efforts at political maneuvering, they touched upon situations of the moment at most ideologically. Still, they are part of Toland's developing philosophy, the pantheistic point-of-view. Once these disclaimers are registered, they constitute a blend of two related contexts, and are parts of the chronologies of the Succession and of the Enlightenment observed at one and the same time.

Toland appears to have been the initial "Freethinker"[32] in England. His confrontation with Convocation in 1702, recorded in *Vindicius Liberius*, is quite literally the history of the birth of this "movement". The question at issue at that time was whether or not Convocation might prosecute the author of *Christianity Not Mysterious* for violating the 1698 Blasphemy Act, until that moment a dead letter. Was not the author an anti-Trinitarian, a Unitarian or even an atheist? It had been charges of this sort levelled against *Christianity Not Mysterious* that had given rise to the Locke-Stillingfleet controversy in 1697. When Toland emerged "vindicated"— which is to say unprosecuted—the predecent to inquire into scriptural and ecclesiastical mysteries had been publicly established. No "mystery" had formerly stood higher in importance than that of the Trinity.

Toland's freedom after 1702 was an ongoing scandal to those Tories who had whole-heartedly embraced the Convocation Movement as the centerpiece of their domestic program, "the Church in danger". During the Nottingham-Rochester administration, 1702–1704, and later the Harley-St. John administration, 1710–1714, "Freethought" was particularly excoriated as outrageous and ever dangerous to the Church of England. Even the Whig press eschewed "Freethought", and joined with Sacheverell and Leslie in branding it a form of "atheism".[33] Only those few radicals who knew of Toland's pantheistic principles dared appear in any fashion enthusiastic for Freethought. It is no coincidence that Collins was receiving stacks of books from Toland in 1713, the publication year of his own *Discourse of Freethinking*.[34]

Associating "Freethought" with "atheism" was the distinguishing mark of the early period. A character in the first act of Addison's *Drummer* delighted his audience, declaiming, "Atheist is an old-fashioned word, I'm a Freethinker, child". Collins averred, in his *Discourse*: "Another trick of the priests is, to charge all men with atheism, who have more wit than themselves; which is what makes them so implacable against Mr. Gildon, Dr. Tindal, Mr. Toland, and myself; and when they call us wits atheists, it provokes us to be freethinkers".[35] Plainly, the key to early Freethought had been Enlightenment anti-clericalism. Freethinkers were the necessary counterweight to "the priests", in company with Bayle and his "commonwealth of learning" constituency directly across the channel.[36] Surely, therefore, the intrinsic connection between anti-clericalism and the Protestant Succession is patent when we consider the importance of Dr. Sacheverell to his Convocation brethren and to various Jacobite causes after 1710. English Freethought was also born in the crucible of revolution.

Concomitant with anti-clerical feeling was the amplification of the "superstition" theme in *Letters to Serena* (1704), the first book of which was entitled *The Origin and Force of Prejudice*, and in which "superstition" was meant as "*pre-judicium*", or any opinion from authority prior to the exercise of reason. An outsider, reason and intellect were Toland's claims to meritocracy, and his only weapons against the entrenched Anglicans of the old regime.[37]

In the letter to Serena above-mentioned Toland opposed "Préjugés" to "la liberté de condamner", baring the very nerve of Freethought. For it must entail the *condemnation* of prejudice, or iconoclasm by civil right. This alleged right to iconoclasm infuriated several of his contemporaries, and has infuriated fideistic commentators unto the present day.[38] Swift, in 1708, railed against Toland's "trumpery". "Toland", he wrote, "the great oracle of the antichristians, is an Irish priest, the son of an Irish priest".[39] For Swift, Toland's taking the sacrament in March, 1706–7, was a cynical affront. As we know from *Memorial of the State*, however (1705), Toland how recognized no contradiction between Freethought and Low Church membership. Certainly, in that book, he interpreted the Latitudinarian Low Church tradition broadly enough so that it was not possibly inconsistent with Freethought.

The humor and significance of Toland's "conversion" was not lost upon his contemporaries. It was a *coup* equal in importance to his besting Convocation in 1702, since no lesser a personage than the Archbishop of Canterbury procured the priest to perform the rite! Letters to Canterbury and the priest in question sketch out the manner in which his "conversion" was accomplished.[40] The outrage of Anglicans such as the future Dean Swift did not avail them. We may imagine the dismay of certain High Churchmen forced to watch helplessly as the man accused of heresy "imputing atheism" in 1702 took advantage of Whig control of the government and the Bench in 1706-7 to have himself baptized and then confirmed. The implications of Toland's Low Churchmanship were inescapable: the Toleration he had proposed in *A Memorial of the State* he had once more managed to exemplify both in practice and in fact. The church accepted his candidacy, yet he espoused views that were atheistic, flouting Tory admonitions that the "Church was in danger". Not only had Convocation failed to prosecute this "Freethinker": it must now suffer his membership within its own ranks. Insofar as he had been admitted, his views were admitted as well. His presence was living proof that Latitudinarianism and Freethought were acceptable to Canterbury and Low Church alike. The ideas of *A Memorial of the State* were now perfectly institutionalized.[41]

Freethought was therefore not necessarily "anti-Christian", as Swift alleged. The Conclusion of Toland's letter to the Archbishop of Canterbury once again identifies Freethought with Gospel Christianity within the Low Church: "I humbly beg the favour of you to permit me to wait upon Your Grace, to offer that further satisfaction I am prepared to give, as well as to receive your paternal advice and directions, which, next to the sacred precepts of the Gospel, I shall esteem the most obligatory rules whereby to frame the future conduct of my life".[42] The Gospels again! Obviously, the Gospels were the limiting boundary for the Freethinker, the sole divine source of truth rather than of "prejudice" that he must admit to. The "right" to investigate historic Christianity did not yet admit a declaration of atheism.[43]

Toland was sincere in his protestations of Christianity, once Christianity was defined according to his own almost non-Christian terms.[44] In this connection a pamphlet published by him in 1705—the year of *A Memorial of the State*—is of some importance in the history of English Freethought. It was entitled *The Primitive Constitution of the Christian Church, With an Account of the principal Controversies about Church-Government, which at present divide the Christian World*. Here, certain implications of *A Memorial of the State* are further worked out. In that book, the Toleration Act had been defended (against Tories and Dissenters alike) on the ground that Low Church, in its Latitudinarian character, had always proven "indifferent" in religious disputes, hence that it was a rational alternative acceptable for all. In *The Primitive Constitution of the Christian Church* this now-official Whig contention is stretched to the limit so as to impute an implicit anti-clericalism even to Low Church. The same writer who, this year, held that English Christianity was essentially identified with the Low Church now categorically informs us that "I do not think...the Clergy to be the Church".[45]

The reason for Toland's near-absolute (if quite logical) anti-clericalism, as it appears here, would seem at bottom not theological so much as openly political:

> Since Religion, Sir, no longer signifies an institution that informs the mind, and rectifies the manners, but is become the distinguishing name of Sect and Party; happy is that man who is not so rigidly narrow, sour, uneasy, and censorious, as his Religion would make him, if it be in a suffering condition; nor so insolent, vexatious, oppressing, and destructive, as it has the countenance of authority. The one of these hates the man who excludes him from publick trust, he severely observes his failings, and watches an opportunity to shake off his yoke: the other will engross to himself all preferments, he unmercifully punishes the exposer of his actions, and keeps him down the more to prevent his revenge. Mutual exasperations must necessarily follow; then Persecutions, Depopulations, Tumults, and Wars. This makes it of the greatest consequence therefore to any good government, that the principal members of it be rightly informed...[46]

These are the pamphlet's opening sentences. The strife between Dissenters and High Tories is denoted clearly, having risen to a head in the 1705 elections. Clericalism is the vice common to both sets of extremists, whether Calvinist or Anglican. Behind either "faction" lurks that fountainhead of all forms of European clericalism, the hierarchical "Catholick Church":

> I do not admit the Church itself to be a Society under a certain form of Government and officers; or that there is in the world at present, and that there has continued for 1704 years past, any constant system of Doctrine and Discipline maintained by such a Society, deserving the title of the Catholick Church, to which all particular Churches ought to conform or submit...Much less do I believe that there was instituted in the Church a peculiar order of Priests (tho' Christian Priests I do allow) no Priests, I say, whose office it is to instruct the people alone, and successively to appoint those of their own function...And least of all will I grant, that either Princes or Priests may justly damnify any person in his reputation, property, liberty, or life, on the account of his religious profession; nor lay him under any incapacities for not conforming to the national manner of Worship, provided he neither professes nor practices anything repugnant to human Society, or the civil Government where he lives.[47]

These words have an eighteenth century ring about them. They are as radical in the sphere of religion as was the Miltonic *Clito* in the sphere of civil liberties, but now they are consistent with the new Whiggism.[48]

Freethought, indeed, ran a close parallel to "Commonwealth" when it came to civil liberties. Toland's strategy was ever radical, and his tactics barely within the pale of more respectable points-of-view. Both Freethought and Commonwealth were "pantheistic"; that is, ideals for a society of maximum diversity and richness, yet held together by a minimum of external authority. The publications from 1705 to 1714 round out Toland's Freethought—notably *Adelsidaemon* (1709) and the pamphlets attacking Sacheverell—yet they are nothing but extensions and amplifications of Pantheism, their philosophic frame.

The Corollary of a General Naturalization

Mention of religious persecution as the central cause of "depopulation"[49] in England seems a common Whig argument after 1705. The Tory party was held responsible for endangering the mercantilist "balance of trade", in that depopulation meant a dearth of ordinary labor, engendering debilitating lags in production and export. In time of war this was as disastrous as defeat in battle, and, by 1713, all attempts to decrease the volume of trade in Britain were tantamount to increasing it in France. For this reason the coalition of Whigs and moderate Tories that year came close to preventing acceptance of the commercial part of the Treaty of Utrecht. A bill for razing the French port at Dunkirk in 1714 was passed for the same reason.

As threats of "depopulation" grew more ominous, cries for a limited or even general "naturalization" emanated more frequently from the Whig camp. John Toland, as might be expected, favored the most general naturalization possible. The xenophobia of landed Englishmen no doubt appeared to him a form of "prejudice" in nationalistic guise. Toland had spent several years in the Low Countries among the Protestant refugees who had flooded into that region during the seventeenth century. He was an emigre himself, having come to England by way of Ireland and Scotland. (Rumor had it, propogated by Swift, that he had been born in Paris.)

Toland did not wish it inferred that depopulation in England in any way ran counter to the constitutional government extolled in his own *Anglia Libera* (1701). This was the usual Tory answer to the Whig claims that religious uniformity was at fault. As he writes in *A Phillipick Oration* "...tis undeniable that the populousness of England and the Seven United Provinces, as well as their wealth and power, do wholly proceed from their form of government; for their trade is but an effect of their liberty".[50] That this statement is in flat contradiction to the earlier claim that England is de-populated in *The Primitive Constitution of the Christian Church*[51] (1705) does not phase him. He is eager to have it both ways to support his hidden agenda.

Toland is always free of inconsistency if we interpret him in favor of a naturalization for the betterment of the *quality* of English labor rather than for a mere increase of names taken in the census. Indeed, his central argument indicates that England was suffering from a shortage of *skilled* labor rather than of labor as such. A growing population is good "for the defence both of liberty and our country...for the consumption of what's imported, and the skillful manufacturing of what's exported";[52] the word "skillful" is chosen carefully.

> For these and like reasons it is the duty of all wise legislators to encourage the coming of all sorts of men to settle among 'em, which must infallibly happen, if they be all equally naturalized, without any condition other but yielding to the civil government, and taking the oath of allegience: and certainly no reason can occur to me, why other foreign nations may not as safely fill the outskirts of London as the French, since they are sure to bring us the same advantages of power, riches, and industry. Their posterity will be all alike reputed natives; and, in my opinion, the greater diversity of strangers, will render any combination against the old inhabitants the less possible.[53]

Having brought himself to say a kind word about the French Huguenot refugees in London, Toland thereafter defended the two groups ranked next in unpopularity, the Palatines[54] and the Jews. His philo-Judaism aroused the splenetic Swift to the following denunciation in 1712: "The time is at hand", sneers the author of *Tale of a Tub*, "when the freethinkers of Great Britain shall be converted to Judaism; and the sultan shall receive the foreskins of Toland and Collins in a box of gold".[55] For answer, Toland countered at once with his *Reasons for naturalizing the Jews in Great Britain and Ireland On the same foot with all other nations, containing also A Defence of the Jews against all vulgar prejudices in all countries*. In this pamphlet a number of Tolandian themes converge. A Naturalization Act is called for; the Jews by any rational account are equal "as any" in the qualities comprising good citizenship; they suffer the "prejudice" of Europeans more than any other people. Above all, their most "inveterate enemies" are the Christian "priests".[56]

Naturalization is yet another "civil liberty" for the Pantheist and must, if reason and not prejudice arbitrate, extend to all peoples! A general naturalization is as logical an extension of Pantheism's struggle for Civil Liberties as Freethought was the extension of its struggle for Religious Toleration. Any country with the maximum number of races and religions within its confines is richest in diversity and in talent, the country of quality. The extraordinary scope of Toland's social philosophy was far ahead of its time. Neither Matthew Tindal, James Foster, Thomas Morgan, The Third Earl of Shaftesbury, Tom Paine, or others of the so-called Deists were free from their measure of anti-Semitism.[57] Even Isaac Newton, whose passionate philo-Judaism has recently been brought to light,[58] does not appear to have been as enthusiastic for diaspora Jewry as he was for the historically remote monotheism of the Old Testament Hebrews.

The Arian Movement and Critical Deism under Queen Anne

The importance of Unitarianism under Queen Anne was still its negative element, the Arian movement. Politically, it was more important to attack entrenched High Anglican trinitarians, and their Tory supporters, than to speculate as to the character of the One.[59] The distinction between Arianism and Unitarianism had become roughly analogous to the distinction between critical and constructive Deism: the former seemed motivated only by a desire to undermine the foundations of orthodoxy. As such, both Arianism and critical Deism were reduced to quasi-political exercises. Unitarianism and constructive Deism, on the contrary, became theological exercises of reconstruction and reform, or substitutes for precisely that orthodoxy Arians and critical deists wished to see demolished.

Whether Toland was a Socinian or an Arian is open to question. That he was a critical Deist is obvious in that critical Deism, during the first decades of the eighteenth century, was an amplification or systematization of Bayle's "ecclesiastical history" of the 1690s, hence, another triumph for the "commonwealth of learning" in Holland. Toland was also a "constructive" Deist; his *Letters to Serena* include a cosmological system of matter, motion, and intelligence; an original fusion of neo-Stoic and Newtonian principles into an Unitarian whole.

Toland had been on record denouncing Arius and Socinus in his Oxford letter to an unknown correspondent in 1694-5.[60] Christ, in that letter, was both consubstantial with the Father yet "true God and man". In 1706, however, Elisha Smith writes Thomas Hearne quoting Toland to the effect that everything as far removed as *Christianity Not Mysterious* (1966) represented only his "Juvenile thots".[61] His constructive Deism, patent in *Letters to Serena*, (1704), and his critical Deism are both, later, seen in (1) his translation of De la Crequiniere's *The Agreement of the Customs of the East Indians, with those of the Jews and other ancient people*[62] and (2) publication of *The Primitive Constitution of the Christian Church*, each printed in 1705. Unitarianism was therefore central to the constructive Deism of *Letters to Serena*, though with necessary pantheistic overtones of metamorphosis and diversity inherent in the Unity; there are no signs of the Trinity, unless matter, motion, and intelligence (the three categories) replace it by analogy. There is no evidence for maintaining this analogy. What seems certain, however, is the almost violent turn from Trinitarian Christianity to Unitarian Deism by 1704, enough to justify the rejection of his "Juvenile Thots". The taking of the sacrament in 1706 does not contradict this increase in sophistication, for Latitude Men of the Low Church, including Tillotson, had rejected the Trinity amongst themselves many years before.[63] All this was an important matter at the time.

The political overtones of Toland's critical Deism and Unitarianism are best deferred to a discussion of certain later works, especially *Nazarenus* (1718) and *Tetradymus* (1720). *Letters to Serena*, aside from the letter concerning "prejudice", requires a strictly philosophical analysis, separate in context even from Enlightenment anti-clericalism. There is concrete evidence available as to Toland's alleged Socinianism, however. The appendix to *Indifference in Disputes*, entitled *Socinianism Truly Stated*, is a translation from LeClerc printed by Toland in 1705.[64] It is prefaced by his bitter rejection and critique of that doctrine, telling us that by 1705 he had abjured it if ever once he had maintained it. Comparing "other Unitarians" to the "Socinians", he writes: "Some other *Unitarians*, you know, render no religious Adoration to *Jesus Christ*, since they do not hold him to be the supreme Deity, wherein, if they do not act more consistently with Piety, yet I think they do with their own Opinions more than the Socinians".[65] Toland, if Unitarian, is therefore no Socinian, or so it would appear. Naturally, he was careful to safeguard his language. Convocation had been monitoring him since 1697.

It is in fact impossible to assert categorically that Toland was a "Unitarian", and had rejected the Trinity, at any rate by 1714. Certainly the esoteric *Letters to Serena* held no brief for the Trinity; it was an impersonal cosmological inquiry. There is no necessary exclusion of an *exoteric* Trinity, however, in Toland's critical Deism, or philosophy of history, save in his insistence that religious evolution in history, from Christianity to Mohammedanism, must surely propel us in a Unitarian (monotheistic) direction.[66] Toland's philo-Judaism was different from Newton's, however, and part of a larger scheme.[67] Moreover, though he had done a good deal of research in religious history by 1714, he did not organize his thoughts for publication until the crisis over the Protestant Succession had been weathered successfully in favor of the House of Hanover.

Imitatio Ciceroni

The hallmark of the Augustan period in English life and letters was Cicero worship. It was particularly a Whig innovation, notable among Commonwealthmen, and turned the great Roman republican into an Englishman, true born. In this regard Toland, when not foremost, was in the van. For radical Commonwealth Whigs, Cicero had emerged first among the official canons. Toland's projected Cicero edition,[68] planned at Epsom, the English Tusculum, promised to be the consummation of his many other canonic editions. He planned it for his friends; it was to be in Latin, so as to exclude the vulgar.

Toland's veneration of "Tully" is hard to estimate; it seems boundless. It is fair to say that, insofar as he might, Toland modeled his very life and actions after certain details of Cicero's biography, copying his writing style, his stoic pantheism, his public spirit, his dual existence in city and country. Ciceronian republicanism defined the Commonwealthmen, whose struggle to drive the revolution beyond limited monarchy was authorized by Cicero's fragment *On the Commonwealth*, translated in part by Toland in *Vindicius Liberius*.[69] Cicero's moral and religious ideas not only re-appear in *Letters to Serena*, but in Shaftesbury's *Moralists*.[70] In *The Art of Governing by Parties* Toland declares; "...Cicero engaged in the same Work that I do now",[71] and in *Anglia Libera*, "I hope to say of England as Cicero did on the like occasion of Italy".[72]

As a political theorist and philosopher, then, Toland, following Cicero, was an "ancient" rather than a "modern". He does not separate politics and cosmology, for instance, but conjoins them as related social patterns; the human are structured microcosmically to the macrocosm of the natural one. For this reason, much later, he glories in the Ciceronian *cosmopolis* of the *Pantheisticon* (1720). The prestige of this ancient Stoical assumption forced him to approach modern problems of political and social philosophy according to the dialectical terminology of "the one and the many", the private or individual interest at once opposed to, and bound up with, the general interest of the group. There must be liberty and there must be order. In *The State of Anatomy of Great Britain*, "commonwealth" will provide the liberty and "monarchy" the order.[73] As in Cicero, liberty and order are not opposed, but are simultaneously interdependent.

The drift of Tolandian Pantheism is perhaps clearer now. It rounds out as a rationalistic doctrine reflecting certain Platonic "innate ideas" inherited from Ciceronian Stoicism, rather than Locke's empirical doctrine which had recently set "experience" at loggerheads with Natural Law and the "common sense". Modeling Pantheism after Cicero rather than after the more rigorous classical philosophers, or after Newton, Locke, and the other empiricists, Toland feels he has struck the proper balance between private and public in an era in which privacy has finally shown signs of coming into its own. He rejects the new empiricism save as an adjunct to, or modification of, the classical theory of *res publica*.

Toland is a "modern" when trying to regenerate the *res publica* of ancient times anew. He is an "ancient" when he is trying to link this regeneration to republican Rome as the model, the authority and the source. Perhaps this is what "Augustan" means. It is "ancient" and "modern" *at once*. The ancient moment and the modern one have merged, anew, as a return. "Great Britain" is the reincarnation of "Ancient Rome", but, unlike the medieval "Holy Roman Empire", it has divorced itself from the Catholic Church. Great Britain was the true, secular "Rome", republican and/or Augustan. In this frame, Cavaliers and Roundheads have been reconciled, and the Wars of Religion at home brought to their long-awaited conclusion.

CHAPTER IV

NOTES

1. H.M.C. Portland, Vol. IV, pp. 289–90.

2. *Ibid.*, pp. 408–10.

3. John Hunt, "John Toland", *The Contemporary Review*, VIII, June, 1868, p. 198.

4. She died young, in 1705. Her mother, the Electress Sophia, also Toland's friend, died after a long life in 1713.

5. Toland, *Miscellaneous Works*, Vol. II, p. 219.

6. *Ibid.*, p. 216. In an unpublished letter from Leibniz, fitting conditions from 1705–1709, Toland is informed that Hanover is opposed to a peace without Spain, and alarmed at Tory feelers in this direction. Leibniz prophecies that "entre autres obstacles, celui de L'hierarchie ne sera pas des moindres"; this tacitly contrasts "L'hierarchie" (identified with Toryism) to the recent Whig "latitude" in *Memorial of the State* (1705). See Niedersachsische Landes-Bibliothek, Hannover, Briefwechsel Leibniz-Toland, without date or other differentiation.

7. *Ibid.*, p. 388.

8. Toland was beaten up in 1709 by several of "Marlborough's toughs", so gossiped Erasmus Lewis of Oxford; we do not know precisely why, nor where. Most likely in Holland.

9. H.M.C. Portland, Vol. IX, pp. 289–90.

10. Harley controlled the Secret Service account through most of 1708.

11. Toland, *Miscellaneous Works*, Vol. II, p. 223.

12. *Ibid., Another Memorial for the Most Honorable the Earl of* ***, pp. 220–238, *passim*, for the complete statement of Toland's politics as of this date.

13. G.M. Trevelyan, *The Peace and the Protestant Succession*, Chapters XII, XV, XVI, XVII. Harley enraged the Hanoverian faction, refusing to support it publicly. He was corresponding with both Hanover and Lorraine.

14. Toland, *Miscellaneous Works*, Vol. II, pp. 231-2.

15. *Ibid.*, p. 232.

16. For the broad implications and issues of the Sacheverell Affair, see A.T. Scudi, *The Sacheverell Affair*, New York, 1939, especially Chapters II and III.

17. Toland, *Miscellaneous Works*, Vol. II, pp. 215-19.

18. Harley was alienated from the Whig leadership after the rise of some of the younger members to power, notably the younger Sunderland (Marlborough's son-in-law) and Robert Walpole.

19. Toland's divorce from Harley seems to date all-too-nearly from Guiscard's assassination attempt on the Lord Treasurer's life. See H.M.C. Portland, Vol. II, p. 678, Renier Leers to Dr. Stratford of Christchurch concerning a letter from Guiscard to Toland, shortly before the attempt, to be used as evidence against Guiscard for treason. Did John recruit the French protestant adventurer to kill Robert Harley? It is possible. Toland about now retreats to Epsom, his country hideaway.

20. Toland, *State Anatomy of Great Britain*, p. 39.

21. G.M. Trevelyan, *The Peace and the Protestant Succession*, p. 196 ff.

22. *Ibid.*, p. 204 ff.

23. Andrew Kippis, "Janus Junius Toland", *Biographia Brittan- ica*, Vol. VI, p. 3972, n. BB. This information copied from Toland's Preface to *A Phillipick Oration*, in which he claims to have discov- ered, from Harley's collection, the manuscript of Schiner's *Oratio Philippica*. It remains a possibility that Toland and Harley invented Schiner's earlier authorship and that Toland "wrote" it in its entirety.

24. From 1710 to 1714; G.M. Trevelyan, *The Peace and Protes- tant Succession*, Appendix E.

25. *Paradoxes of State*, with Shaftesbury, 1702, had introduced the topic before Anne's accession as Queen.

26. Toland, *Miscellaneous Works*, Vol. II, pp. 431–33.

27. Toland's own politics had been as rigid since 1709. Compare this statement with pp. 2–3 of *Reflections on Dr. Sacheverell's Sermon*, 1710, the original of which had been published in Dutch the year before: "We in England are divided into *Whigs* and *Tories*... The one have been unshaken friends to your Republic [Holland], and to the Empire; and the others remain (as before) irreconcilable enemies to all Foreigners, except the French".

28. In late 1711, prior to the creation of the dozen peers, Nottingham joined the Hanoverian Whigs *contra* the ministry. Nottingham, who had an extraordinary career, had long been a "whimsical". This incited Swift, who knew of Nottingham's hatred for Toland on religious grounds, to write *Toland's Invitation to Dismal*; "Dismal" was Nottingham's nickname in English politics.

29. Toland, *Miscellaneous Works*, Vol. II, pp. 428–30.

30. An allusion to Harley's South Sea Company, the infamous "bubble" of 1720, formed in 1711. The share-holders were to be state's creditors, transferring the floating debt of ten million pounds to an enterprise to get underway as soon as the Commercial Treaty was signed. This ploy not only liquidated the debt, but pre-arranged the terms of the Treaty, making it imperative that trade with South America be opened to British ships on the authority of France and Spain. See John Carswell, *The South Sea Bubble*, Chapter III.

31. The Commonwealth Club, notably Molesworth, rallied behind Toland at this most difficult time.

32. J.M. Robertson, *A Short History of Freethought Ancient and Modern*, New York, 1957 edition, pp. 307–308. For Robertson, *Christianity Not Mysterious* means the entry of Spinozism into England, hence a continuation of freethinking in modern times. Also J.M. Robertson, *A History of Freethought*, 2 Vols., New York, 1930, The Preface. After saying "freethought" and "rationalism" are nearly identical in English usage (p. xxvi), he links both to "the right of private judgment (p. xxxv), the pre-supposition of Toland's rationalism in *Christianity Not Mysterious*, contravening ecclesiastical "authority" of any sort. Robertson is suspect as an authority in many ways, yet his studies are central to the history of freethought and circumvent the anti-Tolandian bias initiated by Leslie Stephen and Paul Hazard. Robertson may have been influenced against Toland through contact with Cambridge philosopher Samuel Alexander, who attributes pantheism to Spinoza, albeit wrongly.

33. See the *Tatler*, III, and *Spectator*, 166 and 234.

34. Toland's edition of *Aesop's Fables* (1704) was dedicated to Collins; their friendship was long-standing. One book accepted by Collins in 1713 was a translation of Bruno's *Spaccio della bestia trionfante* by William Morehead, Toland's brother-in-law. F.H. Heinemann, "John Toland and the Age of Reason", p. 56, n. 48.

35. Anthony Collins, *Discourse of Freethinking*, 1713, p. 85.

36. Toland, *Miscellaneous Works*, Vol. II, p. 437. Freethought is anti-party as well as anti-priest, for, as Toland writes Thoresby,

"there are no parties in the Republic of Letters". Thoresby replies (*Ibid.*, p. 440) "I am particularly pleased with one expression of yours, that "there are no parties in the Republic of Letters", for I am...an *Honest man*".

37.   It is incidental though important to note Toland's deep concern for genealogy in private matters. Origins and sources were surmised to constitute proofs relevant to present conditions. In this regard, Toland traveled hundreds of miles to Prague in 1708 to get a certificate of his legitimacy from certain Irish priests there. He was much injured by accusations against him, common after 1702, that he was "the son of a whore".

38.   How else are we to understand Paul Hazard's uncritical hatred of Toland? See *The European Mind: The Critical Years (1680–1715)*, New Haven, 1953, p. 264, in which Toland is "a born scandal monger" of "morbid mental excitement, uncontrollable rage", no originality, and "foaming at the mouth"; all because he is "intoxicated with reason".

39.   Jonathan Swift, *On Abolishing Christianity*, 1708, p. 4 and p. 17.

40.   Toland, *Miscellaneous Works*, pp. 371–73, and pp. 373–76.

41.   It is worth noting Toland did not find it easy procuring the services of an Anglican priest to accomplish the rite of confirmation. A considerable effort to stop him was organized, and the priest in question came under immediate fire from his colleagues.

42.   *Ibid.*, p. 373.

43.   *Contra* E.M. Wilbur, *A History of Unitarianism*, Vol. II, p. 251, this "right" did not admit of "Natural Religion alone". Freethought was yet fideistic to some.

44.   Toland's later work, especially *Nazarenus*, belies F.H. Heineman's insistence ("John Toland and the Age of Reason", p. 56) that he was completely opposed to "every kind of revealed religion which

triumphs in any way in this world". Arguments from Toland's cosmology or constructive Deism are not. Comparison of these philosophical and theological writings, respectively, show Toland struggling precisely to *parallel* the revealed and the natural in one overarching context.

45. Toland, *Miscellaneous Works*, Vol. II, p. 122.

46. *Ibid.*, pp. 120–21.

47. *Ibid.*, pp. 122–23.

48. See above, Chapter III, p. 103, for Bishop Gibson's concise statement of this "new Whiggism".

49. G.M. Trevelyan, *The Peace and the Protestant Succession*, p. 35ff.

50. Toland, *A Phillipick Oration*, p. 21, n. 15.

51. Toland, *Miscellaneous Works*, Vol. II, p. 121.

52. Toland, *A Phillipick Oration*, p. 83, n. 76.

53. *Ibid.*, pp. 83–84, n. 76.

54. Toland, *Declaration Lately published by the Elector Palatine*, Preface, 1707.

55. Jonathan Swift, *A Wonderful Prophecy*, 1712. Printed in *Works*, 1812 edition, New York, Vol. XXIV, p. 85.

56. Cf. Max Wiener, "John Toland and Judaism", *Hebrew Union College Catalogue*, Cincinnati, 1941, p. 235, n. 58.

57. *Ibid.*, p. 215.

58. Frank Manuel, *Isaac Newton, Historian*, Cambridge, Mass., 1963.

59. Philosopher A.N. Whitehead defined "Unitarianism", saying "There is *at most* One God!" Of course, this definition pertains to "Pantheism" as well.

60. See above, Chapter 1, p. 18.

61. Smith to Hearne, Bodleian Library, Rawlinson MSS, C 146 f. 47.

62. See British Museum Catalogue, new series, under Toland.

63. Cf. Roland Stromberg, *Religious Liberalism in Eighteenth Century England*, p. 43.

64. This translation is appended to *Indifference to Disputes: A Letter from a Pantheist to an Orthodox Friend* (1705). There is a copy in the Manchester College Library, Oxford.

65. Toland, *Indifference in Disputes*, pp. 9–10.

66. Toland, *Nazarenus*, 1718, *passim*.

67. For one thing, Toland's thesis, following Strabo, in *Adeisidaemon* and *Origines Judaicae* (1709) was that the Jews were originally Egyptians and that Mosaic institutions among them perished with Moses. Newton held, on the contrary, that the Israelites *antedated* the Egyptians, and that this chronological priority made their law of greater importance theologically than that of the Egyptian religion. Professor Manuel calls Egypt the "pitfall" of Newtonian philo-Judaism. See Frank Manuel, *Isaac Newton, Historian*, p. 133.

68. Toland, *Miscellaneous Works*, Vol. 1, pp. 231–296. This prospectus was entitled *Cicero Illustratus*.

69. Toland, *Vindicius Liberius*, 1702, 142 ff.

70. In Cicero's *cosmopolis*, the moral center to the natural world, Toland and Shaftesbury are prefigured. In all three writers, religion

means the hypostatization of human cooperation. Cicero's *Tusculan Disputations*, echoing Greek Stoicism, asserts that virtue—a divine spark—joins man to God.

71. Toland, *The Art of Governing by Parties*, p. 179.

72. Toland, *Anglia Libera*, p. 173.

73. Toland, *The State Anatomy of Great Britain*, Section II.

CHAPTER V

SUPREMACY AND HISTORY

The Pantheistic System Matured

Toland died in 1722, years before he had finished his self-appointed tasks in political and philosophical exploration. The Preface to *Tetradymus* (1720) informs us he is still in search of the origins of the Commonwealth idea, and it is obvious that *Pantheisticon* (1720) is but the adumbration of a comprehensive system of philosophy. Nonetheless, what remains of his work from 1714 to 1722, reviewed below, reveals a mind hard at solving the problems of contemporary political and philosophical thought, confident of his approach and emboldened to speak out under the new order of the victorious Whigs.

The final eight years of his life reveal a practical, Ciceronian drawing-together of the ideological (exoteric) and philosophical (esoteric) strains comprising pantheism. The publications concerning history (one ought to say philosophy of history), especially *Nazarenus* (1718), were timed and structured to influence public opinion on specific issues of the day. They were also the result of many years independent research in sources of timeless value to the historian, for *Nazarenus* introduced into modern theology the problematic of the first century A.D. Toland thus strove to combine polemic and research for maximum effect in the political situation at home and for the "commonwealth of learning" abroad; that is, in the language of revolutionary ideology or in that of Enlightenment philosophy. Pantheism was dedicated to present and past indiscriminately. It was a method for all seasons, at once practical and theoretical. Reflecting years of discipline and suffering, it demonstrated more importantly a trained political consciousness alert to the dangers and possibilities for reform inherent in the unstable post-revolutionary situation, whether in legislation or in ideas.

The Study of History

With the entrance of the Hanoverians in autumn, 1714, it was now the Whigs' turn to march into the promised land. Their Supremacy would last from 1714 until 1760, although hardly secure until the ascendancy of Walpole in 1722, the year of Toland's death. Prior to 1722 internal Whig divisions were as serious as, formerly, the great division between the two parties, and 1717 marked a severe crisis in administrative organization.[1] After the Fifteen, or rising of the Scots Jacobites, tension eased somewhat throughout a land now sick heartily of war, rebellion, violence. High sounding idealism levelled off to a modest Lockean plateau, and the Commonwealth idea caved in to complete acceptance of what D'Israeli later called the "Venetian oligarchy of the Whigs". Extremists, Sacheverell for instance, soon found out that they were voices crying in the wilderness. The burning question in politics was how far the now triumphant Whigs were prepared to move "backward", toward a genuine, post-Cromwellian reformation of the monarchy.

　　1715 is the major lacuna in Toland's biography. There are but two facts of significance known regarding his reaction to the great victory. First, he presented a "memorial" to an undesignated minister of state outlining a Whig program which, later, was by and large made policy by the entire party. It was published near the end of 1716 as *The State Anatomy of Great Britain*,[2] limning Whig thinking at the Supremacy's outset, a program for action rather than a political theory. Ideas of John Locke, always contested by Toland,[3] came within time to dominate the Supremacy in political theory.

　　The second fact was Toland's concern to close the circle over his *Specimen of the History of the Druids*,[4] begun with John Aubrey long ago at Oxford in 1693. A letter to a fellow member of the "commonwealth of learning", Ralph Thoresby, requests any recent information concerning the Druids the latter might have in his possession.[5]

　　Both these facts, taken together, established a tenuous theme unifying Toland's last years. In politics, he is concerned that the Whigs will secure the Supremacy and crush any real Tory opposition,[6] the time being ripe in 1716 not only for strong but for ruthless action. In ideas, there emerges an interest the in uses and abuses of history, long brewing, but necessarily rendered subdominant during the Succession crisis and during the "heats" over

Sacheverell. Interest in the "use" of history was ever more ideological than philosophical, though the literature itself reads more in the
manner of "philosophy of history", or, as it was called then, critical
deism. History was for Toland an exoteric study; the basis of a
political theory written not for the philosopher, but for the vulgar.
Comparisons of *Nazarenus* (1718) and *Pantheisticon* (1720) vividly
demonstrate the basic distinction between "temporal" and "eternal"
matters. The affairs of the marketplace are explained always with
reference to historical precedent; as whether or not, for example, the
primitive Christian church was gentile or Jewish, or whether or not
the original Mosaic polity of the Hebrews was republican or monarchical.[7] This served to answer Anglican and Presbyterian contenders of the period whose own inherited theories (those of Hooker
and Cartwright) appealed, in scriptural language, to various neo-
catholic forms of "Tradition" in history. The philosophers of the
Socratic Society or "Pantheisticon", however, met in secret, and
rejected completely such quasi-medieval, neo-Augustinian historicism.[8] The philosopher's imagination was classical, eternal, metamorphic. The "pantheisticon" pored over "nature", not history,
separating the spheres in radical manner. Philosophers dwelt in the
classical *cosmopolis*, the Platonic-Stoic overland of history revived
from studying Cicero's *de Legibus*. Among members of this rarified
but intensely emotional group there were no contenders save
emancipated interlocutors of the banquet serenely engaging one
another for the *ratio positio*. Thus the logical *separation* of history
from philosophy is the subject of the *Clidophorus* (1720), a latter-
day key to Toland's entire previous literary production. *Clidophorus*
traces (in history) the struggle which always had marked the
"philosophers" from mere "ecclesiastical historians"; lovers of "nature"
from mere contenders over the *pseudos* of "scripture".

The result of esotericism is a certain ideological unscrupulousness Toland's readers must guard against when evaluating his
incessant forays into history. The line between ideology and research often draws tenuously thin. On the other hand, assumptions
concerning history in Toland were copiously shared with others
within the Augustan climate of opinion. These were assumptions he
considered truth, not propaganda. They were inherent in his thinking as early as *Christianity Not Mysterious*, if not earlier, and were
explicit as early as the first three "letters" to "Serena". As these

assumptions constitute the ground for *Nazarenus*, *Tetradymus*, *The Destiny of Rome*, and the posthumous *Critical History of the Celtic Religion and Learning*, all Georgian writings, had they not best be examined at the outset?

The central fact about history for Toland, and the reason for that obsessive anti-clericalism which constituted the *Leitmotif* of his fairly long career, was the myth, powerful at the time, of human degeneration.[9] It took two related forms; the depravity of human reason and the loss of human liberty. As he wrote in the third "letter", "I believe I may without much difficulty prove, that such as first entertained Designs against the Liberty of Mankind, were also the first Depravers of their Reason".[10] This very basic datum of the Degeneration or fall of man from a primitive Golden Age had been discovered inductively from the repository of history itself. Toland denied that it was an assumption.[11]

Corrolaries of Degeneration in Toland were (1) the fact of a primitive Golden Age,[12] (2) a modern opportunity in England for its relative regeneration (once superstition and priestcraft were exposed and discredited), and (3) a pessimistic disbelief in the perfectability of man.[13]

The first of these corollaries, "primitivism", itself took several forms. Philosophically your Pantheist was paradoxically a "modern primitive", and his secret meetings, the *symposia*, were designed to regain and exercise the primitive faculty, the divine, "natural light" of reason.[14] In the Golden Age, of course, secrecy of any sort had been unnecessary, for reason had been the rule among men. But the "priestly" enterprise for creating the "immortality of the soul", begun in ancient Egypt, soon corrupted this original human pattern of pure naturalistic explanation, driving the beleaguered "philosophers" to ground.[15] Toland's Pantheists were evidence, meeting secretly, that conditions were yet in disorder. Like the seer Pythagoras, whose naturalistic doctrine of metamorphosis had come down through time in distorted form as the religious belief in the "transmigration of souls",[16] Pantheists sought to protect their hard-won return to naturalism, openly declaiming for a scriptural "latitudinarianism", or some other acceptable cover for their now completely non-biblical point-of-view.

There was also a necessary form of primitivism in biblical matters, however. *Nazarenus* ran counter to the Anglican and

Presbyterian conceptions of the primitive church, and, beyond that, to any strictly Christian, trinitarian interpretation of scriptural authority. It was Jewish monotheism, not Christian trinitarianism that Toland discovered yet existing at the source of political history among the corrupted millions, and a "Mosaic", non-Levitical monotheism at that. The Jews, significantly the only still surviving race from among the ancients, were, in Mosaic times (as were modern Whigs opposed to modern Tories) never committed to an absolute monarchy.[17] *Tetradymus* (1720) is in part the declaration for a true *Respublica Mosaica*,[18] prefigured in Toland's writings as early as *Limitations for the Next Foreign Successor* (1701).[19] The book of Samuel reinforced this Old Testament insight, it might well be added, when Israel chose Saul to be King.

Thirdly, there are more than signs in Toland of that sentimental, benevolent primitivism common later to Rousseau and his followers, in which the jaded European saw (or thought he saw) living evidence of the Golden Age in the proto-anthropological rusticity of savages. Toland writes about an undated letter to a fellow member of the "commonwealth of learning",[20] exultantly quoting "An Account of the Indians at Carolina" in which "the honest Indians of that Country" teach the author of the letter, a Frenchman, "to know what Man is in his depraved state". There is "so wonderful an union amongst this People, that you never hear of any disputes or quarrels among them". They are "industrious and laborious", and so forth. "Good God!", writes Toland's source, "What sensible difference I found betwixt the happy quietness and repose I enjoy'd amongst them, and the trouble I meet with daily amongst people, a thousand times more savage than they". These in Carolina will never be Christians, it is true, says the Frenchman, but might that not be better for them, considering the character of most Christians in modern times?

A fourth primitivism in Toland inspired him to write anew his *Specimen of the History of the Druids*, in 1715. In that very strange piece the Druids are portrayed as the *ne plus ultra* of "superstition" and "priestcraft", standing midway in this negative tradition between the Egyptians and the early Christian Catholics, the most demonic of priestcraft's exemplars.[21] All the diabolical techniques of fear and obscurantism concerning the "doctrine" of personal immortality were perfected by these terrible clerics, and their sway over the hapless Celts was absolute not only in religion, but in polity.

Obviously, conversely, the rampant program of unmasking priestcraft in Augustan times gave at least the glimmering of promise for a second Golden Age, a "modern" regeneration of reason and liberty, and a truly genuine hope for establishing Carl Becker's eighteenth century "heavenly city" here on earth. Toland remained ever more pessimistic, however, refusing to embrace the growing and haunting notion of human "perfectability". He was realist enough to recognise the strength of the monarchical, hierarchical and authoritarian institutions of his time, which so tenaciously had withstood the various successive onslaughts represented by the Protestant Reformation, the wars of religion and the English Revolution. Pantheism must lurk hidden underground, content to assail the vulgar with discreet infusions of libertarian ideas as circumstances permitted, reiterating constantly its version of the platonic Great Lie.

The King and his Germans

Toland was supported for a time after 1714 by at least two known Whig patrons, perhaps one or two more. The Commonwealthmen, notably Viscount Robert Molesworth, were interested in his projected history of the Druids.[22] Certain of the new Court Germans, on the other hand, appear to have been prominent sponsors of *The State Anatomy of Great Britain*.[23]

Since 1701, after receiving "medals and pictures" from the Electress Dowager in appreciation for *Anglia Libera*, Toland had made the most of his connections at Hanover, coutributing in a literary way to the cultural life there whenever possible. More than any other British writer he became associated with Hanover's cause. His astonishing philological ability had been recognized at home, on the Rhine and at Hanover in 1701, when, as Lord Macclesfield's secretary, he served as principal interpreter in William III's deputation to that Principality. Some earlier books were overtly flattering to the Hanoverians; *Letters to Serena* (1704), *The Ordinances, Ordinances, Statutes, and Privileges of the Royal Academy, erected by the King of Prussia* (1705). *An Account of the Courts of*

Prussia and Hanover (1705), and *The Declaration of the Elector Palatine* (1707) were all of them particularly fulsome.

For many years, however, Hanoverian policy—especially when enunciated by Leibniz or the Electress Sophia—had been carefully, even fearfully bi-partisan.[24] Elaborate precautions were taken not to offend Queen Anne and the leading Tories through mistakes or signs of partiality toward the opposition Whigs. Tacitly, it was always re-asserted in unofficial messages and acts that the Whigs were the "natural friends" of Hanover, and the Tories forever inimical. This policy gradually changed under George Lewis, Sophia's son, and the Elector *de facto* as Sophia grew suddenly decrepit and older.[25] Disregarding Leibniz, George Lewis had viewed with alarm Harley's and St. John's policy after 1710, considering the "peace without Spain" a betrayal of Allied interests. Hanoverian troops, after all, had fought in Marlborough's armies from the outset! Elevation of the future George II to the Lords as the Duke of Cambridge failed to impress the Elector, for the young Duke was not permitted to come into England to take his seat, any more than the Electress had been allowed to enter after passage of the notorious Naturalization Act of 1705. Information sent back to Hanover by the resident at the Court of St. James, Hans Caspar Baron von Bothmer, convinced George Lewis that his mother's bi-partisan policy had failed and must forthwith be abandoned. The impotence of Nottingham's Whimsicals further deepened this dichotomization of the Hanoverian mind. When at last St. John, as Bolingbroke, got the "peace without Spain" successfully through the Commons, George Lewis told Bothmer to inform the Whigs that his mother's policy no longer obtained. The Elector was now in more than tacit opposition to the British government.

It seems hardly coincidental that Toland's divorce from Harley dates precisely from this jettisoning of the bi-partisan strategy at Hanover.[26] Toland had been defending Harley to Hanoverian agents in London,[27] but he could no longer persist in this after the Elector declared himself. That Toland received money from Whig sources after the packing of the Lords in 1711–12 is evidence that he had timed his desertion nicely. Much of the reason for the plethora of pamphlets from 1712 through 1714 had been motivated by his concern to please the heir-apparent. He and Bothmer appeared to be in close communication. *The Art of Restoring* (1714) excoriated

Oxford to demonstrate beyond a shadow of a doubt where its
author's loyalties now lay, and to atone, if possible, for too long
defending the now "treacherous" Lord Treasurer.

Indications are *The State Anatomy of Great Britain* (1716),
Toland's compendium of Whig legislation which ran continual
editions throughout most of 1717, was sponsored not so much by
the party as by personages at Court. If so, we assume the Court to
have been supporting Toland at least partially in 1715 and 1716,
when the book had been in its various stages of manuscript.
Bothmer, Baron von Bernstorff, and Jean Robethon, all Hanoverian
agents, were at once accused of paying for *The State Anatomy*,
inasmuch as it demanded peerages for all three. In a vitriolic
pamphlet, Defoe impugned Toland for "treason" and for abetting "an
apparent Design among a Party of Men" to "introduce Foreigners
into the Number of our Nobility".[28] *The State Anatomy* had predicted
peerages for George I's favorites by an Act of Parliament, possibly as
a trial balloon for gauging public reaction to the idea. Indeed, the
book seems to have been a trial balloon for the Supremacy itself. In
the words of its principal opponent: "This work has been long
hatching, and had been much talked of many Days before it came
abroad; Pieces and Parts of it handed about, and rehearsed among
the People it is calculated to serve".[29] In a second pamphlet, also
attributed to the now freewheeling Defoe, Bothmer and Bernstorff
were named.

Toland rounded on Defoe in *The Second Part of the State
Anatomy* (1717) as that "Samaritan Whig" who protested to loving
King George I while hating all foreigners! Defoe's *Argument Proving
that the Design of Employing and Ennobling Foreigners...* (1717) had
indeed been racist, more Tory xenophobia than Whig liberality:
"...the author of this foul and rascally stuff", writes Toland, "is the
very man...who wrote the *True-Born Englishman*, a Satyr against the
whole English nation for their contempt of Foreigners". This proved
an effective rebuttal, and some considered Defoe "murthered". The
damage had been done, however, and the King's Germans did not
get their English titles. If Defoe had been discredited, so had Toland.
Later, in his *A Farther Argument Against Ennobling Foreigners in
Answer to the Two Parts of the State Anatomy* (1717), Defoe correctly
sums up: "The Case in short is this, the Design is blown, the Plot is
discovered, and thereby defeated; he thought it was Ripe before it

was so, and brought it out too soon: He knows it well enough, for his own Friends blame him for it, and now he has no Remedy, but to cry out *Jacobitism* and *Treason* in his opposers".[30] That Toland died in poverty five years later, supported only by Molesworth, might have been due in great part to this earlier failure to serve the Court interest. Securing the English titles had been a prime, initial concern of German George for his life-long favorites.

Meanwhile, barely behind the scenes, Harley had his revenge for *The Art of Restoring*. Residing luxuriously in the Tower until June of 1717, awaiting trial, he financed the attacks on *The State Anatomy*. Defoe and Fiddes were his men; Defoe responsible for damaging the non-religious arguments, Fiddes the religious.[31] Risking clear identification with the inglorious retreat of High Toryism in these blasts, Harley seems to have been revenged upon Hanover itself for its having contemptuously rejected him, as George Lewis had, in 1714.

The Whig Program

The State Anatomy of Great Britain, being news, was nevertheless effective. It drew out the opposition on three counts: (1) fear the Dissenters would overnight achieve their religious and civil rights.[32] (2) xenophobic aversion to George I and his Germans, and (3) fear that the Fifteen might justify the future expense of a standing army.[33] It had been Harley's writers who initially voiced these protests, representing the moderate element on the Tory spectrum. In like manner political lines were drawn between the two parties in 1716–17. The Septennial Act had effectively frozen parliamentary personnel in fixed positions so as not to disrupt the balance through the calling of another election. That "balance", of course, was unequal. The Whigs now controlled Commons, the Lords, and the government. They were determined to keep on controlling them.

The Whig Supremacy in domestic and foreign affairs nevertheless required elaborate justification. The number of "Whimsical" Tories had been considerable who stood firm for the Hanoverians in 1714. Many of these hoped for a coalition, and were disappointed when Nottingham alone represented them among the new leaders in the first ministry. To be sure, the riots and uprisings of 1715 played auspiciously into Whig hands, and all Tories were condemned by association with them, regardless of degree. Still, the firm statement of a Whig Supremacy was the signal of doom for the party of Harley and Bolingbroke, now led so tentatively by Nottingham. Toland's *State Anatomy*, awaited by all concerned, commenced with a proclamation to threaten.

In the first place, it was announced, the King's title would no longer be treated in the manner of William III's; that is, *de facto* but not *de jure*.[34] Such distinctions come either from "La Fleche or from Christchurch". It was this Achilles' heel of revolutionary political theory which had enabled Atterbury to rally his fanatical following to defend "the Church in danger" in 1702. Hence the significance attached to the words "Lawful King" in the following statement: "...that never any King will endure, or not execute (*nota bene*) any such persons with his Dominions, as shall deny him to be Lawful King; or go about to withdraw his subjects from his Allegiance, or incite them to resist or rebel against him".[35] The paragraph concludes on this subject ominously, saying "...he, who is not for us, is against us".[36] The die had been cast for a Supremacy. "Divine Right" and "Passive Obedience" were henceforward signs of rebellion in a King's subject.

The words of the Preface were spelled out in the Conclusion.[37] Whigs must heed no "artificial cry, under the notion of a Country party, or any other the like threadbare topick. They cannot but remember that the Tories could never enter, but by the gaps they made for them in their own body". This, for Toland, was an admission. Had he not, following Harley in 1698, preached coalition on precisely this ground, splitting Country Whigs off from those of the Town? The "art of governing by parties" was a monstrosity. It was the rule now, especially in that core of the government, the ministry: "The King is convinced", says *The State Anatomy*, "Whigs and Tories are incompatable in the Ministry; that drawing two ways is making no way at all". All those who want "coalition" now are "trimmers"; "A sort of neutral Gentlemen are much commended by some, but tis by such as know no more of politicks than what's ideal: for those Neuters are real Indifferents, and a Trimmer (which is the name they affect) is like a bird of prey, hovering over two Armies, being ready to feed on the dead of either side". The Whig Supremacy was therefore a matter of proto-Bismarckian *Realpolitik*, a matter of brute necessity. Toland had completely rejected the "ideal" of a non-partisan state, the centerpiece of his writings from 1697 to 1701. Tories are now "enemies" of the King and his government.

The Preface and Conclusion of *The State Anatomy* proclaim the Supremacy; the argument of the book itself presents the Whig state "at one view", foreign and domestic. Later, in *The Second Part of the State Anatomy*, "General Heads" were designated (1) "To show friends and enemies of the Hanoverians at home", and (2) "To show ways for recovering our Honor, Wealth, and Power abroad".[38]

In Section I of *The State Anatomy*, the catagories are two: those who befriend the Hanoverians and those who do not. They are befriended (it is maintained) by Lords, Commons, Army, Navy, Militia, merchants and financiers, gentry, bishops, and by Dissenters. Their enemies, on the other hand, are "inferior clergy" and "peasants". One purpose of this heading was to imply that all animadversions against *The State Anatomy* were *eo ipso* against the Crown. Toland trumpeted Defoe's and Fiddes' pamphlets—"or the Lord of Oxford knows who besides"—as vicious personal attacks not upon himself so much as on George I, forcing Defoe into lamely protesting "There is not one Sentence or Syllable in the Book entituled *An Argument, etc.* which is intended as a Reflection or Disrespect to the Person, or Government, or Conduct of King George..."[39]

The Commonwealthmen, continues Section II, are still friends, for "our Monarchy is the best form of a Commonwealth". But Commonwealthmen "who are either for an Aristocracy or a Democracy" or "for the sovereignty of a Parliament and Privy Council, exclusive of all Regal Government" no longer exist in Britain. "There is no such party at all", says Toland. The word "Commonwealth" is "just as the word *Respublica* in Latin...a general word for all free Governments..." It is not opposed in meaning to absolute hereditary monarchy with "no medium in the case". Everyone sings the praises of a "mixed constitution now, following Aristotle, Polybius, and Cicero. As for the doctrine of "indefeasible Right", it had been "set up at first by a few aspiring Clergymen, to ingratiate themselves with weak Princes, who had designed it inconsistent with the laws: and therefore these Court-parasites represented to the said princes all true lovers of the Constitution as enemies to their power, and as Republicans, or Commonwealthmen, by which they meant men of levelling and Democratical Principles". All this, of course, was entirely contradictory to the author's more radical writings of 1697 to 1701. The old ideal had been outlawed by and subjugated to the Supremacy.

Whig and Tory in *The State Anatomy*[40] are treated as mere subdivisions, like Commonwealthman and Divine Righter, under "friends and enemies of the Crown". The dichotomization is extremely uncompromising: "Whigs", says Toland, "are the asserters of Liberty, and Tories abettors of Tyranny". Following Walpole's lead (after Walpole's consignment of Oxford to the Tower) Toland had been permitted to speak for those in power. Tories will have little to expect in the dark days ahead. The problem is more than political, it is a matter of faith: "A material difference between the Tories and the Whigs is the latter's being civil and friendly to foreigners...whereas the former are their declared enemies (unless you except the French Papists)..." All Whigs, it is concluded, are "Hanoverian" and all Tories "Stuart". Any other subdivisions are misleading save the opprobrious one of "Trimmer". "Court and Country" is a meaningless distinction, for some Whigs and Tories have been both. The Supremacy is further outlined in these hard, unyielding words.

Toland writes on, backed by his Court and parliamentary editors. *The State Anatomy* turns now to that hard core of the High Tory opposition, the universities and the Church.[41] To begin with, England's and the King's friends are *all* Protestants, *none* are Catholics. The King, we are told, was mightily offended by the Pope's public prayers for the Pretender in 1715. In the second place, all English Protestants are friends of the Crown save the High Churchmen, whose "heats" over William III's title initially gave rise to Sacheverell. Quakers are a regrettable exception at the other extreme. The Dissenters, by the way, are to be congratulated for remaining loyal to Hanover following passage of the Schism Act, and now "...railing against the Dissenters is an infallible evidence of the insincerity of a new Convert..."

At this point Toland tips the Whig hand, and goes even beyond conventional dichotomization. He declares that "A Religious Test is a Political Monopoly" save for Catholics (who are cast out from the Toleration *se defendendo*), and the time has come not only for repeal of the Occasional Conformity and Schism Acts—forced through parliament in the last years of Queen Anne—but also of the Test Act, the very spine of the Clarendon Code.[42] Dissenters, under the Whig Supremacy, are to achieve their civil liberty in the process of regaining their religious independence. Toland has taken a giant step beyond the settlement of 1705, and his own *Memorial of the State*, although the same 1705 argument is employed to justify the leap; namely, the public peace. Trouble comes when religion is subjected to a policy of conformity; when "Liberty of Conscience" is violated. England, Scotland, and Ireland will never be at peace, says *The State Autonomy*, until the Presbyterians join the Establishment on an equal footing with the retreating Anglicans. The King's Speech, 22 September, 1714, had stressed "toleration" for the Dissenters (meaning at most repeal of the Occasional Conformity and Schism Acts) but on the secular grounds of "trade and riches". Toland goes beyond this now returning to the old cry for a "comprehension". Partial "Liberty of Conscience" had been tried, he asserts, and had been found wanting, especially since passage of the Act of Union (1706). Now there must be that total "Liberty of Conscience" entailing civil equality for Dissent through a repeal of the Test Act. Certainly another trial balloon had here been sent aloft? Fiddes' *Remarks on the State Anatomy of Great Britain* (1716–17) was the immediate response of "Church" to "our distempered and complaining Sectaries".[43] Defoe's *A Farther Argument Against Ennobling Foreigners* (1717) rails against this framing of a "new Constitution".[44] A religion for Great Britain based on a comprehension was to become the sticking-point for the beleaguered Tory "opposition".

There was a negative corrolary to this program of reform, the suppressing of "Protestant Property" in England; that is, "the independency of the Church upon the State, tho without Transubstantiation".[45] The Whig hand here was tipped again. Convocation, author of this bastard policy, had been branded for a speedy dissolution? The Church had been in danger in 1688, Toland concedes, but never after. It is, however, in danger at this moment, following 1714! Salvation by "Episcopal Ordination", and catch phrases such as "I would rather be Papist than Presbyterian" are hereby out of style. The disgraces of 1704–8, and 1710–13, when "our reputation abroad, and tranquility at home were visibly decaying" must not be re-enacted. Convocation had received fair warning.

Rounding out the domestic program, Toland writes at great speed, taking an axe to that dual taproot of Tory strength, the

universities and common pulpits.[46] Hints are offered concerning the
University of Oxford in particular, and to to "inferior clergy" (gradu-
ates of Oxford) who had long gotten out the vote in the country. The
former, as the foremost supplier of "inferior clergy" to the nation,
was perhaps the essence and source of all present trouble-making
in the land! And this, indeed, was very nearly true. Nowhere, during
the Fifteen, was there more justification for reading the Riot Act
than at Oxford University. "Why may not *Oxford*, for example, be
reformed or purged by a *Royal Visitation* tomorrow, as Aberdeen was
the other day, or *Oxford* itself was at the Reformation"? Whigs
hereby demand "a strictly legal dependence" of universities upon
the Crown", in line with the Act of Submission,[47] and the economic
dependence of all pulpits according to the Statute of Mortmain.[48]

Having said all this, little of which was exactly new or unexpected, Toland then proposed a measure most extreme, and of
which nothing has been heard of since, but which must have struck
a rare note as it rang upon eighteenth century ears. Why, he asks,
may the universities not be nationalized like the Church or the
army? Privately schools are obviously bad, he says, for they tend to
make traditions of the views of the founder "to their own detriment".
Would not an "Act of Parliament" to "change the frame" of the
universities be proper now that Toryism had been proven barren of
all credit? The Dutch, Toland points out, have done just this: "A
History of the Original power and proceedings of the *Curators* of the
Dutch Universities, will be seasonable very soon", the *State Anatomy* suggests. "Schools therefore being instituted for the publick
good, must be kept to their institution by publick Authority".

In sum, the domestic ideas of the early Supremacy appear to be
all suppression, a cleaning out of the Augean stables. In foreign
affairs, however, Toland attempts to draw a more heartening picture
for Whig Great Britain both in Europe and around the world. His
keynote is the mercantilist phrase that "Trade is the soul of our
British world".[49]

Toland's writing on foreign policy is a summing up of the
economic meaning of the English Revolution. It had become apparent to those concerned, London Whigs in particular, that the
Revolution had been, or had become an economic event. This
essential fact transcending even religion and its claims, had emerged
from out of the debates over the Assiento, or Commercial Treaty of
the Peace of Utrecht, in 1713.

Toland, weakest when it came to economic theory—he was certainly less analytic than Davenant, Pollexfen, or even Defoe—had nevertheless followed the Commercial Treaty like a hawk, and eventually came to see in it the underlying crux of things. He had a sound knowledge of mercantilist theory—the "balance of trade" whereby importation of specie must continually exceed export—and he had written on economic matters variously since his *Propositions for Uniting the Two East India Companies*, in 1701. *A Phillipic Oration*, in 1706, had made some interesting comments pertaining to the effects of the Naturalization Act (1705) upon trade, and both *Dunkirk or Dover* (1713) and *The Grand Mystery Laid Open* (1714) had given evidence that their author was becoming more and more concerned about the relation of politics to the Exchequer. It was not until *The State Anatomy*, however, that these ancillary excursions into the mysteries of economics crystallized into sweeping and more important considerations, somewhat original to Whig mercantilism. If the *State Anatomy* is a source of evidence, had there been a proposed change in the nature of the Whig canon concerning "Property"?[50]

Property, surely, was yet a Harringtonian obsession. Toland insinuates to the unsuspecting reader that it was also Cicero's "general doctrine"; "It must be the principal care of him, who is at the head of the Government, that every one be secured in his Property, and that the Estates of private men be not diminished under the pretence of a publick good. Governments and Cities (says he) were constituted chiefly for this very reason, that all men might enjoy their own".

In the *Oceana*, however, "property" meant precisely land, the source of agrarian wealth. In those days, both Republican and Royalist strength had emanated for the most part from the country. By 1716, however, Tory strength was marshalled principally in the country, whilst the Whig forces were located more and more in the town. In accordance with this turnabout, Toland is adamant to assert that "property" meant land no longer; it means money. As now "Trade is the soul of our British world", the old distinction between "landed" and "moneyed" has become specious: "As if the products of Gentlemen's lands were worth anything without money", he expostulates, "or as if they were not more worth, when there's more money"! Revenues, fleets, and armies are paid in coin, not in farm produce. The Venetians are the model now, not the squire-archy. And they, the Venetians, ennobled their merchants accord-ing to merit. As for the Whigs, let it be remembered that the "trading people of this country" are now those in power. Moreover George I, *The Second Part of the State Anatomy*, informs us, is "a perfect man of business"!

The new mercantilist conception of property as money had been found to fit hand-in-glove with post-war schemes for foreign expan-sion. Expansion by "Great Britain", especially the consolidation of Hanoverian and English interests in Northern Europe, was dear to the heart and mind of George I, and, in mercantilist terms, parallel to the interests of the powerful London traders. For this reason agrarianism had become broadly and vaguely associated with reactionaries, Toryism, and Church. Repudiation of agraria, time-honored as agraria was, now came more easily to the Whigs of the Supremacy. Moreover, certain corrolaries to this new canon that real wealth was money more than land devolved; as, for example, the cry to search out and destroy the Scottish clans and rural pockets of Irish Jacobites, and to supplant them with a new trading middle-class empowered to rule particularly in the more backward agrarian counties.[51]

The underlying motive serving the new Whiggism was therefore the economic one. Ways and means became serious matters for diplomacy[52] and war.[53] *The State Anatomy* was the initial salvo for the new expansionism in government policy, commencing with re-establishing the Dutch Barrier system under Stanhope's secre-tariat, and with more aggressive probings into the spheres of influence of the Baltic port of Hamburg. In diplomacy "Our Reason of State", according to *The State Anatomy*, "is, *To support the Protestant interest everywhere...*and...*To keep the balance of Europe equal*". Re-establishing the Barrier System had been patent in the Williamite phrase "balance of Europe". What is new was a general out-going diplomacy of "the Protestant interest everywhere", once the radical Commonwealthman's ideal, but now intensely practical and proper to "Great Britian".

Basic to the new expansionism had to be a vigorous propaganda campaign to discourage isolationist thinking, and promotion of warfare as the surest means to Empire. The giving out of English peerages to foreigners in the old Roman manner meant more than

rewarding a few Hanoverians; it was, in principle, declaring for of the
Whig attack upon Tory xenophobia and conservative Anglo-cen-
tricity in foreign affairs. Isolationism was common not only to
almost all Tories, but to many moderate and conservative Whigs as
well. In the crisis of late 1717, which split Walpole and Townshend
from Sunderland and Stanhope, Sunderland accused Townshend
of Anglo-centric nearsightedness as if it were some sort of political
crime:

> The King is very much surprised [he writes] at the
> strange notion that seems at present to prevail, as if
> the Parliament was not to concern themselves in any
> thing that happens in these parts of the world, which
> he looks upon not only as exposing him to all kinds
> of affronts, but even to ruin: and indeed this notion
> is nothing but the old Tory one, that England can
> subsist by itself, whatever becomes of the rest of
> Europe, which has been so justly exploded ever since
> the Revolution.[54]

The line between Whig foreign policy and Hanoverian self-interest
had drawn imperceptibly thin, but the desire toward expansion and
the traditional mercantilist bullionism were at first not always easy
together, and the extent to which George I might be taking personal
advantage of his new English base of operations was not yet clear.
Use of the fleet in the Baltic was expensive. Toland, writing primarily
for the Court, prior to Walpole's and Townshend's abrupt if tempo-
rary defection from the expansionist line, seemed blind to these
major Whig differences, or else excluded them deliberately from
notice?

The grand theme of the new foreign policy, however, was hardly
mere opposition to xenophobia. It was essentially the lesson Whigs
thought they had learned after suffering passage of Bolingbroke's
"peace without Spain"; namely, that if a good war increases trade,
it is therefore preferable to a bad peace which does not. England,
says Section XI of *The State Anatomy*, must press the Catholic
countries of Europe, and never rest. There must be a barracked
army of at least six thousand on call, ready not only for rebellions
and invasions at home, but for foreign duty. Planned risk of foreign
war is the imperial, "Venetian" hallmark of the new foreign policy.

Dissolution of Convocation in 1718

Following the setback of 1704, Convocation had triumphed steadily in the political sphere. In 1714, however, the Protestant Succession halted Church Toryism dead in its tracks. Sacheverell had meanwhile been raised to the Bench by Bolingbroke as a reward for his successful demogoguery during the 1711 elections. Even after 1714, George I had "gratefully" followed Nottingham's advice that the new government follow a moderate line in religious policy, not seeking immediately to repeal the Occasional Conformity, Schism, or Test Acts.[55] Emotional reactions to these repeals, it was argued, might aggravate the Fifteen into a major rebellion. Dissenters were intensely unpopular among countryside Tories, and the Fifteen had been marked with the sacking of scores of chapels and meeting-houses.

As late as 1717, Toland—the Dissenters were now, in Defoe's words, his "happy minions"—cautioned that an assault on Church was as yet "unseasonable"; he had been so informed by the ministry. He therefore urged patience among "his" Dissenters; their time would finally come. In *The State Anatomy*, however, he had been firm for repeal of all anti-Dissent legislation, including the Test Act.

Behind the scenes measures were being taken in preparation for the onslaught. Nottingham was dismissed in 1716 and the Church deprived of its only real defender within the ministry. Oxford was in the Tower awaiting trial, held hostage in the hands of Whig leaders. His release and acquittal represented a nice bargaining point in the repeals matter, for most Tories and Churchmen were loathe to see him tried and convicted for treason along with Bolingbroke, who had fled to France. The government appeared ready to strike in late 1717. The King's Speech in October of that year called for an ominous "Strengthening of the Protestant Interest", meaning that the time for repealing the Acts was at hand.

Convocation had unwittingly provided the pretext for its own destruction, goaded into action by the absentee Bishop of Bangor, Benjamin Hoadly. Hoadly held views identical with those of Toland both as to the Erastian Church and an individual "Liberty of Conscience" among all Christians. Toland was a layman, however, and Hoadly a Bishop. Convocation could not refrain from acting after Hoadly preached his famous sermon before the King. The text—*John*, xviii, 36—developed all the Erastian and individualist ramifications of Christ's words, "My kingdom is not of this world". Despite the fact that George I publicly, officially approved Hoadly's sermon, Convocation knew that it must censure Hoadly to re-assert its own integrity, and so foolishly if honorably had brought itself into direct confrontation with the regal power. Under these circumstances, Convocation was of course dissolved, not to gather again until the mid-nineteenth century! The time for elevation of the Dissenters to a comprehension and full citizenship had at long last arrived.

In preparation for this showdown, and as a long-standing member of the "commonwealth of learning", Toland had been working assiduously on his *A Critical History of the Celtic Religion and Learning* and on *Nazarenus*; both were major efforts. The former was not yet done; but *Nazarenus* was published in 1718, the year of the dissolution.

Nazarenus' message was that Protestantism was One, a theme old as the *Apology* (1697).[56] The proof was not, however, Unitarian; that is, not directly related to the Arian Movement of the Williamite and early Augustan periods. It was rather historical, bearing on that sticking-point for all Christian churches and sects, the "Primitive Church". Contending for this or that form of original church government had rent Protestantism asunder since the Reformation. Divisions in England between Anglicans and Presbyterians and other sects on this count had resulted in the infamous Test Act, converting all Presbyterians into Dissenters, and depriving a sizeable minority of the populace of their civil liberties throughout the settlement period of the Glorious Revolution. Although Toland had been helpful in shifting Dissent toward the Establishment in 1705, when *Memorial of the State* had linked the party once for all to Low Church, neither he nor anyone else considered this "adjustment" final. *Nazarenus* (1718) was published in 1718 to open wide the Dissent question once again. Not only the Dissenters but that other barely-tolerated minority, the Jews, were central to it's argument. 1718 was the year in which the first Jewish temple re-opened its doors in London.[57]

Christianity Not Mysterious had argued for the unity of Protestantism on grounds of the Gospels alone. Toland, in his concern for the Jews now re-settling in England, realized that any current or future appeal to the Gospels would hardly benefit that minority. He set about re-thinking his entire position *vis à vis* biblical literature. Beginning with *Amyntor* (1699), and evolving in *The Primitive Constitution of the Christian Church* (1713), *Adeisidaemon* (1709) and *Reasons for Naturalizing the Jews* (1713), Toland brought to a culmination non-Christian lines of thinking to prove once for all a Protestant unity in his *Nazarenus*. He extended the meaning of the term "Protestant" to include any group opposed to Rome. Fiddes, in his *Remarks on the State Anatomy* (1716–17), protested against this calling even the Jews "protestants" as "an abuse of Speech", defending the Establishment against "our distempered and complaining Sectaries".[58] After *Nazarenus*, however, it was apparent Toland would insist on an even broader application of the term. His book, involving considerable research concerning the first century A.D., submitted it to the reader that any universal Protestant movement must rediscover itself in the career of the Jews. Jewry must become the rallying-point for all Protestants, superceding the Gospels! History demonstrated that the Primitive Church—that pre-Catholic starting-point for all Protestant churches and sects— had been a Jewish phenomenon through and through, and that the original Jerusalem Christians, prior to the later triumph of Catholicism, had been themselves a sect of reformed Jews, called "Nazarens".[59]

If Toland's evidence weren't valid to some degree, his conception of a Judaic Protestantism would have been little more than an imaginative *tour de force*; rationalizing a general toleration in historical terms. In fact Toland opened a vein of historical research which is still mined, and increasingly so, to the present day.[60] In 1718 the thesis that Protestant Christianity must derive from a return to Judaism and, by so doing, detach itself from all other contenders, was a scandal that required instant rebuttal. Mangey's *Remarks from Nazarenus*, Paterson's *Anti-Nazarenus*, Hare's *Difficulties and Discouragements which attend the Study of the Scriptures*, and Brett's *Tradition necessary to explain and interpret the Holy Scriptures* were rushed to press.

Toland's overall view in *Nazarenus* was that Protestantism was, *ad fontes*, a return to "monotheism" as first practised by the ancient Hebrews, next by the Nazarens, and, after the *diaspora*, by the Mohammedans. The "tradition" was not discontinuous, but bound into one line by our author's investigating the first centuries after Jesus, and through the unearthing of "the Gospel of Barnabas", discovered earlier in the Hague by Toland in 1709. Written in Arabic, the Gospel of Barnabas stood as the missing link between the ancient Hebrews and eighth century Mohammedans through the first century Nazarens. In this Gospel, Toland avers, the essential *anti-Pauline Judaism* of primitive Christianity had in strong probability been finally established. It had been this Judaic Christianity which, later, had undergone various distortions at the hands first of Paul, then, after Constantine, systematically onward from the Council of Nicea.

The description of the primitive Church of the Nazarens (in *Nazarenus*) appeared in structure roughly similar to that of modern Presbyterianism! There had been three "pillars", twelve "apostles", seventy "deacons", and an *ecclesia* or "congregation". This lay-system separated the elders and their appointed managers from the congregation, though beyond this single concession to "church government" there was no "hierarchy". The Dissenters of 1717–1718 appear to have been delighted with the arrangement; Gilbert Dalrymple, in a pamphlet entitled *A Letter from Edinburgh to Dr. Sherlock...In which is An Apology for the English Dissenters with a Word or two relating to Mr. Toland* (1719)[61] comments ironically that the Anglican "Tradition" had been better defended by *Nazarenus* than by Hoadly's "invisible church". In Toland, there had existed at least a primitive structure of *some* sort, *contra* Hoadly and *pro* "Tradition".

The Destiny of Rome (1718) rounds out Toland's commentary on the fate of the three minority groups then suffering under impossible legal restrictions in England. Whereas *Nazarenus* pleaded the causes of Dissenter and Jew, *The Destiny of Rome* sought with equal vehemence to undermine the deteriorating situation of English Catholics. In contrast to a simple Jewish Christianity, *The Destiny of Rome* set upon "Hierocracy, Hierarchy, or Government of Priests, which has so long subsisted in the World". Written by "a Divine of the Church of the First-born" and alluding heavily to "Pufendorf's incomparable Treatise on this Subject, in his Introduction to the General History of Europe", *The Destiny of Rome* prophecies, "...this Papal State is not only now drawing towards its final Period, but you and I...may live to see it totally dissolved and destroyed".[62] There are

four reasons: (1) "the Nature of Things", whereby everything dis-
solves "in a perpetual Flux", (2) the absurdity of princes sharing
their subjects with a "Priest-Prince", (3) the scandal of papal wealth
as against the doctrine of apostolic poverty, and (4) "the fatal
Wounds" dealt Rome by "Those heroic Souls, Luther and Calvin".[63]
Toland's prescription for the *coup de grace* sounds as if it had been
written by Hoadly himself; "All the Princes have to do, whether they
set up National Patriarchs, or other Forms of Church Government,
is to make them in all things dependent on the state: I mean as to
Government and Discipline, for matters of Belief ought to be ever
free and unconstrained".[64] Erastianism in government, individualism in belief; these tenets placed Toland squarely alongside Hoadly
in the Bangorian Controversy of 1718.

The Occasional Conformity and Schism Acts were repealed, but
the Test Act was not. The status of the Dissenters was fundamentally only a little improved by 1720 over what it had been in 1689.
The plight of the Jews worsened; Anti-Semitism provided a sharp
focus for Tory and country Whig xenophobia, and pamphlets soon
appeared such as *A Historical and Law Treatise against the Jews
and Judaism* (1721).[65] At best, Toland's quixotic struggle against
clericalism had helped engineer the dissolution of Convocation and
what remained of the Convocation Movement in 1718. When Atterbury was exiled for treason in 1723, found out plotting for the
Pretender, the political capital from "the Church in danger" for the
defeated side had been, finally and completely, exhausted.

Deism

The relation of critical and constructive deism to the destruction of
Convocation has not yet been analysed.[66] If John Toland is at all an
example, the relation existed and was a significant one. Not until the
dissolution did he dare to make public his most euhemeristic
contentions, in *Nazarenus* (1718), *Tetradymus* (1720), and in *Pantheisticon* (1720). They had been implied or cryptically alluded to,
but might never be published until Convocation was no more.

"Deism" has been defined in various ways, whether sufficiently
or not. In Toland, deism was that part of the Pantheist's frame of
mind having to do not with the parts but with the whole. Pantheism

entire recognizes "diversity" equally with "unity"; a shorthand definition in the *Pantheisticon* sums the entire doctrine up saying, "All Things are from the Whole, and the Whole is from all Things".[67] The deistic *phase* of this doctrine pertains to "the Whole"; the unity of the process abstracted from the diversity. In another writing, the Deity is distinguished by separating the "divine center" from its "attributes".[68] The "divine center", or "Deity", is that which lasts, which is constant, which does not change.

In *Nazarenus*, the divine center of history (Deity working in and through history) was and remained the Jewish tradition, reaching as an unbroken thread from earliest recorded and civilized times unto the present. More especially, however, it was that primitive and entirely original part of Jewish tradition Toland calls the *Respublica Mosaica*;[69] a non-clerical "Commonwealth" instituted by Moses upon his imposition of the Decalogue, the history of which had been imperfectly recorded in the Pentateuch. Buttressing his theme, in *Letters to Serena*, that "Mankind is in all Ages the same",[70] the authority of the Pentateuch is projected hypothetically by Toland from the beginning to the end of time as the marshalling point of history as such, transcending the crucifixion and the gospels, an unending truth throughout human memory.

Toland had this *Respublica Mosaica* in mind as early as 1709, and had promised Leibniz a complete account.[71] Not until 1718 did he hazard bringing his idea into print in English; in 1710 the Convocation movement, parading Sacheverell, had reached the peak of its momentum. When Toland did raise the curtain on the *Respublica Mosaica*, in 1718, he had not yet completed his study of the Pentateuch in Hebrew, either from a want of time or of money, and he states in the Preface to the *Tetradymus* (1720) that a book on the *Respublica Mosaica* was as yet his goal. He complains there about the "impenetrable obscurity of the Old Testament texts of the Pentateuch". He had not lost heart, however, and declared that the discoveries he had made thus far "created in me a higher veneration for Moses" which "superadd the monstrous Traditions of others: and also...those who reject the *Pentateuch* as intirely fabulous, and who will not allow either the wisdom or sanctity of the *Mosaic Laws*".

Toland's historical deism is also clear in his acceptance of the famous "fragment" from Cicero's *de Respublica* quoted in the 22nd Book of *The City of God* (a fragment St. Augustine had put to other uses):

> A government ought to be so constituted, as to be of
> Eternal Duration: and for this reason it is, that no
> kind of dissolution is natural to a Government, as to
> a man; to whom death is not only unavoidable, but
> also very desirable. But when a Government is over-
> turned, ruined, and quite extinguished, tis in some
> sort (that we may compare great things with small) as
> if the whole world should fall to pieces, and to be
> forever destroyed.[72]

For this paradigmatic and primitive "reason" Toland admires "the
Commonwealth of Moses...above all forms of Government that ever
existed":

> You will remember, that I maintain the Plan given by
> Moses, never to have been wholly, or indeed in any
> degree of perfection, established in Judea: and that
> if it once had, it could never have been afterwards
> destroyed, either by external violence of Enemies,
> but should have lasted as long as Mankind; which is
> to make a *Government Immortal*, tho it be reckoned
> one of the things in Nature the most subject to
> Revolutions.[73]

In the exoteric dimension of history, then, Toland embraced a
deism, and had done so since at least 1709.

Pantheisticon (1720) set forth the parallel development in cosmology. In the fourth and fifth "letters" to Serena, Toland had been
extremely reluctant to discuss the "divine center" and had sidestepped the subject maddeningly at every turn, sometimes implying
there was a "Deity", at other times implying there was none.[74] After
1718 and the dissolution of Convocation, however, he was explicit;
the "divine center" of cosmos is in reality "aether", a fine, tenuous
form of matter which runs about *cosmos* like the swift-darting *theos*
of the Greeks—Heraclitean "fire"—and is experienced directly by
man and animals through the nervous system.[75] "Spirit" is in reality
"matter", and *vice versa*. The finest matter is "intelligence", and this
is in turn the "Deity" of constructive deism.

To the extent Toland had modified his philosophy of flux by the
rational mysticism of the "divine center", he had become a "deist",

the political import of which was clear. It was heretical to Anglicans and to Presbyterians alike, because Unitarian and because always "natural" rather than "scriptural". Part of the Enlightenment—the intellectual revolution of return to the presumed natural illumination of primitive times—deism struck at the foundations of the medieval order in politics, at the Trinity, and at the concept of "hierarchy". Psychologically, deism provided also a prestigeous new stability for belief in accordance with Newtonian physics, and promised a natural religion for the scientistic true believers of the onrushing eighteenth century. Toland had in secret forgone his old, biblical religion after rejecting *Christianity Not Mysterious*, some years before; by 1720 he was one of those who sought a new religion more suitable yet equally imaginative for his time, following the turbulent period of "the crisis of the European conscience".

The Septennial Act

Toland appears to have had money enough throughout the Supremacy until he was bankrupted with hundreds of others when Harley's "South Sea Bubble" burst in August of 1720.[76] He was deeply in debt at his death, in 1722, however, and apparently left no will.[77] His papers found no secure repository, and were ultimately "scattered to the four winds".[78] In the mistaken belief that he was destined for a windfall at the opening of the books of the South Sea Company, again in August of 1720, Toland wrote the *Pantheisticon*[79] (1720), the opening paragraph of which heralds the intrinsic sociability of Pantheism and reveals the inveterately political core of the man:

> Man, as a sociable Animal, can neither live well, nor happy, nor at any rate, without the Help and Concurrence of Others; therefore several Societies, nay innumerable, necessarily arose from the very Nature of the Thing. Husbands enter into a strict Alliance with Wives, Parents with Children, Masters with Servants, Magistrates with Subjects, and finally, from the coming together of all those Men with their respective Families, the Union of living in Cities is

formed. Some of these Societies are more, others less
voluntary.[80]

No talk of contracts here, as in Locke, nor of Hobbesian primacies
of force, but a classical socialism, as in Socrates, Aristotle or Cicero.

Death found Toland at Putney (he had taken a house there to
escape the smoke of London for a chronic asthma) where he
recorded himself troubled in mind concerning the Septennial Act.
This momentous legislation, passed as an emergency measure in
1716, and approved by him then in grudging fashion, had, after the
manner of anything pertaining to long parliaments, proven something of a disaster for the Whigs during the first years of the
Supremacy. The party had split in two again, the South Sea
scandals further discrediting it, and an election would soon be
upcoming from which a Tory reaction was anticipated and feared.
Too weary to write, Toland made his last act the republishing of his
Danger of Mercenary Parliaments (1698), with its Harleian arguments for annual parliaments, and its catalogue of long parliament
evils. He managed to eke out a Preface to the new edition, but seems
to have been unable to finish it properly. "After a total Discontinu-
ance of Parliaments", he begins, "the greatest Grievance is Long
Parliaments, and next to that such as are mercenarily bribed and
packed". His advice to the Whigs is to compare "this last Long
Parliament, just expired" with those of Charles I and Charles II, and
from this discern and understand why the South Sea Bubble had
swollen and burst. Corruptions of tenure, seniority, and the private
schemes of placemen had done their work once again. The party was
not to blame. The very nature of long parliaments was responsible.

Near the end, the now Lord Molesworth sent a letter to his friend
of a lifetime:

> ...You will see that I am embark'd in a grand affair, no
> less than standing for Westminster. I have employed
> all my friends as solicitors and runners about, and
> great hopes are given me. I am sorry you are not in a
> state of health to do me service. Believe me, when I
> tell you, you shall fare as I do and if that be not ex-
> traordinarily well, blame not.[81]

Toland's reply may have been the last time he put pen to paper, and, properly, it ended his life on a political note: "...Since you will embark once more on that troublesome sea, I heartily wish you all good luck, and wish I had been able to run for you night and day, which with great ardor I wou'd. I am, with utmost truth and zeal..."[82]

CHAPTER V

NOTES

1. The King demoted Townshend and dismissed Walpole, elevating Stanhope and Sunderland, over the policy of the Northern Sector bearing on Hanover. See Wolfgang Michael, *The Beginnings of the Hanoverian Dynasty*, London, 1936, Chapters XI–XII. Also Wolfgang Michael, *The Quadruple Alliance*, London, 1939, Chapter II. J.H. Plumb, *Sir Robert Walpole*, London, 1956, Chapters IV–VII.

2. See Andrew Kippis, "Janus Junius Toland", *Biographia Brittanica*, pp. 3974–3975.

3. Toland, *Tetradymus*, 1720, p. 190. Toland wrote, "I proceed upon different principles from Mr. Locke, and principles that are better".

4. Andrew Kippis, "Janius Junius Toland", *Biographia Brittanica*, pp. 3974–3975.

5. Toland, *Miscellaneous Works*, Vol. II, pp. 436–440. Dated Sept. 29, 1715.

6. Toland, *The State Anatomy of Great Britain*, 1716, *passim*.

7. Toland, *Nazarenus*, 1718, *passim*.

8. Toland, *Pantheisticon*, 1720, *passim*. Especially the Introduction, pp. 104–107.

9. Toland, *Letters to Serena*, I–III.

10. *Ibid.*, pp. 71–72.

11. *Ibid.*, Preface, I. John Toland, *Critical History of the Celtic Religion and Learning*, 1726, p. 15.

12. *Ibid.*, II.

13. John Toland, *Indifference in Disputes: A Letter from a Pantheist to an Orthodox Friend, passim.*

14. John Toland, *Pantheisticon*, Introduction.

15. Toland, *Letters to Serena*, II–III.

16. *Ibid.*, pp. 57–58.

17. Toland, *Nazarenus*, Appendix I.

18. Toland, *Tetradymus*, 1720, Preface.

19. Toland, *Limitations for the Next Foreign Successor*, pp. 28–29.

20. Toland, *Miscellaneous Works*, Vol. II, pp. 423–428.

21. Toland, *Critical History of the Celtic Religion and Learning*, pp. 47–50.

22. *The Critical History* is in the form of letters to Molesworth. See Caroline Robbins, *The Eighteenth Century Commonwealthman*, p. 126.

23. Daniel Defoe, *A Farther Argument Against Ennobling Foreigners*, 1717, p. 19.

24. Waltraut Fricke, "Leibniz und die englische Sukzession des Hauses Hannover", *Quellen und Darstellungen Zur Geschichte Niedersachsens*, Hildesheim, 1957, *passim*. Also Adolphus Ward, *Leibniz as a Politician*, Manchester, 1911, p. 37.

25. Wolfgang Michael, *The Beginnings of the Hanoverian Dynasty*, Chapter II.

26. Toland, *Miscellaneous Works*, Vol. II, p. 42.

27. *Ibid.*, pp. 231–232.

28. The thesis of Defoe's splenetic pamphlet is in its full title: *An Argument Proving that the Design of Employing and Ennobling Foreigners, Is a Treasonable Conspiracy against the Constitution, dangerous to the Kingdom, an Affront to the Nobility of Scotland in particular, and Dishonorable to the Peerage in general*, 1717.

29. *Ibid.*, pp. 7–8.

30. Daniel Defoe, *A Farther Argument Against Ennobling Foreigners*, p. 27.

31. Richard Fiddes, *Remarks on the State Anatomy of Great Britain*, 1717. Fiddes had been Harley's chaplain until 1714.

32. Defoe also wrote *Reasons Against Repealing the Occasional, and Test Acts, and Admitting the Dissenters to Places of Trust and Power. Occasioned by Reading the 6th Chap. of a Pamphlet called, The State Anatomy of Great Britain...*, 1718.

33. Daniel Defoe, *An Argument Proving that the Design of Employing and Ennobling Foreigners...*, Appendix I.

34. Toland, *The State Anatomy of Great Britain*, Preface.

35. *Ibid.*

36. *Ibid.*

37. *Ibid.*, pp. 102–104.

38. Toland, *The Second Part of the State Anatomy of Great Britain*, 1717, p. 8.

39. Daniel Defoe, *A Farther Argument Against Ennobling Foreigners*, p. 26.

40. Toland, *The State Anatomy of Great Britain*, Section III.

41. *Ibid.*, Sections IV–VII.

42. *Ibid.*, p. 32.

43. Richard Fiddes, *Remarks on the State Anatomy of Great Britain*, p. 29.

44. Daniel Defoe, *A Farther Argument Against Ennobling Foreigners*, p. 43.

45. Toland, *The State Anatomy of Great Britain*, p. 34.

46. *Ibid.*, Section XII.

47. 25 Henry VIII again, by which Convocation could not enact any measure without a licence from the Crown.

48. A precedent for controlling pulpits based on economic sanctions which resulted in limiting preferments. It was modernized in 1736 as the Mortmain Act. See W.R. Ward, *Georgian Oxford*, Oxford, 1958, p. 157–160.

49. Toland, *The State Anatomy of Great Britain*, p. 43. Sections VIII, X, XI, and XV pertain to foreign policy.

50. *Ibid.*, Section VIII.

51. *Ibid.*, Section IX.

52. *Ibid*, Section X.

53. *Ibid.*, Section XI.

54. Archdeacon William Coxe, *The Life and Administration of Sir Robert Walpole*, Vol. II, London, 1798, p. 128.

55. The following summation of church policy under George I closely follows Wolfgang Michael, *The Quadruple Alliance*, Chapter IV.

56. The Dutch model is again apparent in the persistence with which Toland tracked this conception; since 1633 there had been a general Toleration for all save Catholics in the Merchant State, presuming the "unity" of all Protestants.

57. Wolfgang Michael, *The Quadruple Alliance*, pp. 63–65. London Freemansonry also dates from 1718.

58. Richard Fiddes, *Remarks on the State Anatomy of Great Britain*, pp. 29–33.

59. Toland, *Nazarenus, passim*. The relation of this line of argument to both Unitarianism and the Bangorian Controversy is explicit in the Preface, pp. iv–v and xxiv, respectively. Of Hoadly, Toland says: "All the arts of defamation I have enumerated are now jointly put into practice in this nation against one man...I mean the right reverend the Bishop of Bangor".

60. In spite of the fact that the "Gospel of Barnabas" proved to be a late fraud (see Norman L. Torrey, *Voltaire and the English Deists*, New Haven, 1930, pp. 20–21) much work is current dating from Luigi Salvatorelli, "From Locke to Reitzenstein: The Historical Investigation of the Origins of Christianity", *Harvard Theological Review*, XXII, 4, 1929, pp. 263–264; see Hans-Joachim Schoeps' *Theologie und Geschichte des Judenchristentums*, Tübingen, 1949 and L.E. Elliot-Binns, "Galilean Christianity", *Studies in Biblical Theology*, SCM Press, 1956. Eugenio Zolli's *The Nazarene*, Rome, 1951, investigates the meaning of the word "Nazarene" from a Catholic point-of-view. Zolli, a convert to Catholicism, had been the Chief Rabbi of Rome.

61. This pamphlet is important evidence linking *Nazarenus* to the Bangorian Controversy. See especially pp. 33–35.

62. Toland, *The Destiny of Rome*, 1718, p. 6.

63. *Ibid.*, pp. 7–9.

64. *Ibid.*, p. 19.

65. See Wolfgang Michael, *The Quadruple Alliance*, pp. 64–65.

66. There are several treatises concerning deism in general: The best is Leslie Stephen, *English Thought in the Eighteenth Century*, already referred to; Mark Pattison, "Tendencies of Religious Thought in England, 1688–1750", *Essays*, London, no date given, pp. 1–64; S.G. Hefelbower, *The Relation of John Locke to English Deism*, Chicago, 1918; and Roger Emerson, *English Deism, 1670–1755*, 1962.

67. Toland, *Pantheisticon*, 1720, p. 14.

68. Toland, *Clidophorus*, 1720, pp. 87–88.

69. Toland, *Nazarenus*, Appendix I.

70. Toland, *Letters to Serena*, Preface.

71. Toland, *Miscellaneous Works*, Vol. II, p. 392.

72. Toland, *Nazarenus*, Appendix I, pp. 6–7.

73. *Ibid.*, p. 2.

74. Toland, *Letters to Serena*, pp. 232–233 is the ultimate avoidance of the issue.

75. Toland, *Pantheisticon*, pp. 22–24.

76. Toland, *Miscellaneous Works*, Vol. II, pp. 461–475.

77. The following entry appears in Caveat Book 5 for the Peculiar of Croydon, 29 March 1722: "Ne etc. in bonis Johannis Toland nuper de Putney in Com. Surriae defuncti inscio Holman pro intereste Edwardi Hinton cred.". Holman and Hinton are otherwise

completely unknown in Toland's biography. The present writer found no will at Somerset House.

78. Isaac D'Israeli alleges to have seen "some" of them. *Calamities of Authors*, Vol. I, New York, 1881, p. 254n.

79. Toland, *Miscellaneous Works*, Vol. II, pp. 493–494.

80. This is a paraphrasing of the opening paragraph of *Reasons for Naturalizing the Jews* (1713).

81. Toland, *Miscellaneous Works*, Vol. II, pp. 493–494.

82. *Ibid.*, pp. 494–495. Regarding the Septennial Act, see J.H. Plumb, *The Growth of Political Stability in England 1675-1725*, pp. 174–175 (Peregrine ed., 1969). Harley, described elsewhere by Plumb as a "crypto-Tory" and "Whig *manqué*"—his two masks—died in 1724. He might well have been amused at the renewed fuss over "annual parliaments" in 1722.

EPILOGUE

JOHN TOLAND AND AUGUSTAN PHILOSOPHY

Tolandi Peregrinans

There is one remarkable similarity between the careers of Toland and Voltaire. Each waged his messianic battle, often alone, against civil and religious injustice. The great dissimilarity was that, whereas Voltaire rose to an extraordinary eminence, Toland fell into an almost stygian obscurity. Conditions, ripe for Voltaire, were unripe for Toland. This in spite of the fact that Voltaire visited England less than a decade after Toland's death at Putney. The liberties and tolerance of the Augustan period in English history, which so inspired the French Sage of the Enlightenment, had been created in an atmosphere more conservative than either man realized. Toland had paid heavily for attacking institutions and prejudices dear to the heart of average "Briton".

A lost manuscript, *Tolandi peregrinans*, without date,[1] might have revealed much of the man, were we able to peruse it. In a quite literal sense he was a wanderer, a *homo viator*, who travelled more than any ambassador or government agent in his fifty two years. His travel literature was anticipated, printed and read. Figuratively, Toland was the prototype of the alienated intellectual for his period. Irish, probably bastard, classless, an enthusiast, often penniless, he was forced to fall back time and again on a stance of the purest individualism in order to take part in public life at all. *Christianity Not Mysterious*, amongst other things, collapsed "protestantism" into the extremes of individual reason and individual freedom of the will, in opposition to any sort of consensus. Toland's concern for alienated minorities—Dissenters, Jews, Palatines—reflects a deep personal identification with them.

Has too much been made of Toland's "vanity", based on John Locke's personal dislike,[2] on the Pantheist's tactic of secrecy, or on the sometimes unprincipled attempts of a poor man to pay his bills? Once we grasp Pantheism's method—the sense behind the "esoteric" and "exoteric"—this alleged vanity appears in a less unfavorable light. Before the Berlin experience Toland was not entirely in control of himself; he was indeed at times vain, tending to over-react under pressure, and inclined to play the coffeehouse insider. The excesses of *Reasons for Addressing his Majesty*, hastily penned during the parliamentary crisis of 1701–2, were inordinate, even egregious with their claims to close personal influence upon the Electress Sophia and the future Queen Anne. The desire to impress, even to shock, was in the style of an *enfant terrible*.

Much more evident in Toland's *animus*, however, is consistency of opinion and scholarly discipline of the will. The energy to engage himself in the thick of things as a writer, spy, or philosopher seldom lags. The intellectual training and linguistic ability of the man were more than merely sound. His output was astonishing. Revolutionary dedication, when all is said and done, fused and integrated his personality over time, and tamed his neurosis.

John Toland as Political Writer

A study entitled *John Toland als Politischer Schriftsteller*[3] tries to depict Toland as a patriot, misconstruing *Anglia Libera* (1701) as a paean to "England". This patriotism was ostensible only. Toland's reverence for the Dutch Republic was, in context, the more demonstrative. Close study reveals the Glorious Revolution and its Settlement were indeed but the present battleground in an ageless struggle against "superstition" and "tyranny". England and the Dutch Republic were the up-to-date models for religious toleration and civil liberty, even as tridentine Catholicism and Louis XIV's France were still-existing models for the historic opposition. Imitating Cicero, Toland attempted to exemplify his theories in practice. Pantheism was devoid of doctrines with no political meaning. The Gnostic ethics of *Christianity Not Mysterious*, the Stoic ethics of *Letters to Serena*, and the incipient Mosaic ethics of *Nazarenus* and *Tetradymus* were but parts of a developing Augustan philosophy that sought to re-connect the modern world with the lost Golden Age of human reason and human liberty.

This did not merge ideology with philosophy, nor *vice versa*. The "exoteric" dimension of the pantheistic mentality was as "real", as pressing, as the "esoteric". One must descend into the marketplace, attend the forum. The Toland who contested with Defoe, with Swift, and with Davenant was equally as important as the aspiring Olympian.

Toland's political thought was in reaction to the Stuart theory of "Divine Right and Passive Obedience". His answer to "Divine Right" was the "sovereignty of parliament". A Commonwealthman, he was more extreme, and went so far as to postulate "arbitrary Power in Parliaments" against the kingly "prerogative". More important than this, however, was his revolutionist's hatred for "Passive Obedience". Although he did not dare state it openly, the political corrolary to "free-thought" was the right to an active civil disobedience, the antipode of the Stuart theory concerning rebellion. "Liberty of Conscience" meant "civil liberties". Civil authority was as subject to "reason" as ecclesiastical authority. Tyranny had become as inhumane and as "unnatural" as bigotry, and secular tyrants as execrable as clerics.

For this reason, in 1699, he had courageously re-opened the issue of the beheading of Charles I, and attacked "King Charles'" authorship of *Eikon Basilike*, that latter-day canon of Stuart political theory. The Act of Settlement loomed on the horizon, and it was apparent that the unseating of the non-juring bishops in 1688 had but partially disassembled the Stuart machinery. Tories and High Churchmen still balked at the legality of regicide because of tyranny or for any other "just" reason. Toland's *Life of Milton* and *Amyntor* pre-supposed that regicide, under extreme conditions, was a "natural right" of the subject in parliament! The killing of the King in 1649 was his precedent. If Toland emerged unscathed from the controversy, he had verified this precedent, and proclaimed his position successfully in the press. It was a daring ploy he would risk for high stakes on other occasions. That he immediately after enjoyed William III's favor was a scandal. "Liberty of Conscience" enabled this outsider of questionable status to attack the citadel of regal power, the life of the King. But, as he realized, "Liberty of Conscience" coupled with "Passive Obedience" was hypocrisy. The subject in parliament, to verify his "Liberty of Conscience", was entitled to disobey, even to kill.

Ethics

Toland thought himself a true philosopher, superior to Locke[4] and to Spinoza;[5] the peer of Newton and Leibniz.[6] Although posterity has so far repudiated him, close examination of his major work reveals coherence, vast learning, and profound insight.

There was a devout practicality to all his serious thinking, subjecting the purely academic to furthering the Revolution. But, like Cicero, Toland left the forum from time to time for Tusculum, seeking in retreat to compose books of more lasting value than the political pamphlets he wrote for Whigs and Commonwealthmen. Near the end of his life he reminds us, to be sure, that his writings had been to one end; "Religious Toleration and Civil Liberty".[7] Earlier, anticipating the death of Queen Anne, he had added the "Protestant Succession". Finally, at one point, he stated, simply, that "Liberty" had been his ultimate concern.[8]   We have little evidence for disbelieving these assertions, and it is best to interpret his system accordingly, granting him this essential practicality of intention. Toland's thought, then, reduces to an ethics or political theory in support of definite historical ambitions or ends. "Pantheism"is ideological in *purpose*.

"Ethics" is the better term than "political theory" for describing Pantheism, however, if we think of the latter in that Spinozistic sense where "ethics" extends beyond mere conduct into the wider areas of mind, history, cosmos and polity. Toland's system is "ethical" in this sense; he wishes to re-assert that classical "pre-established harmony" which over-arches and sustains all parts or entities of any mind, any history, cosmos, or polity.[9] For Toland the world, if not in actuality a perfect *somehow* (hence "ethical") at least *ought* so to be.

Pantheism was therefore the rationale of an ethical vocation. Never a detached, intellectualist metaphysic, it eschewed mechanistic theories of the day and stressed the role of man in the spheres of his activity, enjoining him to act each day according to the criteria of universal moral laws.

Headings

Toland's philosophical system begins assuming an inter-balanced relatively between two principles, the "divine center" and the "attributes".[10] The "divine center" is one, and the "attributes" are many. These terms are not terminals, or separate modalities, however, unless by abstraction. As Leibniz would say, "they are separate, but not distinct". In reality, constantly, they are literally and physically inter-acting: dynamically, biologically, organismically. The ontological word in the motto "All Things are from the Whole, and the Whole is from all Things"[11] is the connector "from", denoting the eternal relation between the terms, ever *moving* in both directions at once.

Toland's major works thus are interwoven and complimentary analyses of the "general attributes" of mentality, cosmos, history and polity. *Christianity Not Mysterious* is a theory of mind, *Letters to Serena* (the fourth and fifth) a theory of cosmos, *Nazarenus* a theory of history and *Pantheisticon* (and the unwritten *Respublica Mosaica*) a projected theory of world polity. The method in each case is to isolate, amid the welter of phenomena, whichever attribute is in question, then relate it to the "divine center", or "law" of that attribute. Toland is a "Deist", therefore, insofar as the one thing he never permits himself to doubt is the pre-existence or substance of the "divine center" or "law". It is there, waiting to be revealed or uncovered, by assumption. He is a "Pantheist", however, when his concern is more than merely apprehending the divine center; that is, when he wishes to articulate the reverse relation of the divine center "outward", penetrating and articulating the four general attributes in some detail. This is, indeed, the more proper way for the philosopher to proceed, for the importance of the "divine center" and its "attributes" is in their common, hidden dynamic relativity, not in their individual "existences". The former alone is real; the latter is "real" only by a process of bifurcation or furthur abstraction.

The Attribute of Mind

In *Christianity Not Mysterious* Toland investigates the "attribute" of mind, later hypostatized and reified by Immanuel Kant, to the point of obsession, as "the transcendental unity of apperception". The language Toland employs in his enquiry is that of high medieval Thomism woven together with that of Latitudinarian Anglicanism; that is, the early 17th century language of "Natural Law".[12] In the course of pursuing mind in this language he comes to the "divine center" of human thinking in accordance with the crucial neo-Stoic, Thomistic distinction between *synderesis* and *syneidesis* (or of *knowing* the good then, by free will, of *choosing* it)[13] The divine center is forever double; first it is a phenomenon called "the common notions" (KOINAI ENNOIAI),[14] then, second, it is the free choice to abide by these same "common notions" as if abiding by an ethical rule.[15] Together, the "common notions" and the choice for them constitutes the phemomenon we denote as "conscience", which, in one word, is the "divine center" of all our thinking.[16] We acquire our own personal "conscience" by a process, quite naturally, while "learning". This learning or developing process is precisely "Natural Law". As the "common notions" are all moral ideas, the learning process reconciles the claims of our individuality to those of our society; it is an interactive process, mentally considered, and we become moral beings increasingly as the process matures and approaches its end.

There are several interesting themes buried in the history of these ideas from which Toland's theory derives. First, there is much of ancient Stoicism in any conception involving either "Natural Law" or the "common notions".[17] Both terms were essential to ancient Stoic epistemology and ancient Stoic ethics, serving after many centuries, in St. Thomas, to draw epistemology and ethic into one context. Although Toland mentions no names other than that of Origen in connection with these venerable maxims,[18] it is his intention to demonstrate the respectability of his theory by attributing it to that early Father of the Church as a sign of its trustworthiness and persistant usage over many centuries of time.

Another theme Toland's theory reflects is that of the so-called "moral sense", made suddenly popular in the eighteenth century for the most part through Hutcheson's criticisms of Shaftesbury. Toland's was a "moral sense" theory published prior to Shaftesbury's *Inquiry Concerning Virtue* (1699) by three years. Yet, as seen above, almost all Latitudinarian theories of Natural Law—the Latitudinarian moral theology—were "moral sense" theories;[19] neither Toland nor Shaftesbury were unique in re-employing this time-encrusted approach to the phenomenon of mind.

In the course of *Christianity Not Mysterious* Toland carefully weaves together and compromises both Lockean "empirical" and Cartesian "rationalistic" language. There is, in the case of Locke, enough actual paraphrasing from the *Essay Concerning Human Understanding* to explain why Stillingfleet attacked Locke violently for the latter's having "inspired" Toland's book.[20] Indeed, Toland never did escape accusations of "discipleship" to Locke.[21] Overall, however, Toland is vividly anti-Lockean; for both "Natural Law" and the "common notions" are "innate ideas". Locke, ever attacking "innate ideas", must have checked over what Toland had written. As for Descartes, Toland refers to the famous argument (from the *Discourse on Method*) that "God is no deceiver" at least twice,[22] and devotes several pages to explicating "intuitive" knowledge, reminiscent of Descartes' *cogito*.[23] Toland's purpose in subsuming Lockean and Cartesian principles is easily recognizable to any discerning reader, in that it always seems to prove the superiority of his own starting-point. The problem in epistemology raised by Descartes' dualism of "spirit" and "matter", and reflected later in the notorious disparity between "English empiricism" and "Continental Rationalism", is of little or no consequence once one re-adopts a Natural Law Theory. Since the time of the late Stoa both the (Lockean) association of ideas *a posteriori* from a *tabula rasa* and the *a priori* necessity for (Cartesian) "clear and distinct ideas" had both been recognized as supplementary and equal *parts* of Natural Law;[24] that is, binary and complimentary to the learning process. In highlighting Locke's and Descartes' language whenever possible, and in the same context, Toland dramatizes the historical roots of both those languages as merely derived from the more venerable language he was now re-articulating!

Toland's adherence to the "common notions" links him, for students of Deism, both to Herbert of Cherbury and to Herbert's imitator, Charles Blount.[25] Both, remarkably, had understood that part of the Natural Law theory marked out by Christians from Jerome to Aquinas as *synderesis*, or the upward ascent from out of the Platonic cave of ignorance toward the epiphany of "seeing" the Form of the Good. Christian theorists, to avoid the Socratic paradox that "knowledge is virtue", had removed "the Form of the Good", and substituted in its stead the "common notions",[26] thereby necessitating a second, notably "Christian" step in the Natural Law theory; that of morally *choosing* the good, once known, by free will.

All this, however, was recondite to what triggered the uproar *Christianity Not Mysterious* did in fact ignite in England and abroad. What appears to have accomplished that mischief were the more psychologically vivid Latitudinarian and Arminian aspects of Toland's theory, as well as his alleged mishandling of the figure of Jesus, which, opponents claimed, smacked of anti-trinitarianism.

Christianity Not Mysterious is of great interest as the near-perfect systematization of the Latitudinarian mind. In epistemology Toland was radically Latitudinarian—much too radical for the Latitudinarian Stillingfleet—but, being radical, his book shows us the bare-bones logic of the Latitudinarian position. Toland, arguing that there were no truths either "above" or "contrary to" reason, had assaulted certain neo-Thomist assumptions which had been, up to then, more than compatible with Hooker's and Laud's "established" High Anglicanism. In particular, the time-honored Thomistic premise that there was a quasi-substantive difference between "Nature" and "Grace", held comfortably by Jeremy Taylor and other Latitude men, had instantly been wiped out. Natural Law, the connector between Nature and Grace, had once again fused them dynamically together. Toland's insistence on upholding Natural Law—the mean between Nature and Grace in St. Thomas[27]—did not as yet reduce everything to a mere "naturalism", inasmuch as Natural Law required the existence in thought of the terminals Nature and Grace suspended apart,—"separately", if not "distinctly". What it did accomplish, however, was the resultant *synergism* of Nature and Grace,—the creation of a person's "conscience"—precisely in and through the "common notions", and in a stance of a radical Latitude. "Natural Law" in Toland is therefore ontologically more significant than its subsidary terminals of "Nature" and of "Grace". Hierarchy had been modified to the utmost, and this, for many good Anglicans (if not for most) was a disturbing, even frightening innovation.

Another disturbing factor was the dramatic subtlety with which Toland sounded the Dutch Arminian note of freedom of the will when it came to matters of "conscience".[28] Intensifying the Natural Law theme in his book toward a climax or crux, when the Christian, after having grasped the "common notions", must now opt for them, and so begin his career in imitation of Jesus the Savior, Toland had made the freewill principle—*syneidesis* in the old Thomistic language—appear sudden and consummate. He then "reveals" to the reader the very essence of human *nature*, contriving to communicate to him the imperative of a certain obligation to dissent actively whenever the integrity of *any* individual conscience might have been violated![29] This, too, was frighteningly radical. Collective freedom of conscience had long been recognized by Catholics, Anglicans and early social contract theorists, and it was the very prop, at that time, of organized Dissent. But the sheer individuality attached to it by Toland was alarming to all manner of reigning champions of authority. In Toland it had become the individual reason alone, and an individual choice alone, that seemed to matter. No public authority might brook them, at least in theory. Toland's later use of the term "Liberty of Conscience" showed him eager to extend this decision-making required in practice to all individuals when refelected upon in theory as well.[30] Had not Jesus taken a whip to the money changers? Was it not also clear *why*?

Finally, there was little if anything in *Christianity Not Mysterious* to dramatize Jesus as the Annointed One, or the "Christ". Jesus is a model of rationality, and the Gospels are his statement or "Word", but it appeared that his divinity hinged more upon his rationality when all was said and done, rather than his rationality upon his divinity. This, on the face of it, appeared Socinian. Toland extols Jesus as his ethical model, the "son of man", insofar as the latter is the very embodiment of human "conscience" and the "common notions", but claims for his divinity are all but sidestepped. At best Jesus was unique in that he was the only concrete exemplar of Natural Law in history.

The ostensible thesis of *Christianity Not Mysterious* was that "mind" is a Christian phenomenon insofar as reason and the Gospels "agree",[31] the former leading us to the "common notions" according to Natural Law, while the latter "revealed" them in purest literary form. Toland later abjured this good Latitude Man's contention and sought instead to uncover the "divine center" of history in the historic career of the Jews, no longer in Jesus' career.[32] Yet the notion of rationality as "agreement" stayed with him to the end. His definition of reason (or logic) shows us that "agreement" for him was in fact a form of dialectic:

> ...when the Mind cannot immediately perceive the
> Agreement or Disagreement of any Ideas, because
> they cannot be brought near enough together, and
> so compared, it applies one or more intermediate
> Ideas to discover it: as, when by successive applica-
> tion of a Line between two distant Houses, I find how
> far they agree or disagree in Length, which I could
> not effect with my Eye...This Method of Knowledge is
> properly called Reason or Demonstration...and it
> may be defined, That Faculty of the Soul which
> discovers the Certainty of anything dubious or ob-
> scure, by comparing it with something evidently
> known.[33]

Toland's confidence in dialectic remained unbounded, or so it
appears. "*Coincidentia Oppositorum*" was its formulation in the
Pantheisticon (1720),[34] where he conceives it even to be the method
of science. Nothing, he seems to think, is beyond the comparison
process, and, conversely, everything can be sooner or later brought
into universal agreement. One "agrees" by "comparing". Recognizing the limitations of human mentality, however, he ends by stating
that anything beyond our natural capacities of comprehension
is simply not worth knowing: "The most compendious Method
therefore to acquire such useful Knowledge is neither to trouble
ourselves nor others with what is useless, were it known; or what is
impossible to be known at all".[35] We see, therefore, an almost
utilitarian practicality to his fundamental viewpoint in matters of
"epistemology".

What, again, is the "divine center" of the "attribute" of "mind"?
The readers puts *Christianity Not Mysterious* down with the disturbing feeling that there are two contenders for that honor, not one. The
ostensible answer is "conscience", comprised first of the "common
notions" and, second, of freewill or "choice", embodied in Jesus
Christ and revealed by the Gospels. The other contender is dialectic
itself, the swift-darting process of comparison by which, slowly, we
discover and articulate our spiritual environment. Later, when
Toland separated the study of nature from the study of religion—the
"esoteric" from the "exoteric"—dialectic was likened to divine, Heraclitean "Ether" or "Fire", and ascended to its illuminated and

ultimately nameless place at the divine center: "...the Ether, I say, by a wonderful Structure of the Brain thereunto adjusted, and by exterior Objects that act upon the Brain, through the Means of the Nerves of the Senses, and excited therein various imaginations, duly executes all the machinery of Conception, Imagination, Remembrance, Amplification, and diminution of Ideas. This Fire is Horace's 'Particle of divine Breath'".[36]

The Attribute of Cosmos

By 1706, and probably earlier, Toland called *Christianity Not Mysterious* with its outdated, neo-Thomist language, his "Juvenile Thots".[37] Pantheism, his mature "Thots", had by that time been made explicit in *Letters to Serena* (1704) and in *Indifference in Disputes: A Letter from a Pantheist to an Orthodox Friend* (1705). Meanwhile, in *Amyntor* (1699) and *The Primitive Constitution of the Christian Church* (1705) he had commenced a new phase in biblical studies which could culminate later in *Nazarenus* (1718) and in the projected *Respublica Mosaica*. The second and third volumes of *Christianity Not Mysterious*[38] were jettisoned in favor of a plan to search for the "divine center" of history elsewhere other than in the crucifixion of Jesus Christ. The Natural Law theory of mind in *Christianity Not Mysterious*, an epistemology directly related to the ethical, neo-Stoic physics of *Letters to Serena*, was of necessity permitted to stand.[39]

Toland's cosmological system is, some say, Spinozism, but in motion, a nearly perfect re-modeling of the old Stoic cosmology of "self-moving matter". Again, the point of the system, as in *Christianity Not Mysterious*, was to solve existing problems in cosmology while at the same time grounding the entire cosmological enterprise in an historical, traditional precedent of age, respectability, and note. Toland, with his penchant for dialectical "agreement" was determined to be "Ancient" and "Modern" at once. All his thinking revolts at the suggestion that modern discoveries in science and elsewhere might result in a breach with the past. The concept "tradition", while anathema to him if used by churches, sects, or governments, was passionately correct for him in philosophy. Why was this?

The problem of the age in the philosophy of nature had been unleashed by Descartes insistence upon a dualism of "spirit" and "matter", the *res cogitans* and *res extensa* of his own cosmological theory of "vortices". This had been intensified by Hobbes and, especially, by Locke, whose Lucretian materialism had virtually reduced the *res cogitans* to the *res extensa* alone. Locke's psychology presupposed Hobbesian particles entering the box-like apparatus of a mental *tabula rasa*, thereby setting into motion the learning process by a mysterious exercise of efficient causality. Continental rationalists, Spinoza or Leibniz for example, held on to the primal notion of "substance", or an original underlying difference *beneath* "spirit" and "matter" grounding them, and which had marked and integrated the tripartite medieval cosmos of heaven, earth and hell since Augustine.[40]

An early modern attempt at a "middle way", based on classical systems inherited by the Italians of the fifteenth century Renaissance, had been hazarded by Cambridge Platonism.[41] Repelled by Hobbes, the Platonists' emphasis was necessarily on "spirit", which they attempted, seeking the middle, to *materialize* as much as possible. Less extreme than Malebranche, their efforts produced nonetheless an English Malebranche in John Norris, whose *Account of Reason and Faith* (1697) had run fourteen editions in answer to *Christianity Not Mysterious*. Norris, with Leibniz and other of the "continentals", defended a divine intelligence "above reason". In England the Boyle lecturers also worried and gnawed over a middle way and seemed for a time devoted to little other than reconciling the traditional medieval view with various recent Royal Society discoveries, especially after the earth-shaking publication of Newton's *Principia* (1686). Toland's *Letters to Serena* has to be read in this rather turbulent and competitive context.

Toland's "solution" was both modern and classical. A close reading of *Letters to Serena* (and its esoteric companion-piece, *Pantheisticon*) fixes the "divine center" or Deity in nature upon a necessary third *between* Descartes' "spirit" and "matter", which had been known to the Ancients, usually, as "Fire"—Heraclitean "common stuff"—or to the Moderns as "Ether".[42] This notion had its vogue even in the history of modern science. Ancient materialism was revived after Newton to explain the Uniformity of Nature presupposed by the entire scientific enterprise. Toland's re-assertion of this ancient solution was his own attempt to re-establish the so-called "hylozoistic" tradition in natural philosophy. The meetings of the Pantheisticon, or Socratic Society, were to celebrate and to discuss this apparently ageless, supposedly trans-historical vision of the cosmos. The quasi-religious nature of such a study, opposed to the various published, laboratory experiments of the Royal Society, made it "esoteric" or secret. Toland was hardly an atheist—a more devout man in his way is hard to imagine—but he knew from experience that he would be hounded and accused as one if he practiced or wrote about "natural philosophy" openly.[43]

Letters to Serena, then, (the fourth and fifth letters) is an exercise in redeeming the Stoic cosmology, described by Cicero in the *Tusculan Disputations* and *Of the Nature of the Gods*; to outface thereby all modern, scientifically tricked-out cosmological ideas. The entire argument commences by attacking Spinoza for being partly right (his "ethical" view of the cosmos) yet mostly wrong due to his poor accounting of the dynamic, inner, and hidden qualities of things; their essential *bios*. Descartes' theory of vortices is savaged in favor of a plenum,[44] that ancient matrix of self-moving matter in the hylozoistic tradition of the Porch. The continental substance-philosophers are attacked generally as being "mathematicians" or neo-Pythagoreans, arguing naively from the unknown to the known.[45] The object in reviving Stoic materialism, aside from its metaphysical affinity to the reformed Newtonian world of the eighteenth century, seems to have been the practical one of reinstating a suitable ethics. In Stoicism, remember, ethics derived from physics. Toland, rejecting his own naive *Christianity Not Mysterious* for the more mature *Letters to Serena* had in fact rejected Christian ethics for Stoic ethics (later he sought to compliment these "esoteric" Stoic ethics with an "exoteric" Mosaic ethics).

Christianity Not Mysterious, after all, had amounted to a systematization of the Latitudinarian moral theology, and had its roots in the Christo-Stoic Fathers, notably Origen, and in the Thomistic Platonism of Natural Law. *Letters to Serena* is but a transference of this Christo-Stoic ethical interest to a language more in keeping with the Baconian and Newtonian discoveries of the times. This is perhaps interesting, in that it is clear evidence of the bankruptcy of a language. It appears to have been Newton, with his discovery and formulation of the thermodynamic "laws of nature", who had laid

waste the Christian interpretation of Natural Law. At least we may
be fairly certain that he had nearly done so for Toland. Natural Law,
for all "Moderns", while as yet remaining "necessary", was clearly no
longer "sufficient".

There is a genuine sense in which Toland's cosmology is of more
than historical interest. Prior to Whitehead's *Process and Reality*,
Toland's *Letters to Serena* is without doubt one of the few early-
modern theories of nature which insisted upon the inclusion of
biology in cosmos.[46] The "divine center", or "Ether", seemed tailored
to explain all living as well as all mechanical organization. Toland's
imagery in describing the cosmic process was often more biological
than not, reminiscent of Hindu theology, with strong emphasis on
the exchange of matter, through bodies, by intake and excrement.[47]

Toland's biologism, in part at least, harks back vividly to
Giordano Bruno. Bruno, whose doctrine of the "Inward Artist" had
confounded early champions of mechanism over a century prior to
Toland, seems to have been perhaps the greatest single influence in
Toland's education after Cicero.[48] Bruno, like Cicero, derived his
ethical rules from a physical cosmology in the classical manner.
Toland had written a Life of Bruno, had translated the latter's *Of the
Infinite Universe*, had Bruno's *Spaccio* translated and distributed,[49]
and, most importantly, copied the Nolan's secret meetings with the
Elizabethan intelligentsia as the perfect model for his own secret
gatherings, called the "Pantheisticon".[50]

The eighteenth century was soon to become the age and vogue
of the secret society. Aside from political clubs, with which Augustan London abounded, the more philosophically oriented of these
clubbings together were motivated by the approaching French
"Enlightenment", or final anti-clerical debate. Bruno, for Toland,
had been burned at Rome as the first martyr to this cause, and, in
a way, had become the future catalyst toward a last, great intellectual overthrowing of the "dark ages" and the medieval frame of mind.
Although Plato's *symposium* was declared the classical and formal
model for the Pantheisticon, Toland had adopted it because the
Nolan, at the house of the French Ambassador to the Court of
Elizabeth, Castlenau, staged its revival there in honor of the "circle"
featuring Sydney, Hatton, and Raleigh. Toland writes that this
sublime group, taught by Bruno, "saw further than any since (or
perhaps before) into the mysteries of Priestcraft and the extravagan-
cies of Superstition".[51]

We are led to conclude once again that Toland's "Pantheisticon", while meeting in secret to marry scientific discovery to hylozoistic tradition, was motivated not by scientific interest so much as by the more practical concerns of the Enlightenment, the now-raging anti-clerical debate. The "esoteric" philosophy of nature (propounded in *Letters to Serena*) was a non-clerical, freer frame of ethical reference, a substitute for the late and terrifying medieval frame. Nature or cosmos, no less than Christianity, was "not mysterious". It was "intelligible" to the dialectic of "agreement" among the enlightened few.

The Attribute of History

For Toland, history, fundamental to his studies because the reposi-tory of all "tradition", was but an "exoteric" study, a phenomenon of a secondary measure of "reality". Esoterically and ontologically, according to his philosophy of nature, history must of force give way to the ever-recurring circularity of cosmos.[52] By reason of the "uniformity of nature" principle, and by further reason of Toland's primitive formulation of the "conservation of matter" principle, Pantheism was committed hereafter to the proposition that there could be nothing new, ultimately, under the sun. At best, history was either simply fraudulent, or a legitimate distortion of the rules governing what Cicero called the *cosmopolis*. If any invention of "priestcraft" surfaced, it was *ipso facto* a form of *pseudos*. Toland was convinced that Catholicism, Anglicanism, and the various historicisms of Dissent were likewise frauds in this respect. His *History of the Celtic Religion and Learning* (1726) proposed the thesis that the Druids were the inventors of clerical fraud in history, the paradeigmatic case.[53] As for distortion, even the "divine center" of historical time—the career of the Jews—did not escape fraud in this sense. Is not the rabbi a "priest"? The one "tradition" true in history was in fact trans-historical; namely, the hylozoistic round of self-moving matter. This eternal process subsumed history under cosmos, metamorphosis, and "circulation".

One studies history, therefore, as one studies the mirror-image of the real. History is the Platonic "moving image of eternity"; a secondary, "exoteric" phenomenon. It is written for "the vulgar". Yet it is precisely history which *reveals* cosmos to the Pantheist. There appears to be a "conservation of time" principle to Pantheism, as well as a "conservation of matter" principle. As such, all proofs for whatever proposition you may set forth are to be found in history. History is the *dimension of proof*, and must be studied in order that we may separate off three strands; (1) the truth (hylozoistic philosophy) (2) fraud (priestly invention) and (3) the exoteric line of the Jewish model (proper for determining the polity of the vulgar). Underneath this clear but complex view is a common assumption; namely, each of these strands must be carefully separated if the historian is to penetrate to his Source, the veriest primitive starting-point "inside" the time-cycle. Each cycle, apparently, begins in a sort of Kant-Laplace explosion or blowing apart of the strands from their primitive unity. The primitive state, prior to history, is the "divine center" of time before its unfolding, and within the hylozoistic round. It is symbolized in Toland by a hoary seer of Graeco-Semitic origin named Linus. The "original Pantheist" is "Linus, the most ancient, most authentic, and revered Oracle of Mysterious Science".[54] Real time is prior to later recorded or clock "time".

The upshot of this "insight", for practical purposes, is the rule, essential to Toland after he rejected his systhesis of reason and scripture in *Christianity Not Mysterious*, that "There's a wide difference between unfolding Natures Mysteries, and discoursing on Religion".[55] In other words, trans-historical studies of hylozoism are "esoteric", and not to be confused with "exoteric" studies of historic literature or "tradition". This separation is penultimately made explicit in *Clidophorus* (1720). Hylozoism and religion are there to be understood as occurring in *two separate historical contexts*, the former accessible to a few philosophers alone, the latter open even to the vulgar masses. It follows from this there are two sorts of polity "revealed" in history, the former a secret one the members of which are these same few philosophers; the latter polity is open, but its members are the vulgar hordes. The secret polity revealed from naturalistic studies is, of course, the "Pantheisticon" itself, the Socratic Society. The open polity, fit for the vulgar, is "religious" in character and "scriptural" in origin. Toland devoted his later, "deistic" studies to analysing this second sort of polity, and concluded in *Nazarenus* (1718) (though he did not live long enough to properly formulate the conclusion) that it was a certain *Respublica*

Mosaica, the primitive "constitution" of the Jews revealed beneath Mount Sinai and recorded, albeit corruptly, in the Pentateuch.

Toland's historicism resulted in his romantic search for the eternal primitive, and he contributed seminally to this Rousseauesque line of thinking in the eighteenth century.[56] The natural is not the primitive, but the hylozoistic round coursing secretly down through "history" to the present time from the "Source". That which is unnatural, partly a distortion and partly a fraud, has ever accompanied it, comprising as it were two "parallel" traditions, one true and the other *pseudos*.

The ethics of correct historical study rests in this; that the persistent unveiling of frauds brings a few more initiates nearer to philosophy, and that a gradual, prudent and careful destroying of the "exoteric" religious tradition will do much to preserve public order among the restless vulgar. Both purposes, far from ideal, are better than a general decline. As Toland says concerning the Druids, "For Truth will shine the brighter, the better its counterfeits are shown".[57] And the "History of the Druids...is the complete History of Priestcraft, with all its reasons and resorts; which to distinguish accurately from right Religion, is not only the interest of all wise Princes or States, but likewise does specially concern the tranquility and happiness of every private person". How very important to discern "right Religion", then, which, though hardly philosophy, helps us approach philosophy.

Esoteric versus Exoteric Polity

The knottiest problem for any student of Toland is the relation he insists upon between "Commonwealth" taken as *cosmopolis*—the philosopher's homeland examined in the *Pantheisticon*—and "Commonwealth" taken simply as the "commonweal" or general welfare. Each conception is Ciceronian, and Toland entertains both sides of the question, the former in a Miltonic mood (in *Clito*), the latter, as he grew older, in a more mature, disillusioned mood. In *The State Anatomy of Great Britain* (1716) he remembers that there had once been a party for an ideal Commonwealth, but that now there exists "no such party at all". In that opus we are assured that the

Hanoverian limited monarchy is the very best variety of a Commonwealth for all of modern Europe.

Obviously, Commonwealth as an ideal went to ground at the
exact same time Toland began to distinguish "esoteric" from "exoteric" within "Pantheism". Why else extol the ideal *cosmopolis* at the
Pantheists' secret meetings? The Miltonic mood remains alive, but
in secret! Ethically, *cosmopolis* is the only true polity, and, likewise
the only possible criterion for judging the best. Politically, however,
it happens to be out of time.

The ideal Commonwealth thrust aside, Toland pursued his
"exoteric" biblical studies to discover, as he thought sooner or later
he would, a suitable contemporary "myth of the state". He was
apparently dissatisfied with all the present contenders; the Whig
myth, the Anglican, the Presbyterian. Moreover, he did not believe
that he was creating something not there in the first place;

> As the fundamental Law of a Historian is, daring to
> say whatever is true, and not daring to write any
> falsehood; neither being swayed by love or hatred,
> nor gained by favor or interest: so ought he of course
> to be as a man of no time or country, of no sect or
> party...But if in clearing up antient rites and
> customs...any communities or orders of men, now in
> being, should think themselves touched; they ought
> not to impute it to design in the author, but to the
> conformity of things, if indeed there be any real re-
> semblance.[58]

His myth must be discovered from historical research, not formu-
lated, *a priori*, and should be (concerned as it was with the vulgar
and not with the philosophers) of strictly religious origin.

That *Nazarenus* was the summation of many years research in
this line is beyond question.[59] Jewish monotheism had for some
time been a specifically Unitarian focus, and Toland's Jewish
studies link him to that movement. That he was indeed an Arian, if
not a Socinian, appears in the end also to have been without
question. *Christianity Not Mysterious* itself is evidence of a Unitarian tendency. In basing his projected book, *The Respublica Mosaica*,
on a monotheistic progression from the ancient Hebrews to the

Nazarens, however, (and from the Nazarens to Mohammed) it seems fairly apparent that he thought no myth of the state suitable for the vulgar if it were "mysterious" or purely clerical. A Unitarian polity was as far as he was prepared to compromise the ideal, at least near the end of his life. Such a polity would have to recognize kingship and religious services, as in George I's England. But no longer will it stand for the trinitarianism of certain benighted High Anglicans. Evidently Toland thought that Whig Latitude Men were now ready to take the great step forward; adoption of an official Unitarianism would not necessarily destroy the Low Church. Had not Tillotson written that "Nothing ought to be received as a revelation from God which plainly contradicts the principles of natural religion"?[60] And Tillotson, to whom *Christianity Not Mysterious* had been dedicated, had lain dead now for three decades.

Toland's two parallel polities, in sum, were the "esoteric" *cosmopolis* of purely classical origin and an "exoteric", monotheistic kingship of biblical origin. They converge in his thinking about the time of the death of King William III and the near-simultaneous rising of Convocation against him, when, apparently, he moved forward as a philosopher to reject the thesis of *Christianity Not Mysterious* that reason and scripture "agree"; i.e., of his "Juvenile Thots".

Toland's Place in History

Toland's fame has never rested secure. It has depended almost entirely on his contributions to the philosophy of the Enlightenment, and historians of that philosophy, such as Cassirer, unfamiliar with Pantheism, have not heretofore evaluated it with any accuracy. Although it might be erroneous to compare Pantheism with systems of the "great" men of the time—Leibniz, Locke, Bayle, Berkeley, Shaftesbury—still an understanding of Toland raises one's estimation for him while tending to bring the famous ones down a notch or two. It is interesting to note, for example, that Pierre DesMaizeaux chose to edit Toland's miscellany precisely in company with those of Locke, Bayle, Leibniz and Shaftesbury, neglecting Berkeley. Berkeley's star rose later, almost in proportion as Toland's fell.[61] Since the devaluation of deism, with which Toland has been almost exclusively associated, his reputation has suffered most in England and least in Italy and Germany.[62] Italy has only very recently discovered him. The French have evinced only slightly more interest in him than have the English.[63] Though the consensus has been that Toland perhaps deserves more attention than he has received, most remain still fairly puzzled why this should be the case.

Two reasons for taking Toland more seriously deserve comment: first, the metamorphic biologism (hylozoism) of his theory of cosmos is original with him (if related both to Bruno and his friend Shaftesbury). It was long prior to the very modern and very sophisticated biological relativity-systems mounted by Samuel Alexander and A.N. Whitehead in our own time.[64] Second, Toland's historical probing in Nazarenus was arguably the pioneering effort in researching of the crucial first century after Jesus.[65] These achievements, blown up, might at least mitigate his nearly spurious immortality, and entice a few readers to find and open once again at least his major writings. Perhaps, also, it bears mentioning that students of Celtic history could not, until very recently, begin their studies without consulting A History of the Celtic Religion.

Toland is more important than realized hitherto, but not, in the long run, for any of the above arguments. In large measure his importance depends on a possible reconstruction of the so-called "history of philosophy". Granted this reconstruction, Toland (along with other figures whose prime concern was "Enlightenment") ought to attain in future a greater readership.

The history of modern philosophy is still studied as a history of "systems", emanating from several "problems" raised first by Descartes, notably from his metaphysical dualism and its theory of knowledge, which led speculation by the nose until the births of phenomenology, existentialism, and (to a lesser extent) British language philosophy in the twentieth century. There is little doubt Toland participates in this very great development, and there is little doubt also that his role therein thus far has been considered a fairly minor one. But it is equally valid to interpret the history of modern philosophical and scientific systems as part of an even larger "universe of discourse"; namely, the "Enlightenment", or the cultural revolt of the eighteenth century against the medieval, Christian world-view.

In this light, Pantheism was created with an eye to subordinating Cartesianism and the rise of science to what its author rightly considered the far more significant development. Pantheism is particularly the subordination of all reclusive "epistemology" to the street battles of the Enlightenment; it is therefore a system better to reveal to us the points of relation between the scientific and anticlerical movements, hitherto studied for the most part in isolation from one another. There is little doubt these points of relation existed. Almost every scientific breakthrough, once accepted, loosened the hold of the ecclesiastical establishment upon the popular mind. In Toland's case, Lockean faculty psychology and Newtonian mechanics were swiftly fashioned into philosophical weapons; in *Christianity Not Mysterious* and in *Letters to Serena*, respectively, they were wielded to pillory the establishment. Later, in *Nazarenus*, those long accruing findings of the "commonwealth of learning" (always an embarrassment when unearthing childlike similarities between fideism and "superstition") were fashioned into a new and interesting variant of the primitivist theme, ever ultimately harmful to ecclesiastical "tradition". Three blows of this sort delivered in one lifetime against the medieval world-view contributed not a little towards its ultimate discredit. And Toland, with his genius for suspecting and then unveiling the depredations of "priestcraft", had as much to say to his own contemporaries as Voltaire later said to his, for both their vocations were alike attacks upon power, authority and the abuses of reason in contemporary political life.

Toland's Pantheism particularly waged war upon two theories of efficient causality very subtly beneficial to Christianity: the ancient causality of the medieval Aristotelian-Thomist frame of reference, and the more modern, mechanical version of the Cartesian *monde*, reflected especially in the English inductive materialisms of Bacon, Hobbes, Newton, and Locke. This simultaneous attack upon the two equally stupendous errors of "continental rationalism" and "English empiricism" remains the final measure of Toland's importance to modern thought. Both "sides, for him, were complementary modes of fraud, and new dimensions of intellectual tyranny. Both equally served to obfuscate the burning issues. *Letters to Serena* was his simultaneous repudiation of both "schools" of thought, the former represented paradeigmatically by Spinoza, the latter by Newton. Toland's dynamic, metamorphic biologism was, in sum, meant to act as a trap for Christianity from which there might be no escape. Pantheism offered to collapse both the "Prime Mover" and His mechanical "creation" into that primitive "divine center" inimical to both. In Toland, naturalistic *process* is opposed to the all philosophies of *personality* entailed either in the "ancient" Thomist and "modern" Cartesian dualisms. In Pantheism, there are no "realms" of "Nature and Grace", nor of *res cogitans* and *res extensa*". These "realms", if ever they existed at all, were at best "attributes" of the "divine center", parts of the eternal, hylozoistic round. For Toland, both personal deity and mechanical physics were but masks disguising the interests of eighteenth century Christianity, each more or less subtly and cleverly corrupting philosophy itself.

Pantheism commenced with firing off a salvo at the hapless, ever-patient Spinoza. Today it is for some odd reason a commonplace to attribute the creation of "pantheism" to the Watchmaker. But for Toland in his fury, Spinoza was anything but a pantheist. He was a follower of Descartes and prophetic of Leibniz,[66] a continental "mathematician" who had spun out an interpretation of cosmos by *a priori* causation. "It is my present Design", says Toland, "to show that Spinoza's whole system is groundless, which at one stroke destroys whatever is built upon it".[67] In the *Ethics* (Lemma 1, ante-Proposition 14, Part 2) Spinoza asserted that "Motion and Rest are the Causes of all diversities among Bodies", and that meant, (Corrolary 2, Proposition 3, Part 1) that "an affinity of things proceed from Motion and Rest". But Toland was astonished that Spinoza had never developed this theme; in fact, he had contradicted it. When pressed by Henry Oldenburg of the Royal Society, Spinoza pulled back and reduced Motion to "Extension" as a mere sub-attribute: "Extension is conceived by itself and in itself, but Motion not so; for it is conceived to be in another thing, and the Conception of it involves Extension".[68] Spinoza was confused concerning motion, and he promised Oldenburg later that he would "some other time deal more plainly...about these matters".[69] Toland rightly held this to have been an evasion. The *Ethics* had been published posthumously, yet it remained uncorrected.[70] Motion in the *Ethics* meant for its author only "local motion"—this or that change of place—and the want of any *conatus ad motum* had frozen Spinozistic Extension solid and inert. Toland, in rebuttal, insisted with great force that "Motion is essential to Matter".[71] The famed Spinozistic *conatus* had been merely subjective and rational; it pertained to no actual sweep nor motion in the existing material universe. Toland's deeply interior *conatus* made of motion the very first characteristic of every thought, thing, person, or whatever else might exist to be considered. The importance of the point was that "local motion" alone required behind it some sort of transcendent Prime Mover, whereas a principle of general motion did not. Whereas Spinoza had been unable to destroy the concept of a personal God, or would not, Toland was determined to reduce the theological "personality" of God to mere self-moving, sentient "matter".

Toland likewise rejected mechanism, and for the same reason he had rejected the *a priori*. Newton for him was as wrong-headed as Spinoza, for Newton (like Spinoza) conceived of all motion as "local motion", not descriptive of matter in general. Still, it had been typical of Toland to flatter Newton the celebrity, even as he had bludgeoned poor, unpopular Spinoza. "...All Physics", he says, "ought to be denominated from the Title [Newton] has given to the first book of his *Principles*, viz. *Of the Motion of Bodies*".[72] But this flattery is ironical and abusive. For later we read that, regarding "particular Forces and Figures...with their Reasons and Degrees, none in the world is so able as Newton to discover and reduce them into an intelligible System: but as for the general moving Force of all Matter, I would flatter myself, that I have done something towards it in this letter".[73] Newtonian mechanism was as erroneous as Spinozistic "mathematical" rationalism! Both conceived all motion as "local motion". Both made room for the Aristotelian Prime Mover. Both pandered to Christianity, or so it might be interpreted.

Toland's solution to the terrible (if not self-created) epistemological dilemma of European thought is truly ingenious, for all that it has been discarded. In many places he speaks of "circulation": in *Christianity Not Mysterious*, for example; "I am convinced that *Plants* have a regular Contexture, and a multitude of Vessels, many of them equivalent or analogius to those of *Animals*, whereby they receive a Juice from the Earth, and prepare it, changing some into their own Substance, and evacuating the excrementious Parts..."[74] There is no need of a Prime Mover here, nor of mechanism. In *Letters to Serena*, man, the so-called "image of God", is but one of the animals:

> Our Bodies, however we may flatter ourselves, differ
> nothing from those of other Creatures, but like them
> receive Increase and Diminution by Nutrition and
> Evacuation, by Accretion, Transpiration, and several
> other Ways, giving some parts of ours to other
> Bodies, and receiving again of theirs, not altogether
> the same Yesterday as Today, nor to continue the
> same Tomorrow, being alive in a perpetual Flux like
> a River, and in the total dissolution of our System at
> Death to become Parts of a thousand other things at
> once...[75]

Both Spinoza and Newton had missed or passed over the quasi-
biological basis of cosmos, but that was secondary. Primarily, both
played into the hands of the priestly bureaucracy from want of an
adequate biology. There is no overriding purpose for God, church,
nor priest in a "circulating", biological universe. Matter, in general,
moves itself. All modes of existence are metamorphic. Matter is
motion, and motion matter forever and *at once.*

The key to Toland, then, is his attack both on the *a priori* and *a
posteriori* forms of efficient causation, and, respectively therewith,
on both the "ancient" and "modern" versions of the Thomist,
"realist" ideology of the Catholic Church. The Prime Mover and "His"
mechanical "creation" are but complementary forms what amounted
to a mentality of domination and of human bondage. Both "continental rationalism" and "British empiricism" were (and are?) two
forms of philosophical self-deception. This to the present day
remains Toland's message. Implied in this position is that the entire
Kantian enterprise has been a grotesque, even ludicrous "mistake".
"Action" in Toland undercuts both medieval "first causes" and
"Cartesian mechanism":

> Whoever then goes about to explain by their first
> Causes the Origin of the World, its present Mecha-
> nism, or the Affectations of Matter, must begin with
> the first Cause of Motion: for no manner of Variety is
> included in the bare idea of Extension, nor any
> Cause of Alteration; and seeing it is Action alone that
> can possibly produce any Change in Extension, this

> Action of Principle of Motion must be well cleared
> and established, or the System must quickly be
> found defective. If it be only taken for granted, the
> system will be but a Hypothesis; but if proved and
> explained, then we may expect to find greater Certi-
> tude than hitherto in natural philosophy.[76]

"Action" underlies here both any "first causes of the Origin of the
World" and the "present mechanism". The new science ought
instead to be in general hylozoistic, for only hylozoism best and
most elegantly undercuts the fraudulent, tripartite theology of the
Catholic middle ages.

There had been an adumbrated middle-tradition in modern
European philosophy for some time. Giordano Bruno and the Cambridge Platonists had experimented with dynamic systems designed, in their ways, to counter the old Aristotelian hierarchical
"chain of being" and the origins of modern mechanism.[77] Toland was
directly influenced by them, as we know. Yet one cannot say that
Bruno or the Cambridge Platonists were in a position to discern the
problem as clearly as did Toland, later and in precisely causative
terms. The issue itself had become at last dilemmatic and easier to
grapple with.

Toland's cosmos was schematically fashioned to balance those
projected by two philosophical villians, Spinoza and Newton! For
this reason, though he repudiates these acknowledged giants, we
may say that Pantheism takes its own departure equally from the
former's *Ethics* and the latter's *Principia*. Pantheism is an ethics,
brilliantly inaugurated in Spinoza, and its principle of general
motion is derived from and inspired by Newton's chapter from the
Principia, "On the Motion of Bodies". The resulting synthesis,
however, to my mind, is original.

The scandalous attacks on Spinoza and Newton were but the
driving of another nail into the coffin of the Church, now in full
retreat. For Toland, the Continental and English traditions in
philosophy appeared, each one, merely sophisticated upgradings of
the old medieval view.

The significance of Toland's hard-won synthesis was forgotten
in England once it was decided that Church and the scientific
movement could live together according to a purely mechanistic

deism, as in Paley, or when later no incompatibility had been discerned between nineteenth century science and the resurgent tractarian medievalism of Cardinal Newman's "Oxford Movement". In France, *Letters to Serena*, translated by D'Holbach, had meaning only for those *philosophes* whose anti-clerical interest more or less had become the same that Toland's had been earlier in the century.

Toland's importance for his own time, and his relationship to the Enlightenment, rests finally on his assessment of various faltering philosophical traditions in Europe closely related to certain unacceptable institutions comprising Church and State. To correct these errors of intellect and of power in his time, he invented and entertained a vision of a new human being dwelling in a new society. In that utopian vision the cosmos was conceived as a metamorphic, hylozoistic round. The state, ideally, reflected this as a new incarnation of the classical *cosmopolis*. Non-ideally, the state was envisioned, pessimistically, as that limited monarchy taken from the English model which Toland himself had helped fashion while spying, travelling and writing for the victorious Whigs.

Toland had been prepared to compromise his ideal *res publica* to the realities of politics provided that, at the minimum, there remained within the frame of George I's constitutional monarchy some hope for a genuine religious Toleration and set of Civil Liberties—remote hints or promises of a "Commonwealth". As a philosopher, he continued to strive for the ideal while accepting the ashes of this wretched compromise, for he felt that, with the brute fact of the English Revolution, the time for the future emancipation of mankind had at last arrived. Christianity, with its "priests", was on the wane. Toland died the harbinger—perhaps the herald—of a more hopeful time.

EPILOGUE

NOTES

1. British Museum, Additional Manuscripts Division; Add. MSS. 4295, f. 43. The title is contained in a list of manuscripts Toland had lent out.

2. Locke to Molyneux, May 3, 1697, printed in John Locke, *Works*, Vol. 9, 1823, pp. 415–416. Also Molyneux to Locke, May 27, 1697, *ibid.*, pp. 421–422.

3. Anna Seeber, *John Toland als Politischer Schriftsteller*, Freiburg, 1933, *passim*.

4. Toland, *Tetradymus*, 1720, p. 190 seq.

5. Toland, *Letters to Serena*, 1704, the fourth and fifth "letters".

6. Toland's *Letters to Serena* attacks all the prominent continental "mathematicians" in philosophy, including Descartes and Leibniz, for spawning the notion of a trans-natural Substance, central to Spinoza's *Ethics*.

7. Toland, *Tetradymus*, 1720, p. 223. "*Civil Liberty* and *religious toleration*, as the most desirable things in the world, the most conducive to peace, plenty, knowledge, and every kind of happiness, *have been the two main objects of all my writings*".

8. *Ibid.*, p. xx.

9. Toland, *Letters to Serena*, 1704. Letters four and five, *passim*.

10. Toland, *Clidophorus*, 1720, p. 88.

11. Toland, *Pantheisticon*, 1751, p. 14.

12. Toland, *Christianity Not Mysterious*, pp. 57–60.

13. Toland, *Christianity Not Mysterious*, Section II, Chapter 4, *passim*. Cf. H.R. McAdoo, *The Moral Theology of the Caroline Divines*, p. 72 ff. Cf. W.R. Sorley, "Synteresis", *Dictionary of Philosophy and Psychology*, edited J.M. Baldwin, pp. 655–657.

14. Toland, *Christianity Not Mysterious*, p. 118.

15. *Ibid.*, pp. 61–62.

16. *Ibid.*, p. 60. Toland states this obliquely; "...tis the Perfection of our Reason and our Liberty that makes us deserve Rewards and Punishments".

17. See Eduard Zeller, *Outlines of the History of Greek Philosophy*, New York, 1950, pp. 231, 237f.

18. Toland, *Christianity Not Mysterious*, p. 118.

19. See John D. Wild, *Plato's Modern Enemies and the Theory of Natural Law*, Chicago, 1953, pp. 132–133. Professor Wild lists five criteria for recognizing Natural Law. The fourth and fifth criteria together constitute a synthetic "moral sense".

20. For two flagrant examples compare Toland's *Christianity Not Mysterious*, p. 13 to Locke's *Essay Concerning Human Understanding*, Book IV, Chapter VII, Locke's number 18; then *Christianity Not Mysterious*, p.12 to *Essay*, Book IV, Chapter XVII, number 14.

21. In the Bangorian controversy (1717–18) Bishop Hare of Worcester reiterated and amplified Stillingfleet's charges. See Toland, *Tetradymus*, 1720, p. 190 ff.

22. Toland, *Christianity Not Mysterious*, pp. 30 and 31.

23. *Ibid.*, pp. 12, 13, 15.

24. See Eduard Zeller, *Outlines of the History of Greek Philosophy*, pp. 230–233 on the Stoic logic.

25. H.R. Hutcheson, *Lord Herbert of Cherbury's De Religione Laici*, New Haven, 1934, p. 35; Blount translated this work as *Religio Laici*. For references to the "common notions" linking the Deists to the ancient Stoa, see J.L. Saunders, *Justus Lipsius*, New York, 1955, p. 88n.; also H.A. Wolfson, *The Philosophy of Spinoza*, Vol. II, Cambridge, Mass., 1948, p. 119 n. 1.

26. See especially R.J. Henle, S.J. *Saint Thomas and Platonism*, The Hague, 1956, *passim*.

27. Saint Thomas Aquinas, *Summa Theologica*, Part II (First Part), Q.XCI, article ii. See Carl Becker, *The Heavenly City of the Eighteenth Century Philosophers*, New Haven, 1960, p. 3.

28. Arminianism was widely if popularly linked with freewill theories in Toland's day. See Roland N. Stromberg, *Religious Liberalism in Eighteenth-Century England*, Chapter VIII, *passim*. Especially, p. 114.

29. Toland, *Christianity Not Mysterious*, Section II, Chapter IV, pp. 61–62.

30. Especially in *Anglia Libera* (1701) and *Reasons for Naturalizing the Jews* (1713).

31. Toland, *Christianity Not Mysterious*, p. xvi.

32. Toland, *Nazarenus* (1718), *passim*.

33. Toland, *Christianity Not Mysterious*, p. 13.

34. Toland, *Pantheisticon*, 1720, p. 38.

35. Toland, *Christianity Not Mysterious*, p. 76.

36. Toland, *Pantheisticon*, pp. 23–24.

37. Bodleian Library, Oxford. Rawlinson Manuscripts. C. 146, f.47. Letter from Elisha Smith to Thomas Hearne.

38. Toland, *Christianity Not Mysterious*, pp. 174–176.

39. The Stoa, Toland's model, derived logic and ethic from physics. Toland, knowing this, appears to have unable to do otherwise himself.

41. Substance is patent in Spinoza. For those who contend Leibniz is free of this notion, the following is quoted, written by Leibniz with reference to Toland's materialism: "It must be admitted...that there is some *substance separate* from matter...Even the existence of matter depends upon it, since one does not find anything in the concept of matter which carries a reason for its existence with it". Translated and quoted in Leroy E. Loemaker, "On what is Independent of Sense and Matter", *Philosophical Papers and Letters of Leibniz*, Vol. II, Chicago, 1956, p. 897.

41. See Ernst Cassirer, *The Platonic Renaissance in England*, New York, 1953, *passim*.

42. Toland, *Pantheisticon*, pp. 23–24. The inadequacy of mechanical causation, which reserves a place for "Fire" or "Ether" at the center, is stated in *Letters to Serena*, pp. 232–233.

43. In this context, Goethe's *Faust*, I, scene 16, "in Martha's garden", bears reading: Faust's speech to Gretchen concerning "God" is pure Toland.

44. Toland, *Letters to Serena*, pp. 176–177. Toland uses Occam's razor to eliminate the Cartesian assumption of a void in space, upon which the vortex theory depended. For Toland, as for the ancient Stoics, motion and a plenum were not contradictory notions, but complementary.

45. *Ibid.*, pp. 179–180.

46. See Helene Metzger, *Attraction Universelle et Religion Naturelle*, Paris, 1938, pp. 107–111. Cf. A.N. Whitehead, *Science and the Modern World*, New York, 1925, p. 58 seq. Also Margaret C. Jacob, *Newtonians and the English Revolution*, Cornell U. Press, 1976, *passim*.

47. For example, Toland, *Letters to Serena*, pp. 188–189.

48. Toland, *Miscellaneous Works*, Vol. I, pp. 316–349, for Toland's own translation of Bruno's *Of the Infinite Universe*, the *locus classicus* of this doctrine.

49. William Morehead, *The Expulsion of the Triumphant Beast* (by Giordana Bruno), 1713. The only known copy of this translation is in the Manchester College Library, Oxford. Morehead is thought to have been Toland's brother-in-law.

50. Toland, *Miscellaneous Works*, Vol. II, pp. 376–381.

51. *Ibid.*, pp. 376–377. It is interesting that in this same letter concerning Bruno's *Spaccio* the "unalterable Law of Nature" is employed "against the mysterious, speculative, unpracticable, and changeable Institutions of all other kinds" (p. 378). Toland discovered the *Spaccio* in 1696 (see F.H. Heinemann, "John Toland and the Age of Reason", p. 56, or Pierre Bayle, *Dictionnaire*, edited de Chaufepie, Vol. I, Amsterdam, 1750, p. 453) and *Christianity Not Mysterious* was printed that same year.

52. Toland, *Letters to Serena*, p. 192; also *Pantheisticon*, pp. 16–17.

53. Toland, *Miscellaneous Works*, Vol. I, pp. 8–9.

54. Toland, *Pantheisticon*, p. 14.

55. *Ibid.* Introduction.

56. There was a second English edition of *Nazarenus* in 1732, and a French translation, *Le Nazareen*, Londres, 1777. Both were anonymously printed.

57. Toland, *Miscellaneous Works*, Vol. I, p. 16.

58. Toland, *Miscellaneous Works*, Vol. I, p. 15.

59. *Ibid.*, Vol. II, pp. 314–317. Toland claims to have been preparing a manuscript on the *Book of Job* in September, 1695.

60. Quoted by Leslie Stephen, *English Thought in the Eighteenth Century*, Vol. I, p. 78.

61. G.A. Johnston, in his *The Development of Berkeley's Philosophy*, London, 1923, says that Berkeley's "general philosophical position is intended to be, in the main, a criticism of Toland". See pp. 341–342. If so, Berkeley's growing popularity may well have contributed to Toland's obscurity.

62. Typical of English opinion of Toland is that of the influential Sir Leslie Stephen, for whom Toland is "poor Toland", a disciple of Locke. See *English Thought in the Eighteenth Century*, Vol. I, pp. 93–115, German writers such as Lechler, Berthold, Zacharnack, Fensch, Seeber, and Muff, on the other hand, have collectively monographed almost all the main facets of Tolandian writings.

63. Sayous, Nourisson, and Lantoine have written on Toland as deist, philosopher of nature, and "freemason" respectively. Helene Metzger compares him to Newton.

64. Samuel Alexander's *Space, Time, and Deity*, London, 1920, and A.N. Whitehead's *Process and Reality*, Cambridge, Mass., 1927, are based on conceptions similar if not identical to those of Toland in *Letters to Serena*. It is perhaps enough here to state that Toland, Alexander, and Whitehead are all philosophers of "organism", or biological process.

65. See Luigi Salvatorelli, "From Locke to Reitzenstein: The Historical investigation of the Origins of Christianity", *Harvard Theological Review*, XXII, 4, October, 1929, pp. 263–264. Also David Patrick, "Two English Forerunners of the Tübingen School: Thomas Morgan and John Toland", *The Theological Review*, LIX, October,

1877, pp. 594 f. Vico did not publish his *New Science*, it should be noted, until 1725, three years after Toland's death.

66. Spinoza follows "his Master Cartesius". See *Letters to Serena*, pp. 135–136. Page 152 of the same calls Descartes' system "at best but an ingenious Philosophical Romance"! Leibniz had written "On What Is Independent of Sense and of Matter", in defence of Substance.

67. *Ibid.*, p. 145.

68. Quoted in *Letters to Serena*, pp. 145–146. Interestingly enough this was the first letter of the famous series between Spinoza and Oldenburg.

69. *Ibid.*, pp. 154. This from Spinoza's final answer to Oldenburg concerning motion, the seventy second letter.

70. *Ibid.*, pp. 154–155.

71. Stated in the title of the fifth "letter" to Serena.

72. Toland, *Letters to Serena*, p. 202.

73. *Ibid.*, p. 234.

74. Toland, *Christianity Not Mysterious*, p. 75.

75. Toland, *Letters to Serena*, pp. 188–199.

76. *Ibid.*, p. 141.

77. Toland, Bruno, and the Cantabrigians were all philosophers of a plenum. In *Letters to Serena*, a plenum was meant to replace Descartes' theory of vortices. It squares with the plenum in Bruno's *Book of the Infinite Universe*, translated in Toland, *Miscellaneous Works*, Vol. 2, pp. 316–349. Ernst Cassirer's *The Platonic Renaissance in England*, London, 1953, p. 140, quotes Ralph Cudworth, foremost of the Cambridge men, attributing "all events in the

universe to a "Plastick Nature" or plenum, somehow forming events from within.